T0329079

VICE AND VIRTUE

Men of History, Great Crooks for
the Greater Good

BY THE SAME AUTHOR

Le Médecin devant ses juges, with Pierre Macaigne and Bernard Oudin. Robert Laffont, 1973.

Divorcer. La Table Ronde, 1975.

Mon intime conviction. Robert Laffont, 1977.

Plaidoyer pour Marseille. Ateliers Marcel Jullian, 1979.

Quand la justice se trompe. Robert Laffont, 1981.

Par le sang d'un prince: le duc d'Enghien. Grasset, 1986. (Académie Française award winner; Femina Prize for Essays, 1986.

Toursky et le commencement du désert. Seghers, 1986.

Le Crépuscule des juges. Robert Laffont, 1988.

Les Insurgés. Flammarion 1990. (Académie Française award winner)

Le Juge et l'Avocat: dialogue avec Simone Rozès. Robert Laffont, 1992.

Le Procès du roi. Grasset, 1993.

Anthologie des poètes délaissés, with Pierre Dauzier. La Table Ronde, 1994.

La Justice des bien-pensants. Flammarion, 1995.

Anthologie de l'éloquence française, with Pierre Dauzier. La Table Ronde, 1996.

Ma Vérité sur le mensonge. Plon, 1997.

PAUL LOMBARD

VICE AND VIRTUE

Men of History, Great Crooks for
the Greater Good

Algora Publishing
New York

Algora Publishing, New York
© 2000 by Algora Publishing
All rights reserved. Published 2000.
Printed in the United States of America
ISBN: 1-892941-08-2
Editors@algora.com

Originally published as Le Vice et la Vertu © *Editions Grasset &*
Fasquelle, 1999.

Library of Congress Cataloging-in-Publication Data 00-008790

Lombard, Paul, 1927
    [Vice et la vertu. English]
    Vice and virtue : Men of History, Great Crooks for the Greater Good /
    by Paul Lombard.
    p. cm.
    Includes index.
    ISBN 1-892941-08-2 (alk. paper)

    1. France--Moral conditions--History. 2. Political corruption--France-
    -History. 3. France--Politics and government--Moral and ethical as-
    pects. 4. Celebrities--France--Attitudes. I. Title.
DC36.1 .L66 2000
172'.2'0944--dc21

                        00-008790

Algora Publishing
wishes to express its appreciation
for the assistance given by
the Government of France
through the Ministry of Culture
in support of the preparation of this translation.

New York
www.algora.com

TABLE OF CONTENTS

To Caesar.

Chapter 1

A Brief Chronicle of Anti-Heroes

Should I start my irreverent chronicle all the way back at the time of the Flood? Let's just digress for a moment in Greece and Rome which, in addition to great benefits, bequeathed to us many dubious practices. "A great many politicians do not deserve really the name, for the politician chooses fine actions for their own sake, but many adopt this kind of life only out of ambition and to grow rich,"[1] wrote Aristotle. He went on to decry a certain number of evils from which we still suffer. "Most men are more avid for material goods than for honors . . . One need not fear being short of money when one is absolute master of the State."[2] Less naive than Plato and Xenophon (who portrayed Sparta as the paragon of all virtues), the philosopher asserts that Alcibiades went over to the enemy; Demosthenes gave in to Arpolos' gold, and Aristogiton sold himself to the highest bidder. Athens was the first to implement a "clean hands" operation, requiring politicians to justify their public expenses before a court of 500 citizens whose sentence could be confirmed or annulled by the judges of the *demes* or the *thesmothetes*.

These democratic jurisdictions, predecessors to our audit agencies, were perverted by sycophants, professional court witnesses who threatened to denounce the rich if they resisted their underhanded requests. "They launch libelous charges against the wealthy in order to have a chance at confiscating their goods."[3] Sycophants are still causing trouble.

When Rome conquered Sparta, the face of Antiquity changed but corruption remained. Candidates ruined themselves trying to be elected as proconsuls; they plundered their provinces. Verres, the gauleiter of Sicily, was sentenced to death after a devastating indictment by Cicero, and the *Verrines* became famous.

This virtuous rigor did not prevent Quintus, the great orator's own brother, from writing *A Little Manual on Election Campaigns* for his use. "When seeking a magistrate's position, you must be scrupulously sure of two things. Both the devotion of your friends and your popular support must be based on benefits and services rendered." A better description cannot be found for the relationship between populism and corruption — primary causes of the decline of Rome, according to Montesquieu: "They introduced the custom of corrupting people with money. Crassus, Pompey and Caesar were champions."[4] This triumvirate had many illustrious successors.

What is corruption? We have yet to define it. It requires a passive recipient and an active tempter, for this form of delinquency cannot be one-sided. The legal system takes a particularly severe approach to it; but the (French) penal code is impotent. According to the lawyers and their legalistic jargon, corruption exists when a decisionmaker modifies his choice in exchange for undue advantages. Corruption is synallagmatic, it imposes reciprocal obligations on both parties. Don Juan corrupts Sganarelle by associating him with his seductions. Sganarelle corrupts Don Juan by seconding him in his undertakings and accepting his pledges. But this reductive sense confines the concept too narrowly. One can be corrupt and still stand by his initial decision, if that is ultimately to his own benefit. One may corrupt others in the interest of his fatherland, his party, his company, and still maintain — the supreme stage of permissiveness — a clear conscience. An appallingly diverse spectrum of examples exists.

One form of corruption mixes private business and the public interest. Coeur, Concini, and Richelieu elevated this to a virtual religion where the sacred vessels were communicating vessels.

The corruption of magnificence drove Fouquet, the Sun King's financial superintendent, to flaunt his wealth under the exasperated gaze of the monarch. He would have done better to play it down, like Mazarin, stowing it away in the cellars of Vincennes under the vigilant eye of the Swiss .

With the "corruption of lucidity" Mirabeau narrowly missed preventing the Terror; he nearly gave France a constitutional monarchy that would have changed the face of the world.

The "corruption of extralucidity" enabled Talleyrand to pay his bills every month by making deals with Austria, Russia, Prussia, and England. But it also enabled him to prepare the Congress of Vienna, which limited the disastrous consequences of the Corsican megalomaniac. Talleyrand may have had a limp, but he was by no means lame.

Edgar Faure embodied the "corruption of intelligence." He played such a brilliant *tour de force* in the 4th Republic that his greatness underscored the smallness of others. He transformed this evanescent but productive regime into a mere Lilliput. When Charles de Gaulle took center stage, Faure maneuvered to lay the foundation for the France of tomorrow, while the General gave yesterday's France its final illusion of grandeur.

"Corruption of the heart" is the most contagious. François Mitterrand corrupted France through disenchantment. He set out to change society but he left the old structure in place, crumbling, greedy, and egoistic, only now less generous, less interdependent. Money became a cancer during his reign. I do not know the truth about the esoteric bank accounts and other allegations. . . and, frankly, nobody else knows, either. For the moment, Mitterrand is one of those men who has left no one indifferent and yet whom no one can admire completely.

Corruption is the spawn of two evil mothers: the weakness of humanity, and the inadequacy of our institutions. Montesquieu noticed that, long ago. "There are two kinds of corruption. One, when people do not observe the laws; the other, when they are corrupted by the laws. The latter is an incurable evil because it lies within the remedy itself." The present age should consider this warning. There is no salvation if the law does not teach us to prefer public interest over personal passions, as Robespierre observed. Protecting goods, honor, and life, when tragedy is in the wind, it gives license to steal, and to kill — in the name of sacred love of the fatherland, for example. In so doing, it perverts virtue, corrupts it.

Any regime that intends to be incorruptible becomes malevolent, by taking the place of God in the choice between Good and Evil. Popular democracies are no exception. Limits on competition, managed consumption, nationalized ambition — all our navigation buoys on the course of happiness — have led to the black market, to the single party and to the reign of the Mafia. Their corruption, embodied in power, gives Benjamin Constant's pessimism its potency: "Mankind is foolish, and is led by rascals. That is the rule."

Utopia itself is condemned to bring about corruption and to corrupt itself; even justice cannot escape this curse. The establishment of an international tribunal charged with punishing war crimes and crimes against humanity constitutes a decisive projection of the law. For its severity to be neither corrupt nor hypocritical, the community of men will have to judge with identical rigor the torturers of small, vanquished peoples and the torturers of the great victorious nations.

But let us return to corruption and to its anti-matter, virtue. Should "virtue" be written in the singular, or plural? This is a question of ethics, not of grammar. If Virtue comprises all the virtues, no weakness would be tolerated and the cabinet ministers would have to be beatified before attaining their positions in the marble halls of the capital. The man of power must be virtuous; that is not a question of conscience alone but also of prudence. If, on the other hand, virtue is diluted, the statesman can be satisfied with just one quality and ignore those that are foreign to the matter at hand. Then, is he entirely virtuous, half-, or one-quarter virtuous? Lucky Socrates, who could say: "I am truly fortunate. I seek a single virtue and find myself amidst a whole swarm of virtues." Of course, he died from it.

The conflict between perfection and pragmatism generates many painful paradoxes. A judge on the take, who accepts money to acquit someone who is innocent and who does acquit the person is just, but not honest. Another, who spurns all bribes, listens to his inner convictions and condemns the innocent person, is honest but is not just. We ask magistrates not to be irreproachable but infallible — irreconcilable adjectives.

During the long cohabitation between politics and money, among the men who made France, the virtuous ones were rare. Often, the most effective were the least presentable and their contribution was measured by the scale of their lapses.

The allure of gold and the fascination of power were inseparable under the *Ancien Régime*, where the king set the pace and confounded the public till with his own coffers. This example carried in it the seeds of a generalized corruption, reaching first the ministers and the king's favorites, who forgot that the King was the State and that, by acting in his image, they became abusive servants. However, of the great corruptible figures presented in this work (except for Concini, who was condemned *post mortem*), only two had to account for their actions: in 1453, Jacques Coeur, who was so imprudent as to try usury on his sovereign; and Fouquet who, in 1661, had impudence to dazzle the great king with his own wealth. The others, having made their fortunes, lived to see a tranquil old age. France was easy on those who served it while relieving it of its assets, as long as their merits outweighed their shortcomings.

Moreover, they hardly dissembled their delinquencies and these great men knew how to handle their failures. Danton, Morny and Clemenceau never claimed to be feeding their factions' bank accounts. However, one cannot play that way anymore, and today's politicians are militant in manifesting their disinterestedness. It is the party and the party alone that must appear to benefit.

Today, we face corruption of the third kind. For decades the French government practiced laissez-faire, the Parliament kept its mouth shut, and justice closed its eyes, for both the better and the worse. The political parties, as vast enterprises without capital and with no one standing guard over the accounts, were condemned to institutional begging; they experienced the dilemma of Jean Valjean — steal or die.

When the time came to elect a President, nothing was spared in the effort to ensure the triumph of the providential man (something France had been lacking since Napoleon III). Now, that "nothing" was paid at a high price. Public forums and republican banquets had given way to the public relations industry (expensive advertising campaigns) under the impotent gaze of the Minister of Justice, who should himself have passed around the handcuffs. Relentless competition between the factions led to the cohabitation. The Constitution of France in its ripe age has difficulty regulating the relations between the citizens and their elected officials, and greater difficulty regulating those of the executive, the legislative and the judiciary.

In 1995, France had three million unemployed, the offence of begging was beginning to rear its head, the links between the economy and politics were putrefied, and the alarm clock of populism was about to go off. Thus the outlines of the new French trouble were drawn. A new and necessary therapy appeared; but it was a therapy that, in the long run, may turn out to be pernicious: the revolt of the judges.

Illegitimate because they were not elected, the judges proclaimed themselves the saviors of a drifting ethical system. How much has changed since I, as an adolescent, first visited the Chancellery. In the Ministry of Justice, petitioners were jostling each other. "How do you recognize the magistrates?" I asked the assistant prosecutor who was accompanying me. "They wear white gloves," he answered me, "and they crawl on their bellies to move up the ladder."

It's not like that anymore. The servility of the judgeship has been replaced by jealous independence. Today's judges live in autarchy, and they assume the right to make up for any deficiency of the other powers resulting from the universal vote. Threatening the fragile balance of power, they claim theirs is supreme over all the others. Our judges decided (and who could blame them for it?) to apply the law without taking account of the personality of the delinquents nor of the apparent purity of their motives. For them, abuse of public funds, forgery and secret payoffs remain condemnable, even if the money ends up in the right bank account or makes it possible for a company to enter a new market that requires upfront payments.

France during the Liberation wearied of the spectacle of poor wretches, brutally shorn and paraded naked under the public's gibes and catcalls. Today, I am fed up with TV images of those who have been indicted, exposed to the public scorn. This spectacle masks the responsibility of the Republic and its leaders, who left the financing of political parties (the drive train of democracy) in a vacuum for decades. The spectacle diverts attention from the complicity of a whole people, who never wondered, who never asked, how were these ruinous election campaigns financed? To make an exhibition of this criminality that we all tolerated is pernicious, and all the more so given that it is accompanied by the devaluation of the fundamental guarantees. The burden of proof is reversed, room for doubt no longer benefits the defendant, the secrecy of the jury's instruction is ridiculed and we speak about the great principles only with the respectful tones reserved for those who are already deceased.

France's Third Republic consecrated the separation of the Church and the State. The Fifth one must separate politics and money. But does appearing to be virtuous make one virtuous? Molière showed us otherwise. The purity of morals is an ongoing combat. To achieve it, the powers must cease clashing.

Were the great corruptible men in our history perverted by institutions that were already polluted? Or did they degrade healthy regimes? Is there collective responsibility for corruption? May your visit to this portrait gallery enlighten you (and give you the strength to resist pernicious requests). In moments of temptation, may we all forget Talleyrand's last sally: giving his word to Louis-Philippe, he murmured: "It is the thirteenth time, Sire."

Footnotes

1. *Ethique à Eudème* (1, 5 121a23).
2. In *Politics.*
3. *Ibid.*
4. *Grandeur et décadence des Romains.*

Chapter 2

JACQUES COEUR

Jacques Coeur, 1395-1456, was an immensely talented merchant and advisor to King Charles VII of France. He oversaw royal finances and held great influence throughout Europe, lent extensively to king and nobles., was charged with treason and died in exile.

"His diligence and activity were transformed into public affairs and sources of profit and of glory for his King."

Juvenal des Ursins

"Righteous ministers," misled by scrupulous magistrates or by vindictive adversaries, crowd the corridors of history. In 1315, Enguer-rand de Marigny, Philippe the Fair's banker,[1] was sent to the gallows in Montfaucon by Philippe's successor, Louis X the Stubborn, who found his wealth and arrogance annoying. Two centuries later, Jacques de Semblançay, financier to Louis XII and François I, was hanged at the same location for having dipped his hand into the public coffers.

Rather than go into the detailed history of these two unfortu-nates, we have chosen an esoteric adventurer whose varied facets have too often been ignored: Jacques Coeur.

Some years ago, at Senlis, the old royal residence, one might still find a delicate old lady who was a direct descendant of the famous banker. She displayed the escutcheon (azure with a horizontal band of gold, charged with three black seashells, flanked by three crimson hearts) chosen by her ancestor at the time of his ennoblement in 1440, under the reign of Charles VII. She claimed to be the last of her line, and a note of sadness sounded in her voice, muffled by the memory of past glories and evaporated privileges.

How well did this final, proud heiress know her ancestor, who was suspected, questioned and tried, in the mid-15th century ("the autumn of the Middle Ages," as the Dutch historian Johan Huizinga so nicely called it)? The pivotal era, hesitating between the obscure clarity of robust times and the luminosity of the Renaissance, when Christendom left behind the shadows of religiosity, and cast itself free from the heavy symbols of its cathedrals. This was no longer the time of the crusades but of trade and adventurers, glorifying the empire of mortals, preferable to the hypothetical kingdom of God. Man put himself to the service of man, and Jacques Coeur served himself, his monarch and France.

While the rest of Europe was lost in a Gothic swirl, Italy, reviving its ancient glory, produced the majestic domes of its basilicas, replaced the vertical thrust of *ogive* arches with forceful horizontal constructions and opened the windows of its buildings to the so-greatly desired light. In France, nothing modern was to be found, as the country was splintered between the various factions and their armies. The Hundred Years War, whose seeds were planted the day the Angevin dynasty of the Plantagenets acceded to English throne England some three centuries earlier, would come to an end only in 1453.

The 15th century of Jacques Cœur was a twilight era where the thunder clouds of the Reformation were gathering (even if it was not until 1517 that Luther nailed his famous theses to the great portal of the Cathedral of Wittenberg). Humanism started to emanate from the universities of Bologna and Padua, where Marsile Ficin would translate Plato, the Greek philosophers and the great hermetist texts of the dawn of our era, and offered to the West the priceless gift of free thought, that fragile seed of liberty.

The 15th century of Jacques Coeur saw the advent of the great commercial and financial empires: Flanders, Genoa, Florence and Venice (which were already in conflict). But the new capitalists, builders of this first Renaissance, were not French. In Paris, no one was ending one day as a tradesman and starting the next day as an untouchable, a money prince or a doge. There were no all-powerful mercantile dynasties in the country that, under Charles VII, was painfully trying to recover from a fratricidal war and to affirm the authority of a broken-down State.

Ambitious commoners became entrepreneurs (without ceasing to be agents of the king), and this duality made them into workmen for national unity, founders of a long lineage proper to France. Coeur participated at the beginnings of a centralization that would culminate in

Jacobinism. He helped Charles VII to fill his counting houses, to levy taxes, to institute and run monopolies, without ever neglecting his own interests. He was not the only one to accumulate honors, nor the only one to lose them, but he was the first Frenchman to enter the legendary ranks of bureaucracy and corruption.

"With a valiant heart, nothing is impossible;" such was the motto of this high-roller. The scandalmongers claimed that, in the secret chambers of his Bourges[2] mansion, Charles VII's *argentier* (steward of the royal purse and court banker) enjoyed this insolent saying: "Jacques Coeur does what he wants / And the King does what he can." He was mistaken. The intrigues of the court, the fickleness of the monarch, were stronger than his vanity. In France, the politicos always end up having the last word, even if the contractors and the judges seem, for a moment, to be winning the day.

When Jacques came into the world in about 1440, Charles VI (the Mad, but also the Well-Loved. . .), who mounted the throne in 1380, was still reigning. His father, Charles V (the Wise),[3] had caused the English and their Burgundian collaborators some trouble, thanks to Du Guesclin, a promoter of patriotism and a captain who had a big mouth and a big lucky streak. But Charles VI was declared incompetent and his uncles were quick to take over his authority and his money. In 1400 (having temporarily regained the right to rule), he massacred his comrades-in-arms during a fit of delirium. This paranoid schizophrenic was hearing voices (and he was not the only one), while two cruel parties, the Armagnacs (favorable to the throne — they claimed) and the Burgundians, clashed. Since the times of French historians Michelet and Lavisse and the duettists Mallet and Isaac, they have been considered traitors in the pay of England, with a hidden ambition to recreate Lotharingie, that middle empire wedged between France and Germany provided for in the Treaty of Verdun in 843. Charles the Bold was the last representative of this party and this imperial dream was put to rest by Louis XI.

Charles VI's insanity brought to power his wife, Queen Isabeau of Bavaria. This malicious and salacious Gothic heroine fell into collaboration with England and the bed of Henry V, the sovereign immortalized by Shakespeare's tragedy. In 1415, the French were crushed at Agincourt (now called Azincourt), through the foolishness of the French commander-in-chief, who sent in knights on horseback, in heavy armor. They were soon pinned down under a rain of arrows, and then, once on the ground, had their throats cut by the English men-at-arms. This stunning butchery gave the Crown of France to "good King Harry,"[4] who became, through the Treaty of Troyes in 1420, regent and heir to the kingdom.

But that was without reckoning on Charles VII,[5] holed up in Bourges, the shrunken capital of his truncated State. This apathetic and ungrateful sovereign would become the liberator of the territory. Without an army, without a penny, but with the assistance of God (at least, so he pretended to believe), he would end up imposing his views and become "the Victorious." A providential trinity supported him: Joan of Arc (who also heard voices, but not the same ones), Gilles de Rais (the marshal and pedophile), and Jacques Coeur, financial funambulist, commercial juggler and spectacular speculator; his father, a furrier, was a member of the bourgeoisie, that third estate that the nobility considered to be the Third World.

In 1418, the future Charles VII escaped assassination at the hands of the Burgundians and fled Paris.[6] Twenty thousand dead: an excellent repeat of Saint-Barthélemy and the September massacres. Having taken refuge in Bourges, the dauphin brandished, without much spirit, the amputated sword of France. All his attempts to rid himself of the Englishmen and the Burgundians were useless until spring 1429, when the good Lorraine, the shepherdess so dear to Péguy, revived the dispirited army's morale, liberated Orléans and offered Valois its first victories. The war would only be won much later, thanks to Dunois, victor at Formigny in 1450 and at Castillon in 1453. But, for the French, it is the Maid of Orléans and the Maid alone who cut down the Englishmen. Chauvinistic memory forgets how brief was her intervention and how varied her fortunes — just two years — and her defeat before Paris.[7]

Before distinguishing himself in white collar delinquency, in his first rendezvous with justice Jacques Coeur displayed his preference for common law. Charles, whose Treasury had been drained dry, was scraping for every *ecu* he could find, and running up against a stone wall of short-sighted lenders. Jacques Coeur was not so timid; he responded to every appeal from the kinglet, thus winning (in the absence of friendship) his capricious confidence.

Since 1429, the sovereign had conceded the minting of Bourges currencies to a certain Ravant the Dane. When Jacques teamed up with Le Danois, the two accomplices, considering their margin too narrow, scorned royal decrees and decreased the proportion of fine metal contained in each coin, pocketing the surplus. This devaluation created a "true-counterfeit" currency that threatened France with a financial Agincourt. Once the ruse was discovered, Charles punished the culprits for their sins and condemned each to pay a fine of thousand gold *ecus*, (properly measured, this time), and to restitute their illicit gains. A good prince, he then granted the perpetrators "letters of remission," prohibiting that they should be "hounded or molested in the future" for this indelicacy. A few years later, deeming that one does not manage high finance with high ideals, he would name Ravant "General Overseer of the Currencies of France" and, fantastically, would offer to his former associate the directorship of the Bourges mint (among other responsibilities), where he would continue, all fines duly paid and bitter cups of shame duly swallowed, his erring ways.

The small city with its narrow ramparts was confining to one such as Jacques Coeur. Choosing between the gentle countryside of Berry and the mirage of a mythical Levant, he quickly transformed himself into a buccaneer of international trade. He made his way south to Montpellier and Lattes, embarked for "far-off lands," visited Alexandria, Beirut, and Damascus, and pushed on until Famagusta, in the island of Cyprus, the country of Aphrodite where the delicious figs melted in the mouths of the vestals.

The Venetians and the Genoese, who had no scruples about trading with the Infidels, charted his course. Everywhere he went, he inventoried the wealth of these, and the needs of those, and discovered that the Orient was willing to exchange silver and lead for an equal weight of gold.[8] In 1432, he made his way to Corsica, dangerous territory for foreigners (and fatal, for a generation of Frenchmen contemporary to Napoleon Bonaparte). Outside of Calvi, his ship foundered and an Aragonese troop despoiled him of his goods. A few years later, Coeur would receive from the king of Aragon an indemnity of twenty-seven livres, scant compensation for the priceless experience brought back to the lands of Berry.

1432. Upon his return, he created a vast firm — a vertically integrated enterprise, in economists' jargon — that was astonishingly modern. It encompassed both trade and craft activities, raw materials extraction and processing, and it redeveloped the silver, lead and copper mines in the Lyons area that had been forsaken since the Roman empire. His enemies claimed that secret formulas enabled this magician to smelt metals more easily, and permitted this devil's douser to unearth unsuspected mineral deposits.

This was not an evil spell but a blessing, not enchantment but investment; and at the head of his protean conglomerate, Jacques Coeur became the first French importer-exporter. His local representatives traded (in a capitalist form of barter) metals, cloth, wool, furs, and hides for the wealth of the sun: spices, silk, velvet, precious stones, exotic wood, ivory, perfumes — all the delights of the court. Given the rapacity of the ship-owners, Coeur made up his own fleet. He ordered a galley to be built by the Genoese and, thumbing his nose at the Italian rights, had it reproduced by his Languedoc carpenters. To reduce the cost of sailing crews, he asked the king to restore serfdom and to authorize "impressment," which gave him the right to forcefully take onboard his ships the wharf-side loafers, vagabonds and bums. This priceless advantage granted by a sovereign who had waged war just a few years before against private militias, "plundering hordes and vandals," enabled him to set up shop across the entire breadth of Europe. Ship-owner, counterfeiter, speculator — nothing much was left for Cœur to do but to become a banker.

Currency trading, the close cousin of usury, is the most profitable of all. Without the right or the title to conduct such trade, the merchant extended advances to the kingdom's grandees and, every time he needed a favor, he also granted loans to the sovereign himself, who was always trying to scrape up more cash. Such devotion does not go unrewarded, and the emoluments accumulated. 1437: the King entrusts to him the Paris mint, where he is charged with striking good coins, including the "big Jacques Coeur," appreciated for its stability. Behind the public figure, the racketeer builds his fortune on the royal funds. Incorrigible, according to his nephew Jean de Villages, he adulterates ingots of silver, forged at a low price and exported at a high price, thus plundering the Treasury right under the nose of the King.[9] 1438: he becomes Minister of Finance and Superintendent of the House of France. 1440: Charles VII, guided by an ephemeral sense of appreciation, makes him a nobleman.

Rich, famous, and titled, he decides to have a suitable setting for his success built in Bourges. His mansion, the outrageous expression of his pride, a delirious manifestation of humanistic imagination, immortalizes his visions in stone. Nothing is left out from this weighty frenzy: Joan of Arc, in a battle scene, dominates the campanile of the mistress tower; under a marble baldaquin, Charles VII on horseback heads off to war; statues and stained glass panels glorify the exploits of the master of the house and illustrate the history of the era (for example, a parodic high relief depicting a swirling tournament of peasants mounted on donkeys, a satire of chevalieresque manners foretelling Don Quixote).

1442. Charles calls him to join his Great Council. What good are honors when the political sap is rising? The never-satisfied one accepted with enthusiasm, made himself indispensable, and became a permanent fixture in an assembly whose members had, until then, had sat in alternation. Caught in the snares of an ambition that was without limits but not without means, he believed he was crafting for himself a future as a minister by mixing his affairs with those of the kingdom. This power, bought at the price of gold, would lead to his becoming (once again, unofficially), Secretary of State for Foreign Affairs. Charles VII, knowing his influence in the Mediterranean basin, sent him on mission to Genoa, accompanied by Juvenal des Ursins,[10] with the charge of trying to bring the Republic under French suzerainty and assimilate its port into the bosom of his enterprise. Betrayed by Janus de Campofregoso,[11] he advised his master to organize a punitive expedition to rectify the cited offense and to ensure ongoing trade relations. Preoccupied with the need to bring an end to the interminable Anglo-French war, Charles was unaware of this proposal and the banker, ignored, made the Languedocian populace repay his "diplomatic expenses."

This failure did not prevent the King from entrusting a still more delicate task to him: to allure the Eternal City, out of countenance with Bourges since the "Pragmatic Sanction."[12] The Sanction gave the throne the upper hand over the princes of a Church emancipated from the scepter of the Holy See that was under pressure from the unfair competition of Felix V, the anti-pope of Lausanne. Coeur persuaded the schismatic to retreat, in exchange for a cardinal's miter and the tempting function of legate. Nicolas V legitimated him, blessed his trade with Islam[13] and named his son Jean bishop of Bourges. A nice title for a nice, if young, man.

Not to be outdone, Charles VII gave Coeur dominion over the states of Auvergne and Languedoc, where he raised the tax as he pleased to meet his insatiable needs. He ensured the prosperity of Montpellier and required of its inhabitants a quantifiable recognition. He was responsible for administering the royal monopolies, and he took over certain wholesale operations.[14] Seller and buyer, supervisor and supervised, he had all the leisure to speculate in salt, an invaluable food product, and to steal from the State.

But this money-man was also a man of ideas who wanted to modernize France, to equip it with a system of taxation and justice that would be both worthy of France (and practical for him). His reforms already presaged Richelieu and even the interminable rhetoric of the barristers did not escape his analysis: "As for lawyers, who plead their causes often times too long and prolix with prefatory remarks, linguistic flourishes and circumlocutions, an accumulation of facts and reasons without cause, let us desire them and command them to be enjoined, on their oath, that henceforth they be more brief and, if they fail in that, make amends through arbitration." As a lawyer myself, I have to say, "Touché."

1449: Jacques Coeur financed the Normandy campaign, negotiated the surrender of the English,[15] brought triumph to the colors of France, and called down upon himself the morbid jealousy of his king.

Soon, Charles VII gave way to his envious passion. 1451: a terrible year, an accursed year, a year of downfall. The arrogant mansion of Bourges dims in the mind's eye and the austere cell where the discredited banker will soon be pacing begins to take on its contours. Soon, the richest man in Europe (even his Italian rivals could not match him)[16] would become a prisoner of the State, shuttled from one prison to another at the whim of his King. Everyone and everything conspired in his undoing: debtors hoping for a moratorium; envious rivals irritated by his ostentation; the ambitious seeking to take his place. Coeur, who had thought himself impervious to scandal mongering, calumny, and intrigue, was eminently mistaken. On the very day that he was arrested, July 31, he wrote to his wife "that [his] status was still good and relations towards the King as good as ever. . . the King is a great King, just, grateful. . ."

That day, Charles met with his advisors at Taillebourg, home of de La Trémoille, our adventurer's sworn enemy, who had already returned to grace after his English treason. Charles announced his decision to try his famous clerk who, alerted by the rumors, forced open the door of the Council and delivered himself of a haughty self-defense. He offered to remain in prison "until justice be served." He could hardly have been more conceited or more imprudent. The King, who had just borrowed

20,000 livres[17] from him, had the goodness to accept this suicidal proposal, and Coeur was condemned.

Among the counts of the indictment, he was accused of assassinating by the poison the King's mistress Agnes Sorel, who died in childbirth and who had made him her executor. Jeanne de Vendôme, a woman of doubtful reputation, had originated this eccentric accusation; she found the King a ready listener. When the justices realized that the suspicion was not sustainable, they changed the charges from assassination to corruption and the offense from criminal to financial.

Three trials, symbolic of their time, marked the reign of Charles VII: Joan of Arc, Jacques Coeur, and Gilles de Rais. The porous boundaries between the judicial and the religious, the tendency to presume the defendant guilty, and the use of torture to extract confessions (a practice that is still enshrined in our law courts), prolong our legal Middle Ages. The Maid of Orléans, the banker and the Marshal of France experienced the same pains, the same terrors; and all three wavered before the fires of martyrdom.

Jacques Coeur, led into the torture chamber in March, 1453, naked and bound, caved in, in his turn. "I would have thought that I deserved better treatment and a different form of reward for the services that I have rendered. I have told you the truth; *but I will say whatever you want me to say.*" He hardly discussed the thirteen points of the indictment, a mixture of fantasy and partial truths.

Any defender (but none was provided) would have easily set aside the circumstantial incriminations. "Supply of harnesses to Saracens and non-believers." The court pretended to be unaware of the royal and papal authorizations to trade with the Orient. The charge was sustained. "Restitution of a Christian slave to his infidel Masters." This "great and enormous crime" was explained by the King's desire not to compromise his agreements with Sudan and Egypt. The charge was sustained. "Forcibly embarking on board his galleys honorable people," including a young German pilgrim who drowned in despair. How could they prosecute the defendant without implicating his accomplice, the King? Hadn't he authorized him to impress "sailors"? The count was sustained. For good measure, they dredged up the old scandal of 1429 with Ravant the Dane, paying no heed to the letters of remission that protected the counterfeiters from legal pursuit. The count was sustained. This was a court for settling accounts.

Not all the charges were of the same nature, and the financial side of the case was of a different proportion: illicit export of money, gold and bullion to Muslim countries; traffic of currencies with the image of the *fleur de lis* but of insufficient quality; breach of trust against the merchants of Genoa, Provence and Catalonia, "by holding for an unreasonable time considerable sums that were due them;" embezzlement connected to the administration of tenant farming to the detriment of his associates and of the Crown; illegal procedures in the exercise of his mandate as Commissaire of Languedoc, "under the pretended authority of the King" and "without his seal and assent;" fraudulent payments to the Treasury by means of devaluated money; exchange and accounting charges made in his capacity as the sovereign's banker and to his detriment. All counts were sustained. And rightly so, this time. The defendant, declared guilty of lese-majesty and conspiracy, did not come out as badly as he might have done, since the commission of instruction failed to make reference to his support for the *Praguerie*,[18] a revolt fomented by the Dauphin, who was tired of waiting for his father's death so that he could attain the throne.

When the defense lost all hope, and proceedings were filed, as his final and fragile hope Jacques Coeur evoked "the benefit of the clergy," claiming, in his appearance before an ecclesiastical court, that in his youth he had taken the first degrees of the clergy. It took the judges a year to decide to reject this exception, since the crime of lese-majesty concerned royal justice alone.[19]

April 1453: the Court (made up of the members of the Council, of princes of the blood and some small-fry lawyers) met in Lusignan, where it handed down its judgment. All the accused's goods were to be confiscated to the profit of the Treasury; 100,000 ecus in damages to be paid to the Crown; a penalty of 300,000 ecus. While waiting for these sums to be paid, the condemned was to remain in prison, to make honorable amends with a ten-livre candle in hand, on his knees and dressed only in a chemise, and to publicly acknowledge his faults. (This humiliation is replaced, today, by the television news, which places the stocks in everyone's own living room.) It would take seven years for Dauvet, the Attorney General charged with auctioning off all of Coeur's estate, to come to the end of this monumental sale (which brought to light still other offences not revealed by the trial). Visualizing such events, one understands better the severity of his friend Juvénal of Ursins: "One should better call him a thief who robs a person who is stuck in a box."

October 1445. The prisoner escapes and, after picaresque adventures, reaches Rome where he is welcomed by Nicolas V, who remembers him. 1456: when his successor Calixte III organizes one last crusade, Coeur offers his services one again. Commander of a galley, he makes a stopover in the island of Chio,[20] where a malignant fever carries him off toward other shores.

A precursor of modern capitalism, a Richelieu without political vision, a Mazarin without a ministry, greedy for power and mad for money, Coeur was in the wrong century and the wrong location. Instead of being born in Venice in the 16th century or Paris in the 19th, another place, another time were selected for him. Under His Most Serene, the Restoration, the Second Empire or the Third Republic, he would have been able to allow his bountiful imagination to spur his polymorphic talent. If his king had been Charles X instead of Charles VII, he would have become one of the great businessmen, working the universe to their best interests. Jacques Coeur, a character by Brauquier,[21] Levet[22] or Balzac, was not made for the legend of the centuries, but for the trading floor, the great steamers, the French trading posts in the Indies, the Suez Canal. There, his genius would have prevented him from becoming this tainted adventurer, the prototype of a certain form of corruption which, similar to the Hundred Years War, still has not ended.

Footnotes

1. This same Philippe the Fair, who was served by the powerful order of Templars (bankers of the Crusades), decided to seize their inexhaustible treasure. In 1307, he had 138 knights Templar arrested. The trial lasted until 1314. Thirty-six were condemned to death by torture, fifty-four were burned at the stake.
2. Bourges, in the heart of Berry, the very center of France, was also Charles VII's residence from 1322-1337.
3. Born in 1338, crowned in 1364 and deceased in 1380.
4. Nickname given to Henry V by his subjects which adored this generous and courageous king.
5. Born in 1403, died in 1461, he succeeds his father in 1422.
6. The same year, the young Jacques Coeur married Macée de Léodépart, daughter of the provost of the merchants. She would give him five children who all remained faithful to him in misfortune.
7. Born in 1412, she died at the age of nineteen.
8. Damas and Alexandria traded with India and China, where silver had more value than gold, the Chinese having adopted silver plated mono-metallism.
9. Coeur had a secret forge in Rhodos for producing counterfeit money.
10. Archbishop of Rheims, Chairman of the Parliament, this great moralist, a faithful friend and severe critic of Jacques Coeur, was immortalized by Jean Fouquet in a portrait highlighting the subject's common sense, intelligence and ostentatious sobriety. This was an ugly man who never claimed to allure, but always to convince.
11. Chief of the faction that wanted to drive out the new doge, Bernarbo Adorno, supported by King Alphonse d' Aragon. In exchange for military assistance, he promised to place Genoa under French government in the event of victory.
12. 1438.
13. Papal authorization was required to export to the Orient metals liable to be transformed into weapons that could be used against Europeans.
14. Organizations responsible for the salt supply.
15. Simply a question of money.
16. He had at least 30 manors, the largest being Saint-Fargeau.
17. To repurchase the jewels of his beloved Agnes Sorel.
18. Named after the Hussite uprising in Prague.
19. The judgment was not rendered "in the name of the king," but "by the king," who signed it himself in the Council.
20. Immortalized later by Delacroix in his *Massacres at Chios*.
21. Leon Brauquier was a poet, 1900-1976, whose complete works were published by La Table Ronde in 1994, under the title *I Know Remote Islands*.

22. Author of "Postcards," the original edition of which was prefaced by Valéry Harband and Leon Paul-Farque.

Chapter 3

ELEONORA AND CONCINO CONCINI

Concino Concini, a member of Marie de Médicis' entourage when she headed to Paris to wed King Henry IV in 1600, married Marie's foster sister and became the most powerful figure in France.

> "He was pleasant in his person, a skilful rider and good at all other exercises; he enjoyed the pleasures and particularly gaming. His conversation was gentle and easy, his thoughts were high and ambitious."
>
> Le maréchal d'Estrées

> "Eleonora, a kind of dark dwarf with sinister eyes like coals from hell."
>
> Michelet

It's a thin line between legend and history, and those who record events modify the plot according to their inclinations and the influence of dubious testimonies. They celebrate the "good," from the Pierre Bayard, the peerless knight, to General de Gaulle, and they denigrate the "bad," from Ganelon (in the Chanson de Roland) to Pierre Laval (who led the Vichy government in collaboration with Germany during World War II; he was later executed as a traitor to France). Under their paintbrushes, the French epic looks like a long fresco painted by irreproachable men who defied all the rascals and connivers. They distill, for the centuries that follow, a view that has been arranged so as not to be disturbing. Woe to all contrarians who risk threatening this order. Written by the winners, history is inevitably partisan, and populated by actors that are necessarily portrayed inaccurately. Private diaries, annals, autobiographies, memoirs and introspection, all perverted through charity, for fun or out of partiality, encourage lies by omission and cheap truths in the parade of time, that vast purgatory where the children of the fatherland change their roles according to the coterie in power and the whims of public opinion.

Does Concini, so reviled and hated, deserve to appear among the corrupt men who built France? Corrupt he was, and more thoroughly so than any other. However, his mark is found on the golden book of the great national causes. In 1617, when Louis XIII was in his sixteenth year (in those times, kings and assassins were precocious) had his aides execute Concini, he killed (as an Oedipal figure) his mother's favorite and, as a politician, punished the imprudent being who had humiliated the monarch as a nurseling. A nurseling the King would remain all his life: Richelieu was his godfather; Concini, his stepfather.

This Florentine, who embodied all the cunning of Italian comedy, seems to step out of a novel by Michel Zévaco re-written in black humor by Shakespeare: intrigues, treason, plots, hired killers, nothing is missing in this existence driven by money, ambition and leadership of the State. Most historians, except for Helene Duccini,[1] have decried the memory of an adventurer without morals. Philippe Erlanger goes after him with a vengeance, denouncing him as an agent of Spain, duplicitous and regicidal, the key man in the famous and dubious plot that made Ravaillac an assassin. Posterity, impelled by xenophobic hatred, blackens his origins in order to make it easier to explain his villainy.[2] It has invented a Concini who emerged from the swamps of Florence where the Arno releases vaporous hints of the Lagoon and has transformed the son of the count of Penna, Secretary of the Grand Duke of Tuscany, into a commoner off the street. He has been charged with all forms of licentiousness and gambling, deeply in debt and ready to do anything to wipe the slates clean.

His bawdy contact with France soon would be followed by a second, more honorable one: the marriage of Marie de Médicis, niece of the Grand Duke, with Henri IV. That skirt-chaser might have had a right to expect a more glorious union but his fiancée's uncle had played a decisive role in the deals made with the pope to obtain the annulment of his nuptials with Queen Margot. And then, the Medicis were rich and France was deeply in their debt. A marriage for money ensures peace within families and prosperity for the couple better than fleeting unions of romance and the heart. Thus, the dowry was fixed at 600,000 ducats, 350,000 payable in cash plus the settlement of all outstanding accounts.

October 1600: the hymen was consecrated by proxy in the cathedral of Florence and eight days later, the Queen and her retinue — more than a thousand people — departed for Marseilles where, after a furious attack by waves whipped up by the mistral, the small squadron arrived on November 3. Amongst the accompanying mob was a Florentine girl, the new wife's hairdresser. With a long bony nose on a thin face surrounded by crisp hair, her gaze did not leave her mistress. She was called Eleonora Dori and in this extraordinary saga, she will hold the role of confidante — in the sense of Racine: an Oenone who is always ready to give to the sovereign that she dominates wise and useful councils.

On Friday November 17, Malherbe arrived, and his ode of pump and circumstance to Marie de Médicis, upon her welcome to France, certainly did not earn him the indulgence of Boileau. The recitation hardly finished, the Italian entourage turned back toward the peninsula, leaving to just a privileged few the task of escorting the sovereign to Paris. During this interminable advance on the capital, Eleonora was charmed by a handsome and noble Italian— *il signor* Concini.

How could such a man-about-town be satisfied with this "sad owl that flees the light"[4]? To ask such a question is to forget the charm of certain nocturnes and the interest an ambitious man has in ensnaring such a royal favorite. This professional seducer, with the false airs of Henri IV[5], did not live off women but thanks to them, and would practice indirect procuring while becoming the protector of a Queen by the means of her hairdresser. The King, who quickly understood his wife's weakness and her love of money, took a dim view of Eleonora's suitor. He ignored the letter of introduction sent by the Grand Duke of Tuscany: "He belongs to a family that is very well regarded by Their Highnesses and he would like to settle in France and will serve there with fidelity and diligence to gain the good graces of His Majesty." Concini would secure his position only by persuading the Queen to tolerate the presence at the court of Henriette d'Entragues, one of the King's innumerable mistresses. On July 12, 1601, the King granted his union with Eleonora.

That day, the irresistible rise of the most shameful couple of France began. The bride, having become a lady-in-waiting, always present, always heeded, had rooms close to the apartments of Marie de Médicis. Concini, superintendent of the House, was named first royal equerry. In 1603, their son Henri was born; his godfather was a prince of blood, his godmother, the queen herself. In 1607, their daughter Marie arrived. The Princess de Condé and Henri IV carried her to the baptismal font.

When Concino was entrusted with the task of choosing among State office-seekers, he constrained the applicants to pay "considerations;" this trading in favors, carried out with the assistance

of Eleonora and with the complicity of the queen (the primary benefici-
ary of these *combinazione),* enriched the Italian trio. When the civil lieutenant to the Parliament of Paris died in 1609, Marie left it to her favorites to find a successor. President Le Jay had to pay 150,000 livres, not
counting the "pins"[6] intended for the queen's pincushion (she was a
frightful gold digger[7]).

This all-consuming passion clarifies the role of Concini: there
were no State markets, no transmission of taxes, no fines paid, on
which Marie did not receive a generous commission. The system almost broke down when Antoine Allory, declared the highest bidder for
"the collections from the five large farms" for 886,000 livres, was victim
of too obvious a racket. What was his by law on one day, was denied
him the next day by whim. To the Duke de Guise, who expressed his
surprise, the sovereign off-handedly answered, "See the Marquise and
straighten it out with her." When Eleonora received the plaintiff, she
presented her logarithms: "I have calculated, Sir, the income that your
duties will bring you: 600,000 livres per annum. Thus, it is appropriate
that you bring a consequent amount up front." He proposed 30,000
livres. A paltry sum. "You jest," she countered. The Queen, called upon
to lend her assistance, took refuge behind her laconic refrain: "Speak to
the Marquise." A few days later Pierre de La Sablière, a man who knew
his way around, secured the account for a sum of 60,000 livres for the
royal pins and 10,000 livres per annum throughout the lease.

But the auction was not over. Allory insisted: 36,000 livres for
the pins, 60,000 livres on the future benefit. Eleonora found this proposal outrageous. The Chamber of the Accounts got involved, and
came down in favor of the one who had been scorned. On the injunction of Marie de Médicis, the King's Council ordered the magistrates
"to bypass the verification of the lease, notwithstanding any contrary
opposition." The tight overlap between government funds, the queen's
pin money, and the interests of her favorites set loose a villainous
mechanism that upset the people and outraged the princes.

History would serve the couple's intentions well. On May 13,
1610, Marie de Médicis received the Crown of France. May 14: Ravaillac attacked the King. May 15: The Queen was named regent of the
kingdom and the *"lit de justice"* (the Parliament), which ensured the triumph of Concini, who, seated to her left, became in three days' time the
most powerful man in the country. "If you had not known me in my
degradation," he admitted one day to Bassompierre,[8] "I would try to

hide it from you. But you saw me in Florence, debauched and *scapilatte* (dissolute), sometimes in prison, sometimes banished, and generally without money." The dissolute was out of the picture, the parvenu held the regent under his spell and France under his scepter. In July 1610, he was admitted to the Council and the Queen authorized him to draw promissory notes on the Treasury for any amount and for any recipient.

He had everything that a man can wish for, except popularity and peace at home. An avaricious woman of petit-bourgeois tastes, Eleonora kept an eye on her collection box and piled up her gold. Florence, Genoa, Venice, Antwerp, Augsburg, all havens for those guilty of embezzlement, were put to use in sheltering from inquisitive eyes more than 1,800,000 livres. It was a fortune: the budget of the entire kingdom was 20 million livres; that of the queen, 400,000 livres. Eleonora pressed her husband to end his party in France and to return to the lenient peninsula. But money isn't everything; Concini (like today's speculators, gilded by Wall Street and its offshoots) was looking for more prestige. For 330,000 livres, he purchased the marquisat of Ancre and assumed the title. In spite of Sully's opposition (he was still a minister) and that of Nicolaï (head of the Court of Auditors), the regent — generous with her subjects' money — subsidized this acquisition and exempted the new marquis from paying the feudal and seigniorial rights. Condé launched his barb: "He had the Comté of *Penna*,[9] he has acquired the marquisat of *Ancre* [rhymes with "ink," in French] Now, he only needs a paper duchy." There would be little need of that.

February 1611: Concini is appointed king's general lieutenant in Picardy, which he wants to make his fief and, in case of trouble, his fortified camp. This *scapilatte* who, as he was leaving his birthplace, said, "I want to see how far fortune can carry a man," was gaining territory: Péronne, Roye, Montdidier, the citadel of Amiens were in his control. Seizing the depths of France did not distract him form the thought of Paris, the capital of his ambition.

He bought from the Duke de Bouillon, for 200,000 livres, the rank of first gentleman of the Chamber, with the right to sleep in a room close to the young King's, and not far from the regent's apartments. This was too bold a step and the peers, who had tolerated his sacking of France's finances, rose up in indignation to see such a good-for-naught contaminating the tabernacle of French legitimacy. This Italian presence insults the King, they insisted, and compromises his mother, whose reputation is sullied. Concini had to capitulate, and he moved out.

The following year, Marie took her revenge. She offered her adviser a parcel of land at the edge of the Seine, alongside the palace, to build a mansion. A bridge, dubbed the "bridge of love," enabled him to gain the intimacy of the sovereign with dry feet. The French adore conducting open heart surgery on their kings, and Marie de Médicis and Concini posed an enigma to historical voyeurism. Was this copious Rubens, whose fleshy form was in decline, seduced by the intelligence and brawn of her compatriot?[10] We are hardly giving out prizes for virtue, in this book, but it appears improbable to me, in spite of the salacious Parisian rumors suggesting that Ruggieri, the astrologer, had succeeded with his potions, formulas and horoscopes, to awaken the attenuated senses of the royal widow and to tantalize the explosive temperament of Her lover.

1613. Seeing that he could not become Constable, Concini, the soul of military commitment, took advantage of the death of one of the kingdom's six marshals and satisfied himself with the more modest rank, becoming Marshal of France. The revolt of the nobles, the bane of Louis XIV's adolescence, makes us forget the smaller rebellions that preceded the Fronde rebellion that darkened the ripe old age of Marie de Médicis and the role played by the Italian — who was savior, for a time, of French national unity. The high and mighty, jealous of this con man whose courtly gowns would supplant their armor, conceived a plot. Marie was called a usurper, for not having summoned the Estates General (the only body qualified to constitute the Council of Regency) upon her husband's assassination. Their head, Henri de Bourbon, Prince de Condé (with his beautiful wife Charlotte de Montmorency, who was easily persuaded to join the cause), aspired to a national destiny. He had plenty of pretexts for raising the ragged standard of aristocratic rebellion: pro-Spanish diplomatic policy; the excessively pious Queen's support for the ultramontanes and the papists; the ambassador from Madrid with his ghoulish entourage; the abandoned policy of cooperation between the Catholic powers and the Protestant states. These objections formed a facade, insidious and populist, to encourage "all good Frenchman" to send Marie, the Iberian marriages[11] and the foreigners all to the devil.

But the reality was more materialistic. The privileged few were up in arms against increased tax pressures, falling pensions, the devaluation of sinecures, and the requirement to share their power with parvenus. "Wayward in every sense, prodigal, selling men and reputations, prostituting all the orders of the kingdom . . . where there is no more reward for virtue since favor and money have are all that matter to these people who grow rich without working, off the blood of the people."

The dukes set up a resistance, and after Condé, Nevers, Mayenne, Bouillon, and Longueville went underground in their provinces, demanded that the matrimonial plans be abandoned; and they dreamed (already then) of attacking the Bastille to seize the treasure set aside by Henri IV.[12] Lastly, they demanded a meeting of the Estates General. In January 1614, they let their guns do the talking, and the French civil war raged again. The capricious performance of the weapons gave each camp both successes and reversals, without either side getting the upper hand. Since peace could not be obtained by force, Concini, ever pragmatic, decided to buy it.

April 14, 1614. The Sainte-Menehould treaty put an end to the confrontation. It cost the Crown a million livres and an indemnity of 450,000 livres to be divided between the rebels to cover their expenses. This treasure chest, added to the two million livres received by Condé two years earlier, demolished Henri IV's deflationary policy; soup with a grimace replaced the chicken in every pot. October 27, 1614, the Estates General met: 140 deputies from the clergy,[13] 132 delegates from the nobility, and 192 representatives of the third estate[14] gathered in Paris; they were seated separately. The nobility, supported by the majority of the clergy, opposed the prevailing power with a redoubtable unanimity. The third estate, which wanted a king who would be "emperor within his kingdom," found itself supporting the monarch, who was recalled to his duties by the spokesman, Robert Miron. Kneeling, as custom decrees, he did not, however, grovel: "Excessive expenditures reduce the people to feeding and grazing like animals . . . the poor work ceaselessly, sparing neither their bodies nor their hearts, that is, their lives, to feed the whole kingdom." Then, he challenged Louis: "Who gives Your Majesty the means of maintaining royal dignity, covering the necessary expenses of the State, inside as well as outside the kingdom? Who gives you the means of raising an army? Who? The ploughman."

The confrontation begun that day would go on for a century and a half. When the third estate proclaimed, "The three Estates are three brothers, children of their common mother, France," the nobility flung back this answer: "There is no fraternity between us and the members of the Third Estate. We do not want the children of the shoemakers and cobblers to call us brothers. There is as great a difference between us and the others as there is between the master and the servant." Figaro, and Diderot's Jacques le Fataliste, would answer to this nonsense. The Estates General of 1614 prefigured those of 1789, where the King's procrastination, his brothers' complacency, his wife's deficiencies, and the blindness of a whole caste are explained by their confusing the end of the 18th century and the beginning of the 17th. Louis XVI thought he could treat his delegates as Marie de Médicis did hers, and extricate himself with a few vague promises. He did not understand that the Revolution was inevitable once the Third Estate converted itself into a National Assembly and competed with him for legitimacy.

Marie de Médicis — illegitimate regent that she was — was saved by the separation of the Orders, and by the cunning of Concini (more effective than the genius of Mirabeau). He enabled the power to make commitments that were purely formal: ending the *paulette*,[15] abolishing payment for government posts, reducing the pensions, fighting to reduce the corruption and punishment that would make examples of those guilty of embezzlement.

"Promises make fools merry." None was kept, and the regime came out stronger after this close brush with danger. Deluded once again, Condé denounced the Italians as liars and railed against the aspirations of Spain, who obstructed his monarchical ambitions, and called for the departure of "the Marshals of Ancre," who were responsible for all these woes.

A few months before the nuptials in Bordeaux of Louis XIII and Anne of Austria in December 1615, the insurrectionists attacked and their revolt devastated the countryside again. "The soldiers of both armies are ruining the country . . . they force themselves on girls, even in the churches, and then they tie them to the trees, as food for the crows. . . That cannot go on," Bartolini wrote to the Grand Duke of Tuscany, "God must step in." In the absence of the Eternal, Concini, considered to be a pantomime of a soldier, confounded the scandalmongers and thrashed Condé's and Longueville's troops at Clermont-in-Beauvais. Flattering writers would transform this great miscreant into "a real war chief," "a good servant of His Majesty;" and he began to dream again of the attributes of constable. While waiting to receive his stripes, the marshal, shaken by the attempted murder from which he barely escaped, allowed Villeroi[16] to treat the plenipotentiaries with a questionable generosity, and the treaty of Loudun depleted the Treasury still further: Condé received 300,000 livres; Vendôme, 100,000; Luxembourg, 500,000; Sully, 300,000; Rohan, 200,000; Mayenne, 300,000.[17]

This reward for rebellion only strengthened them in their cause, and the dukes did not hold back in crucifying the accursed couple. "Ambition, Sire, and the insatiable avarice of the Marshal of Ancre and his wife are the sole causes of the evils from which we suffer . . . it is the ulcer that has practically spoiled and infected the body of your State . . . The remedy, Sire, is in your hands . . . drive out the Marshal of Ancre, his wife and her followers from your sacred presence and that of the Queen your mother, and allow justice to punish the many crimes of which they are guilty towards your State." The little people, enflamed by this defamatory campaign, followed the example of the blue-bloods and covered "Les Conchines" with insults. Graffiti was scrawled all over the walls of their house on rue Tournon, which was baptized by the hate-filled imagination of the writers, "principality of Lucifer," "brothel district," "kingdom of the Demon," "sewer of the savages," "home of the heartless."

This alliance between a certain slice of the aristocracy and the rabble flushed out the quarry: the game was up for the Marshal, for Eleonora and for this particular form of absolutism; it was the last refrain in the song of feudalism. Cunning keeps death at bay, and Concini, the royal favorite spoiled by good fortune, transformed himself into chief minister, giving birth to the vision that was refined by Richelieu and Mazarin. A great politician, he restored monarchical power vis-a-vis the protesters. As an irony (of which history is so fond), this corrupt figure surrounded himself with collaborators above all suspicion: Barbin, the upright Controller of Finances; the incorruptible Mangot, the original Mr. Clean and Minister of Justice. For Foreign Affairs, he called upon a certain Armand du Plessis, a young prelate aged thirty-one. This war ministry would put an end to the disorder: "If need be, we will resort to force and to violence; but complete obedience will be obtained from everyone. . . We now regard the war as having been declared. The Queen-Mother is prepared to risk all for all," wrote the Venetian ambassador, a diplomat-spy, to his government.

Concini thus took in hand the affairs of France. Italian-style. He brought on his own undoing — by saving the regime, he lost his own cause. To allow the Sun King to rise tomorrow on Versailles, he decided to put Condé in the shade. The prince, who already considered himself regent in place of the corpulent Marie, conspired quite openly but he was fishing at the edge of Rubicon instead of crossing it. When he went to the Louvre, the marshal of Ancre (in a shocking breach of the rules of hospitality) had him arrested by the Swiss guards. The King's cousin reacted the same way as the Duke de Guise ("They will never dare," he said, before being stabbed by Henri III's men). This noble insouciance led the chief of the rebellion to the Bastille, happy to have escaped alive from the trap. His arrest was not just a stab in the back, it amounted to a coup d'etat and the insult to the nobility provoked the sacking of the beautiful house of Concini. "The damage was great, paintings, gilt carvings, marbles, clothing, linens, furniture, tapestries, vases, medals of gold and silver, and an infinity of those beautiful curiosities that the Great Ones have in their cabinets."

January 17, 1617. The King summoned the rebels to surrender on pain of being declared lese-majesty and incurring the rigors of the law. February 12: The princes retorted with an insolent injunction to their sovereign. "Seeing the extraordinary favor accorded to this foreigner who gives away the government of your territories, relieves the old principal officers of your council and your Parliaments, and snatches from their very hands the titles of honor that their age, their virtue and their merit had earned them, to set up in their places his own creatures, unworthy people, inexperienced in conducting a State *(so much for the young Richelieu)* and people born into servitude *(so much for Barbin, the commoner)*."[18] These gestures hardly affected the marshal, who wanted to finish off the putschists. He had English troops waiting in Picardy, Brittany, and in Normandy; and everywhere, in Nivernais, Champagne, Ile de France, loyal troops and Swiss mercenaries (recruited at great expense) were defeating the noblemen's troops. Victory seemed close at hand, and Concini regained Paris to impose on the rebels a treaty that would have enabled France to avoid the Fronde, the *real* rebellion.

The young Louis XIII decided otherwise. It was repugnant to him to see a foreigner become the benefactor of the French monarchy; he did not wish to be so indebted to a villain. Egged on by Charles de Luynes, his dear friend, he was anxious to be rid of his mother's favorite. Between the two deputies, the fight was unequal — while Concini dominated the queen, Luynes held sway over the King. The first was capable of every form of cunning, the second, of every baseness. With the help of his brothers, he took the lead in the plot of which Vitry, courtier and future marshal, would be the secular arm. The King, central character in this tragedy that was played "inside the Louvre and under the very nose of the Queen," called Concini to his office to allow his henchmen to arrest him. "And if he resists, Sire?" The monarch stared into space.

The morning of April 24, 1617, in the bosom of the château, a desacralized haven, Vitry hailed the marshal. "In the name of the King, I arrest you." In the confusion that followed, five shots were fired at close range; two missed, one struck him between the eyes, a second lodged behind his ear, and a third slashed his throat. His body was hacked by the swords of cowards who hoped to share in the glory of this assassination. "In words choked with tears and joy," Louis incoherently congratulated his accomplices. "I am a King now, I am your King. I was before, but I am now and will be, so help me God, more than ever." Then, he started over. "You will say to my Court and my Parliament that Concini was killed while resisting those whom I had commanded to arrest him." This was no longer a matter of justice served, but of murder.

Concini's corpse was torn from the tomb and dragged through Paris to the general jubilation. The rabble, and higher people too, added their own touches: hands and feet chopped off, back and belly branded with red-hot iron — the cock was de-cocked and his attributes, stuck on a halberd, gave one last impression of virility. Since Antiquity, the spectacle of death has been an entertainment, and the grimaces of victims, the contortions of anguish, make spectators squirm with pleasure. While the people were dancing with a corpse and indulging themselves in incredible scenes of cannibalism, Eleonora, still alive, was in despair. In the anteroom to the Great Beyond, she learned that Parliament had decided to try the marshal and his heritage at the same time they would be trying her.

The charges were far-ranging. Against Concini: breaching the external and internal security of the State, illicit weapons sales and, needless to say, corruption. Against Eleonora: abuse of public funds, trading in favors[19] and, of course, sorcery, which made her liable to torture. This accusation, which we first encountered while discussing the affairs of Jacques Coeur, was used then the way charges of tax evasion are used today. It is a way of getting to those who believe they are immune to prosecution. The investigation proceeded as anticipated, and revealed worrisome practices on the part of the marshal's wife: relations with the devil — surprising in such a pious woman; fear of evil spells; inexplicable healings. But the prosecutors especially reproached Eleonora "for having protected Jews who had been persecuted for publicly practicing their religion." That was all that was required to see this wretched, hypertrophic woman, remanded to her executioner after a mockery of a trial. "The Court has declared and does declare the aforementioned Concini, and Galigaï, his widow, guilty of divine and human lese-majesty; and in reparation, it has condemned and does condemn the aforementioned Concini *in perpetuity* and the aforementioned Galigaï to have their heads removed on a scaffold to be built for that purpose in the Place de Grève, in this City of Paris, their bodies and heads burnt and reduced to ashes." Then, to allow the assassins to touch the fruits of their crimes, the square hats commanded "that their feudal possessions and their personal belongings be "immediately removed and incorporated into the domains of the Crown of France, their holdings and belongings having been acquired from this kingdom are hereby confiscated in the name of the King."

When she learned her fate, Eleonora said simply, "*Oh ime, poveretta,*" then, in the cart encircled by a howling mob, she murmured: "So many people just to watch a poor victim passing by." Contrary to du Barry, another adventuress, she did not beg the executioner to grant her one last postponement.

For how much difference to such prolongations make to posterity? Collective memory and the authority of the court make any revision impossible and the caricature will continue to take the place of the portrait. Concini and Galigaï have entered, for all time, the hell of French national imagery. The author of this book will not achieve anything, and the readers will blame him for trying to excuse the inexcusable. However, it is not my fault if history is an anamorphosis whose events reach us through the deforming prism of the humors of those who recompose it.

The legend of Concini, blackened by the pride of the great and the jealousy of the small, was woven by a nationalism that cannot tolerate the thought of an Italian looking down on, or taking the place of, good Frenchmen. "Italy was the forge where all the sources of our misfortunes were hardened, where all treasons, disloyalties and perfidies were conceived," fulminated a pamphleteer. In Louis XIII's funeral oration, a monk, Father Lingendes, spoke in praise of murder: "On April 24 1617, on the bridge from the Louvre, in response to the ongoing refusal to obey the orders of the King, fire and iron were employed to cut the root of so contagious an evil, which threatened the security of the entire kingdom . . . a monstrous colossus of Fortune was reversed by not allowing it any chance to grow." This frightening apologia drowned out the timid whisperings of a few courageous contemporaries: d'Estrées, Héroard,[20] Bassompierre, who stigmatized "the stunning death sentence against the Marshal's wife, on the pretext of magic with which she never meddled."

Not until the 18th century will we hear a real plea: Voltaire's. In his *Essai sur les moeurs,* the advocate of tolerance recriminates the Parliament that takes orders, condemns "a cruel injustice," "a rage of hatred endorsed by the judiciary, to mask approval of murder with a legal cruelty. There was no cause for reproaching the Marshal's wife; she was the queen's favorite, and that was her only crime." This generosity went un-echoed. The historian Michelet, the great hallucinator, traces a sooty portrait of Eleonora "the witch:" "A kind of dark dwarf with sinister eyes like coals from hell. . . She believed that anyone who stared at her was casting a spell on her. She always wore a veil for fear of the evil eye. France, bright and merry, a country of light, must have been odious to her. She must have become darker and more perverted with every year, and become more and more malicious." Vigny, jealous of the images painted by Victor Hugo and Alexandre Dumas, succumbed in his turn to the contagion. In *La Maréchale d'Ancre,* he repeats on his own account Sully's calumnies and makes Concini the emasculated accomplice of Ravaillac. Thus literary error exonerates, once again, the miscarriage of justice.

Footnotes

1. *Concini: grandeurs et miseres du favori de Marie de Médicis*, Albin Michel, 1991.
2. *Concini.*
3. The French particularly hated the Italians; at the beginning of the century, there were pogroms in Marseilles against the "Babis" — as the southern French called the people of the peninsula.
4. According to Michelet's description in *La Sorciere*.
5. See the portrait of Concino Concini, copied by Denis Cocq in 1834, in the museum of Versailles.
6. "Pin money": a nice name for not so nice a practice. This is what they called covert payoffs.
7. "Inventory of the Queen's purchases of diamonds" is a detailed statement of her expenditures for jewels, covering the period when Marie lived in France until 1631.
8. François de Bassompierre, a marshal faithful to the regent, would later be sent to the Bastille for twelve years by Richelieu.
9. Concini was a count of Penna, "Penna" in Italian meaning feather.
10. Concini, who enjoyed all forms of entertainment, was passionately devoted to sports. In his *Memoirs*, the marshal of Estrées says he is "pleasant in his person, skilful with the horse and all the games..."
11. Marital unions planned in order to cement the new alliance between France and Spain: Louis XIII was to marry Anne of Austria, daughter of Philippe III; Elisabeth, daughter of Marie de Médicis, had been promised to the duke of Savoy but would instead marry the prince of Asturies, heir to the Iberian throne.
12. Seven million livres patiently accrued during the reign of the good king.
13. Where Richelieu sat and was selected to read the notebook of complaints.
14. In this assembly of commoners, 121 were royal officers, including 114 in the judiciary.
15. A tax instituted by Henri IV, allowing positions to be passed down to one's descendants. This innovation was a setback for the aristocracy, who were increasingly excluded from the administrative offices of the kingdom.
16. The Regent's Secretary of State , favorable to the aristocrats; Concini did away with it.
17. Never mind the governorship of Berry, the harbor office of Bourges, the city and the château of Chinon for Condé, and the maintenance, by the Crown, of the men-at-arms of these unrepentant factions.
18. The King's would remember this insolence.
19. For the sake of clarity, I am using terms borrowed from modern law.
20. The young king's doctor.

Chapter 4

RICHELIEU

Armand-Jean du Plessis, Cardinal and Duke de Richelieu, 1585-1642. Controlled King Louis XIII from 1624 onward; instituted royal absolutism, reducing the nobility's power.

> "Through uncommon industry, one managed to persuade the Huguenots to accept the peace agreement out of fear of that of Spain, and the Spaniards to make peace, out of fear of that of the Huguenots."
>
> Richelieu, *Memoirs*

> "Gold and money are the tyrants of the world."
>
> Richelieu, *Testament*

Richelieu. R as in rigor, religiosity, and rapacity. The Great Cardinal was Evil incarnate — according to the romantic vulgate dispensed by Alexandre Dumas[1] and Victor Hugo — while the king, who represented Good (and a certain weakness) enjoys our compassion. A pleasing image for one, a repellant image for the other; these are misleading views reinforced by the flourish of capes and swords. How much could the authors of *The Three Musketeers* and *Marion Delorme* retain of the era that had sunken into grandiloquence and embroidery, how much depth could they give to this inflexible man who gave birth to the France of the Great Century, "the most beautiful kingdom after that of Heaven"[2] and who embodied every contradiction: measure, violence, grace and restraint, corruption, misery?

Richelieu, that steely kill-joy, invented and imposed absolutism, the basis of his *Political Testament*. That document, the final text of which was pulled together three centuries later from disparate sources, was disseminated under the table and Voltaire refused to believe that it was penned by the *Eminence Rouge*. "The reader can hardly summon enough patience to read it, and it would be ignored if any less famous name had been attached to it."

Far from the rigid program of instruction that legend suggests

Richelieu promoted, he taught Louis XIII the love of power and the need for a centralizing monarchy. Using and misusing the word "Reason," he saw himself as master of the land and the seas, the arbiter of fine speech, the founder of the Academy, the referee in the quarrel between Corneille and Scudéry,[3] the go-between in the ambiguous loves of the king, the dictator of French unity. The ultimate political man, and a mediocre dramatic author,[4] he confused epic breath with historic breadth. In fact, his tragedies were not particularly interesting. His admirers were those who cared more about his warlike virtues than his theatrical virtuosity; the stage on which he displayed his true worth was France itself.

For in order to control everything and to satisfy his passion for money, the basis of his power, he brazenly commingled his funds with the public funds and inaugurated a new form of delinquency, patriotic corruption. "We have always said that finance is the life blood of the State... Gold and silver are the tyrants of the world, and although their power and their dominion are unjust, there are times that are so irrational that we must submit to their domination and there are times when things are so disturbed that it is impossible not to suffer their entirely insupportable yoke." This pious and abstruse maxim did not prevent him from falling into financial foolishness and did not prevent the historian Daniel Dessert[5] from condemning him for "double talk." But is it duplicitous, indeed? With the cardinal, double talk was the same as straight talk and, at the time, there was no distinction between the interests of a first minister and those of the State. This crossover enabled him to take his place among the corrupt officials who were necessary to a kingdom that, consequently, was deeply in their debt. His tentacular system (already outlined under Sully) met four requirements: *to restore the grandeur of the State* that was mocked by the egoism of the feudalists; *to give the law enough force* to subjugate them; *to ensure the rise of the commercial and industrial classes*; *to found an autocracy resting on continuous confrontation*, to reduce Austria and Spain, to play as equals with the maritime powers, England and the United Provinces (the Dutch Republic). These obsessions would ensure France's supremacy in Europe and prepare the advent of the Great Empire.

The royalty installed by Richelieu, inherently bellicose, could survive only in and by war; one cannot appreciate the epic and the mishaps of the Bourbons without referring to the cardinal doctrines of permanent conflict. War was the lifeblood of a necessarily aggressive regime. When it stopped, the state, lacking logic and justification, would disintegrate. Toward the end of his reign Louis XV, aware of this curse, thought to implement reforms to head off the implosion (Maupeou,[6] as Chancellor, temporarily got the better of the Parlements, overriding their attempts to block the proposed reforms), but Louis' innovative course was cut short by his departure in 1774 for, at best, Purgatory. Louis XVI would do well in America but, yearning for complete harmony, he ended up dying of his pacifism. The red hats, condemned to perpetuate the policies of the crimson gowns, would confront all of Europe, shedding blood in order to impose happiness (a new idea) upon it.

The Little Corporal, ultimate heir to the Great Cardinal, would follow his example; but Waterloo put an end to this typically French confusion between size and terror. Terror was imposed by Richelieu through his secret police, who comprised all forms of duplicity, with louts and hooligans from all over the kingdom. To ensure his own safety and to terrorize the terrorists, he surrounded himself by a personal guard: 120 light horsemen, 100 men-at-arms, 200 musketeers. In Alexandre Dumas' trilogy, they would pursue the outraged Constance and hound Buckingham, the Queen's intransigent and calculating lover. To end the internal squabbling and to destroy the ruling cliques, he got rid of the pious party, in November 1630, on of the Day of Dupes.[7] The King, called upon to choose between his mother and his minister, made the right choice and sided with Richelieu. Family feeling yielded before the interests of the State, and an astonished Marie de Medicis was obliged to take the path of ingratitude and exile. To recall the nobles to prudence, he forbade public duels (in remembrance of his brother Henri, slain in 1619 in one of those imbecilic combats that were decimating the country's elite). After the cardinal's death, the nobility would again fall into this ruinous jousting. "Since the regency, 940 gentlemen have been killed in duel," the marshal of Gramont would write. This number is artificially low, for it was customary to lie to the families in order to spare them concerns over the eternal well-being of their dear departed.

Richelieu's policies were followed from 1624 — the year he came to power — until 1815, when the monarchy would be weakened in peace. His logic was not that of Reason, as it was understood in the 18th century, but a rationality that was close to that of Descartes or St.

Thomas, who sought to dominate the world by concentrating on relentless principles. Voltaire, in the introduction to his *Century of Louis XIV*, would speak of "the lack of outstanding performers in every aspect of State governance" to explain the cardinal's role. Nietzsche was thinking of him when he wrote, "The 17th century suffers from man as a sum of contradictions. . . it seeks to discover man, to command him, to exhume him." Was Richelieu the first enlightened despot? Tirelessly seeking divine protection, he added a pinch of the Good Lord to his Testament dedicated to the king, preparing the way for Bossuet and his *Politique tirée des propos de l'Écriture Sainte* (*Politics derived from remarks in the Holy Scriptures*).[8] His method is a systematics (more than a system), and we must return to his personal history to understand how, in order to govern, he gained control over such a breadth of power and such a wealth of gold.

In the 16th century (that of the wars of religion), the Richelieus were a minor lineage and their name, that of the manor owned by the du Plessis family in Berry, was not in the least outstanding. They belonged to the weak provincial nobility, scraping together a living out of their rents, and making their home in a very modest place. The grandfather, married to a Rochechouart, of illustrious stock but of its weakest branch, derived little advantage from this alliance. His son, François du Plessis, the future cardinal's father, married Suzanne de La Porte, daughter of a lawyer at the Parlement of Paris. Was it a poor match? Not necessarily. The lawyers were, at the time, a considerable power (may God never allow that again!) and the dowry of 10,000 livres improved the standard of living but left the young groom mired in an anonymity that he aspired to escape.

After the "purifying" massacre of St.-Barthélemy, the Catholic factions were disemboweled, while the Huguenots led by Henri de Navarre transcended tragedy and set out again on the attack. Tumult! François du Plessis, clairvoyant, sided with the future Henri III, who named him grand provost; then he served Navarre and became captain of his guard. Five years after Armand's birth, God, indifferent to the whims of the century, called François to Him with his military stripes and his debts intact, thus depriving him of the ecumenical triumph of Henri IV. Du Plessis' wife was forced to pledge the ring he was given as a knight of the Holy Spirit to cover the funeral costs. The bishopric of Luçon, the only jewel in a poor patrimony, a "blessing of Divine Grace" according to the Testament, hardly changed the family circumstances. "Impoverished nobility is such a great pity," wrote Armand who, shortly, would only be looking back at yesterday's miseries. After the father's death, the roles were distributed between his three sons: Henri, the eldest, joined the court; Alphonse, the second, the Church; Armand, the youngest, the king's army. Everything seemed to have gone according to tradition. But let's not discount the mystic powers, the spiritual agitator of era. The future prelate gave up his seat, forsook worldly life, and died of his ecstasies. To preserve this one advantage for the family, Henri IV named Armand to take Alphonse's place as Bishop of Luçon, in 1606. He was only 21 years old, and needed a papal exemption to allow him to take the mitre. Thus he departed for Rome, added a year to his age, deceived the sovereign pontiff, and obtained his authorization before confessing his lie. "This boy will be a great deceiver," His Holiness predicted.

In "the muddiest bishopric in France," the young man revealed his exceptional qualities: as a reformer, diplomat, and administrator of hearts and goods. He reminded the religious denizens of Fontevrault of their vows (to the eminent satisfaction of the queen mother), converted Protestants, and restored order and piety in his diocese. Luçon was his first draft; later he would work on all of France. Varied and ambiguous, virtuous and in love with things of nature, he composed a curious work: *Instructions and maxims that I have given myself to guide my conduct at Court.* I heartily recommend this Stendhalian breviary for the perfect *arriviste* to anyone who frequents the Elysée and Matignon. It was quite useful to Armand upon his arrival at the Louvre, where Marie des Medici and her Italian *camarilla* were engaged in a power struggle. At the Estates General of 1614, where the bishop Jean-Pierre Camus distinguished himself (a friend of François de Sales and a great overlooked writer), the young du Plessis presented the book of the clergy's complaints. Cautiously visionary, it criticized the medieval prejudice against having the servants of God direct the affairs of Caesar. When the parliamentary turbulences were over, he served the regent, looked after her favorite, spied on everyone, and waited for his moment to come. In December 1616, thanks to protection Eleonora Concini's protection, he became Secretary of State in charge of Foreign Affairs in the transitory cabinet cobbled together by her husband.

After Concini's assassination, the disgraced cardinal shared the exile of the queen mother and supported her in her bellicose attempts against her son; but he soon realized his error. "Those who fight against a legitimate power are half-undone through their own imagination," he would say, after his reconciliation with the king. Upon the death of Luynes, his intrigues paid off. Cardinal by 1622, he managed to get into the exclusive Council in April 1624, was its leader by August, and five years later became chief minister. "I won the prize by turning my back to it, like the oarsmen," he conceded in his Testament. A man of God, he demolished the separatist Protestants; a man of the church, he subjected it to the king; a man of order, he crushed the troublemaking princes; a statesman, he engaged the power in a regenerating war against Spain; a man of money, he combined his personal accounts and the Treasury. In short, he played politics.

Before he attained these honors, Richelieu, penniless, had disputed bitterly with the other legatees over Henri's heritage. He has even been accused of having invented false creditors to his brother's estate in order to bilk the real ones. Pessimists and certain financial analysts say that great fortunes thrive on accounts where mud is mixed with gold. Here is where Richelieu's found its first fertilizing compost, and in less than twenty years, this poor young man would become the richest person in the kingdom. What is the income of a cardinal, or a chief minister? The Council paid him 2,000 livres; his ministry, 20,000; his title, 18,000. The *Ancien Régime*, provider of emoluments of all kinds, knew nothing of the separation of goods and functions. All his life, Richelieu would take advantage of this license, piling up ecclesiastical benefices, land, offices, and government posts. His Eminence, having become the salutary plunderer of the kingdom, sank into an austere opulence, in the name of the God of poverty.

He began by getting his hands on land that enabled him to become the equal of the impoverished great feudal lords who were constrained, from 1623 onward, to sell him their estates at discounted prices. The château and the county of Limours, the royal domain of Montlhéry (which he would sell shortly thereafter at a profit of 300,000 livres), the "small holdings" of Plessis-Billebault, Vaux, Chambronne, the Angennes mansion in the St.-Honoré district in Paris, the seigniory of Baussay, and those of Moray, Avert and St.-Luc, Mirebeau, Beaufort-in-Valley, Ile-Bouchard, and Bois-le-Vicomte. According to the inventory drawn up after his death, the cardinal invested more than five million livres in land holdings, concentrating in his hands a vast portion of the country (the body of which he felt he personified, leaving to the king the symbol). When Richelieu became a landowner, France was dispensing usufructs again and shared the bounty with him. In 1631, the seigniory of Faye was renamed "Richelieu;" and he laid out the contours of the new city, with the architect Jacques Lemercier. To populate his duchy-peerage, he exempted it from the salt tax, giving it an advantageous fiscal status that transformed it into a kind of tax-free zone, beyond the reach of the gluttonous collectors. However, candidates were hardly competing to move there, and Richelieu remained a deserted burg, in spite of the audacity of its design. "The plan, along right angles, was implemented according to the most rational principles, thus forming one of the most coherent examples of small urbanism,"[9] as the celebrated art historian, Sir Anthony Blunt, would write. It was a stark contrast to Paris, still dominated by its Gothic turrets, its malodorous alleys, and general disorder, the "embarrassments" that would inspire the lively writings of Boileau.

While land confers titles and income, ecclesiastical benefits, even if they fail to sanctify, enrich their holder. The cardinal, dreaming of a Gallic Catholicism of impressive severity and rigor (this would find its ultimate and excessive expression in Jansenism), joined in the ultramontane aspirations of the Queen, Anne of Austria, but without neglecting the attractions of the profane. This was an odd duality in a sincere and pragmatic believer who tied his cash box to the Middle Ages and his mind to the political requirements of his own century. What is a benefice? According to canon law, it is an income inseparable from a dignity of the Church. When the young scatterbrain de Guise wanted to give up his emoluments to marry the princess of Gonzague, Richelieu gave him a lesson in arithmetic. "Think this through seriously; you have 400,000 livres of incomes in benefice; you intend to give them up for a woman. How many others would agree to give up 400,000 women to keep the money?" He himself did not give up anything, and piled up bishoprics, abbeys, priories: Ile-Chauvet, Moreille, Redon, St.-Benoît-sur-Loire, St.-Sauveur, St.-Martin-de-Tours, Pontelevoy, St.-Pierre-de-Châlons. . . All the Saints of the calendar. At Cluny, one of God's strongholds and hostile to the king, he had to resort to *lettres de cachet* to impose his way. His greed was not restrained by any Lent; to disarm those who would reproach him, he answered: "I wish to increase my benefices as much as I can. . . so that those who come after me will have occasion to pray for me." Failing to ensure himself a place at the right hand of the Father, he was frantically raking up the goods of our Holy Mother, which enabled him to play as an equal with the high-ranking dignitaries, adversaries of his religious and political vision, and to blend, once more, his interests and those of the kingdom. They would be merged still further when he launched out to attack the offices.

According to Loyseau, an office is "a dignity with public office, which implies a delegation of the sovereign's authority." Their venality, abolished the night of August 4, gave way to a trafficking that had been growing since François I. Power, which always needs more money, expanded the number of positions in order to take in the corresponding fees. Richelieu, after Concini and before Mazarin, became an intermediary in this lucrative and not very admissible practice, thus adding abuse of power to embezzlement. 1619: He is named superintendent of the House of the Queen Mother; 1621, her grand chaplain; 1623, President of the Council. Until the estrangement in 1630, Marie de Medicis heaped him with benefices, including the Petit-Luxembourg, near to her own palace. (This debatable success of pseudo-Italian style, minus the charm and harmony, was built by Solomon de Brosse. Today it is the seat of the Senate, where the wise leaders of the Republic sit.) During this epoch, Richelieu was collecting governorships. Le Havre, Honfleur, Harfleur, Brouage, La Rochelle (which he entered, October 30, 1628, wearing armor as a triumphant victor), and Nantes, offered by the States of Brittany. Joseph Bergin bridles about it: "The governors' income was not limited to their official salaries. Much more important were the coincidental, even hidden and illicit, receipts. States, cities and corporations were in the habit of currying the favor and the goodwill of their governor through substantial gifts. The governors did not hesitate, either, to take their share of the taxes or to find their own illegal royalties. They extorted bribes from officers and from others requesting their protection."[10] But Richelieu was no ordinary extortionist. When he extended his power, he was consolidating the unity of a country that was prey to the personal interests of the Great and to the schismatic tendencies of the Protestant areas. His corruption did not sap the authority of the State, it reinforced it.

This accumulation of offices, this seizure of lands, was accompanied by a geopolitical and tactical desire to control the seas and to position France as a rival of mercantile Holland and soggy England. In 1626, over the opposition of certain Parliaments, he became "grand master and general superintendent of navigation and trade." This new charge, which he had fought for savagely, enabled him to pocket anchorage fees from every ship that landed and departure fees for every ship that left, plus a percentage on the revenues from shipwrecks, sinkings and confiscations from smuggling. This was the first time since Jacques Coeur that a French statesman concerned himself with international trade, and the king gave him a quasi-monopoly over the littoral, where the essence of his governorships were located. This policy was not supported unanimously; a Superintendent of Finance called the Cardinal's House, the Navy and the Artillery (which he ran), "the three money pits of French finance," whose lack of transparency was criticized by the Chamber of Accounts. Richelieu paid little heed to this tempest in a salt water glass. "I never received a penny from my sea-related responsibilities," he claimed with a straight face.

Majordomo of the Crown, he did not balk at seizing its heritage. Faithful to his obsession, "everything for me, thus everything for the State," he acquired, through assumed names, goods and properties "corporal and noncorporal"[11] that belonged to the king and which were considered inalienable but which, for centuries, His Majesty had been trading.[12] By "Richelieu-izing" them, the cardinal took control of a new part of the French patrimony, which he nationalized by privatizing it. Never satisfied, he penetrated the General Farms, charged with collecting taxes[13] (an inexhaustible source of profits), the better to drain the State's accounts. This avid tax collector would take advantage of the opportunity to inject a little order and justice into a corrupt administration and to reduce a tax inequality that would be fatal to the *Ancien Régime*. This corrupt figure (we should call a spade a spade) would go after corruption with a vengeance — an obsession with purity characteristic of the classical age — and in 1632, ordered the decapitation of, among other indelicate operators, Louis de Marillac, guilty of embezzlement in his governorship of Verdun. He purged the kingdom's blemishes by blood, for "it is easy for the bad to spoil the good through contagion."

Such cynicism in a great sinner who punished others so severely upsets Bergin again. "Without substantial additions to his known resources, he would have never been able to make the investments that he made starting in the mid-1620's. And if one adds to these investments an ever-increasing household budget, the hole to be filled becomes a gulf."[14] To reduce Richelieu to the rank of a common racketeer, to make him, as does Montesquieu, the worst citizen of France, to accuse him, with Retz, of having transformed the monarchy into "the most scandalous and most dangerous of tyrannies," is to ignore his strategy, where personal enrichment consolidated the authority of the State. When he received considerable sums from the Treasury, thanks to "payment orders" over which the Chamber of Accounts had no right of inspection,[15] he would use part of them to bribe the foreign courts swarming with his paid spies and his hirelings, and to maintain the hostility of the Protestant princes against Vienna and Madrid.

The immense fortune he accumulated — some 20 million livres — earned the Great Cardinal a post mortem trial. His victims, returned from exile, released from the Bastille or coming out of their carefully constructed shells, spoke their minds and the conspiracy of mediocrity and resentment would have the last word. The King pretended not to remember the Cardinal-Palace,[16] a sumptuous gift made by his minister while he was alive, nor the cardinal's will that allotted vast domains to him, plus a million and half livres, works of art, and the "Richelieu" — the legendary diamond that was worth 400,000 livres alone and that was the object of so much covetousness.

These generous gestures would not protect his heirs from Louis XIII's greed during the five months that remained to him on this planet, and then from that of Anne of Austria, who became regent. The Crown seized a million livres,[17] confiscated another million that the Treasury owed to the cardinal and, on the pretext of depreciation of the currency, constrained the duchess of Aiguillon, his testamentary executor,[18] to pay an additional sum. On the whole, the heritage was reduced by five million livres, for Richelieu-the-State had to be retrieved by the King-State which, soon, would become the Mazarin-the-State, when France moved from the influence of a corrupt genius to the influence of a corrupt talent. Early in his reign, Louis XIV picked up an old idea that had been abandoned under Anne of Austria: the constitution of a Court of Justice charged with examining the accounts of the late Eminence.[19] Embezzlement, abuse of public funds, forgery and fraud. . . It was all there. The cardinal was guilty — inevitably guilty, since the king needed money. His memory was slapped with a 500,000 livre fine, and the duke de Richelieu, his principal heir, had to pay.

This harsh and antipathic giant, whom Malherbe said "exceeded humanity," was understood neither by his contemporaries (who saw in him the terrifying specter of authoritarianism) nor by the royalty (which he filled with fear), nor by France, through the romantic vision of the 19th century. "Certain men are hills that rise among mankind," Guillaume Apollinaire later wrote. Richelieu was a mountain, a solid mass. "I do not undertake anything without having thought it through very well; but once I make a resolution, I go until I reach my goal; then I step back, I brush away any traces, and then I cover it up with my red cassock." Indeed, he covered everything: gold, abuses, the corpses of his adversaries. Everything, except the grandeur of France.

Footnotes

1. In fact, by his "writing workshop," directed by Maquet.
2. According to the philosopher Grotius, in a dedication with Louis XIII.
3. In 1636 and 1637. Scudéry belonged to the Guise coterie. Paradoxically, in the argument around *Le Cid*, the king and his chief minister approved the play, in spite of the pro-Spanish sentiment which it exalted and the power of the aristocratic factions that it vaunted. Going further, the Academy wanted to censure Corneille.
4. He liked to think that he was the author of these plays — *Mirame, L'Aveugle de Smyrna, Tuileries* and *Europe* — of which he drafted the broad outline, to be fleshed out by various co-writers, Corneille in particular (who was thus reduced to the role of scribe). This poverty would not escape Rostand, who would comment to de Guiche: "Your verve amuses my uncle Richelieu... / Expert that he is / He'll just fix up a line or two for you."
5. *Argent, pouvoir et societe au Grand Siecle*, Fayard, 1984.
6. As chancellor, Maupeou began to replace the hereditary *noblesse de robe* with appointed, salaried judges; he also denied the Parlement of Paris the right to veto royal edicts, which enabled his finance minister to implement a tax reform.
7. November 10, 11 and 12, 1630. The queen mother rescinds all of Richelieu's responsibilities in her House and dismisses all his protégés. The court is convinced of the cardinal's disgrace. It is wrong.
8. Richelieu reputedly reserved this divine guarantee to the political sphere. With regard to his morals, rumor has it that he was quite debauched. During evening parties at his niece's home, he re-drafted the *Theses of theology* learnt on the benches of the Sorbonne as *Theses of love*, in a parallel stylistic form.
9. *Art et Architecture en France: 1500 a 1700*, Macula, 1983.
10. *Pouvoir et fortune de Richelieu*, Robert Laffont, 1987.
11. The grounds, seigniories, forests, buildings and royalties were corporal assets; the rights belonging to the King, as suzerain and sovereign, were incorporeal.
12. With the right to buy them back, which shows the supposed precariousness of these acquisitions.
13. The farmer disbursed, in advance, a fixed sum to the Treasury and pocketed the difference on what was actually earned.
14. A word that often comes up in *The Testament*.
15. Even today, the Prime Ministers for the Fifth Republic are the only ones accountable for the secret funds.
16. He didn't even wait for his suffering minister to die, before moving in.
17. That is to say the amount of the rights of the ports of Brouage — now

silted up — and Le Havre.

18. In *Le Brevaire du politicien* attributed to Mazarin, one may find this wise maxim: "Never accept the task of executor."

19. Curiously and prudently, the King preferred not to sully the memory of "the little cardinal," and the magistrates did not examine the far more scandalous fortune of Mazarin.

Chapter 5

MAZARIN

Giulio Mazarini, 1602-1661, Italian-born French cardinal and statesman. Succeeding Richelieu as prime minister, he completed the destruction of the feudal nobility's power, strengthened France and laid the basis for Louis XIV's success.

> "Upon the throne sat a gentle, benignant man, a man who did not want anything, who was in despair because his dignity did not allow him to be as humble before everyone as he would have liked to be."
>
> Cardinal de Retz

Twenty-six years after Concini was eliminated, history gave birth to a new *scapilatte*. A cardinal, he was never a priest. As a politician, he deserved the nickname "the Florentine." A foreigner, he took power thanks to a regency, and thanks to him France became the premier European power. A thief, matchmaker, and statesman, his skill in intrigue enabled him to build the greatest fortune of the *Ancien Régime* (after that of Orléans, who partly financed the great Revolution).

His memoirists — Retz, Rochefoucauld, and the Great Mademoiselle[1] (who will figure more prominently later in this chapter) — his most ardent enemies, makes him out to be Volpone, forever anathematized in *Twenty Years After*. This perfidious hatred associates the cardinal with the brotherhood of the sodomites who never die out but who never reproduce, scorned by Bussy-Rabutin in *La Guerre Amoureuse des Gaules*. Anne of Austria herself, to protect her reputation that was tainted by the scandal-mongering, cast doubt on the inclinations of her favorite. "He does not love women," she confided to the severe Madame de Hautefort. "He is from a country where they have inclinations of another nature," propagating an abusive generalization originated by the marquis de Vallière: "Who sacrifices to two Eros? In Spain, the monks; in France, the Great Ones; in Italy, everyone."

Released from the yoke of Richelieu, the princes, exiting prison or returning from exile, thought that power was within their reach. This bonfire of egoism would take six years to die out, six years of anarchy during which the princesses and the precious, disguised as heroines by Corneille, played at the tragi-comedy of revolt. The Great Mademoiselle, the duchesses of Longueville, Chevreuse and Montbazon, muses of confusion, became the great men of the Fronde through weariness with being women, and they condemned it to failure because they were. During this time, Paul de Gondi, future cardinal of Retz, dreamed of stripping the man of his surplice and of taking his opulent place. He was not the only one who wanted to drive out the oppressive influence of Italy, which reigned over taste and guided the artists. Since Primatice[2] and the school of Fontainebleau, French art had been dominated by a foreign esthetics that it would have done better without. The literary gallicanism of Richelieu, the paradoxes of Corneille, the rigor of Descartes, the hieratism of Poussin (citizen of Rome though he was), transformed the codes of creation and France, delivered of foreign values, became a reason, a face, a nation.

This Mazarin of "low extraction" was hard to tolerate; his dubious origin made the whole city laugh. It was said that his father was an innkeeper, a porter, a stableman or, worse, that he was a recently converted Jew.

> *No one knows who this runt may be,*
> *Or who his putative dad.*
> *Where did this fakester come from;*
> *Is he is noble or something more sad...*

To soften these harsh tongues, Mazarin coined an illustrious heritage, whetting the imagination of the heraldry buffs with species by no means imaginary. The doges of Venice and Genoa registered him in their golden book, without requiring much evidence. In spite of his panegyrists' efforts, Mazarin probably comes from a lineage of the minor Sicilian nobility. His father, Pietro Mazzarini, a steward in the service of Colonna (one of the top families of Rome), married Hortensia Bufalini, goddaughter of the prince his employer; then, upon her death, he wed an Orsini, a plump princess. Our hero, Giulio, the eldest of six children, educated by the Jesuits, studied law in Spain (a superfluous science), and then Castillan, which would turn out to be quite useful for him in seducing Anne of Austria.

Would the good fathers make this gifted boy into a splitter of theological hairs? The temptation was great, since the Spaniards were so impressed by the Italian talent for cheating. Only his faith remained to be proven, but was that really necessary to enter this Company of Jesus that was relieved of the mystical exaltation of Ignatius Loyola, and that had become the front line against the Reformation? In any case, Mazarin decided to serve His Holiness without joining the black gowns and from 1622 to 1627, as a captain in the pontifical army, he held the garrison at Valteline in the valley of Grisons, a strategic passage between northern Europe and the South, where the troops of the Pope Gregory XV were acting as U.N. soldiers. As liaison officer, then Secretary of the apostolic nuncio of Milan, he was at the center of the conflict that once again set France and the Habsburgs against each other.[3] On October 26, 1630, under the walls of Casal, the belligerents faced each other and a choreographed, courteous and fatal battle was about to begin. The fuses were already lit and the muskets were about to open fire. Suddenly, in a swirl of dust, a rider emerged, clearing a passage between the two parties. Mazarin, archangel of reconciliation, held up a crucifix and bellowed with all his might a cry that seemed stunningly out of place: "Peace! Peace." The soldiers exulted, the Generals resigned themselves, the swords were returned to their scabbards. The pope would commemorate the event by having an obedient artist represent his plenipotentiary as a St. George defeating the dragon of war and would appoint him "Minister of His Holiness."

Six months before this peaceful exploit, Mazarin had become acquainted with Richelieu in Lyon. This meeting between His Intransigence and the *combinazione* was a thunderbolt. "The Cardinal is one of those who, in turning you down, charms you even more than those who grant your desires," wrote Mazarin. He would remember the lesson well. In 1631, the aging autocrat presented him to the Queen, Anne of Austria, in terms of a rare boorishness, according to Tallemant de Réaux. "You will like him, Madame. He is like Buckingham." When the King offered him a few ecus in reward for his assistance to the secret service, he refused them. For the first and the last time Mazarin, the supreme luxury for one who has sold his soul, gave the illusion that he could not be bought. He did not exhibit the same decency with Urban VIII and accepted, without waiting for anyone to beg him, the canoni-

cat of St.-Jean-de-Latran, the holder of which does not need to be ordained but only tonsured. He sacrificed his beautiful hair for the violet
cassock that the title of Monsignore conferred on him, and an emolu-
ment of 500 ducats. To be a representative of the Holy See and at the
same time Richelieu's agent was not, even for a virtuoso of the double
cross, an easy task. Cardinal Antonio Barberini, chief of the Spanish
party to the Vatican, was on his guard and his mistrust was heightened
when Louis XIII set out to make his favorite the papal nuncio to Paris.
The pope, who was not very eager to give up his profitable neutrality,
politely hid himself away, and his refusal threw the double-agent into
the arms of France.

1640: Mazarin, "the canonized Frenchman," left Rome, where he
had no future, and arrived in Paris, equipped with "*lettres de naturalité*,"[4]
which made him almost a subject of the King. Pressed by Louis XIII,
the pope finally granted him the hat and, at the age of 39, Jules Mazarin
became His Eminence, the cardinal.

Less than a year later, Richelieu gave up to God his inflexible soul,
leaving no successor. The King, before leaving the kingdom of earth in
his turn, in May 1643, summoned Mazarin and his Council and, bright
mark of favor, designated him the godfather of his eldest son, the future
Louis XIV. *Après moi, le chaos* — a Gallic maxim, the fear of everyone in
power. Louis XIII, who remembered the turbulent reign of his mother,
Marie de Medicis, was wary of his Spanish wife's intermittent fidelity
towards France and instituted, through his will, a regency council.[5]
But the ambition of the living obliterates the desires of the dead, and
Parliament, being unaware of his last will and testament, gave full
power to Anne of Austria. To the amazement of all, she named Mazarin, the creature of the so-hated Richelieu, chief minister. Just for the
transition period? Everyone thought so, and everyone was mistaken.
"The man from nowhere," with cunning intelligence and ostentatious
humility, would rule France for eighteen years.

This unexpected promotion may be attributed to the mediocrity
of his rivals, his calculated neutrality in the quarrel between the
Condés and the Vendômes, and the Queen's favor. Time had not yet
dimmed the imposing presence of the dynamic forty-something nor
slowed the pace of his limbs dissimulated so modestly under the silk of
Tartuffe. The devout Queen, forsaken by the wandering gaze of the late
King, the regent felt her interminable frustration melting under the
silky gaze of the prelate. Puritan history, chagrined by the weaknesses

of the great, attributes to them an imaginary virtue and an unearned reputation for austerity. The relations between Anne of Austria and Mazarin, however lacking in mystery, still disturb scrupulous hearts. Friendship, nothing but friendship, such historians claim (in agreement with Madame de Motteville, according to whom the Queen always met with the cardinal with the doors open, far from the shadows and closed door of the alcoves). This saintly certainty would be belied by the Palatine princess who, in her broken French, would reveal the existence of a secret marriage.[6] The passionate correspondence exchanged between the regent and the cardinal during his exile leaves no doubt about the strength of their feelings and the nature of their intimacy. "Our two hearts are united by such bonds that, you yourself have agreed with me more than once, they could be broken neither by time nor by any effort whatsoever," wrote "the Royalist pig wop from the Third Republic" to Charles V's grand-daughter on October 27, 1651. "It is a strange thing for this child (*it is of he that we speak*) to see himself married and separated at the same time, and that obstacles to his marriage continue to present themselves." The Spanish princess answered him with the extreme enthusiasm of the Devout Portuguese. "There are words that betray the disorder of one's heart and almost of one's mind," Victor Cousin would say.

"The holy family," as that unreliable Condé would call them, soon ran into the hostility of the Great Ones, the Parliament and the people. Everyone was fed up with Satan's Cardinal. The Fronde, before turning up the volume, expressed itself with plumes, and the Mazarinades set a new record in the history of calumny. More than five thousand tirades are collected in thirty volumes with revealing titles,[7] giving rise to Voltaire's lines:

Kings cease being kings when they abuse their authority. Subjects are released from their oaths when the kings contravene theirs.[8]
What is a King? A man who is always wrong, a master who never knows his trade. A prince? A criminal that no one dares to punish.[9]

Mazarin remained impassive in the face of all this abuse. As Madame de Motteville wrote, "He used these insults the way Mithradates used the poison which, instead of killing him, finally became, over time, like food to him." "Enough talking, let's do it," he used to say, adopting in advance Chamfort's maxim: "The government of France is an absolute monarchy tempered by songs."

1648. The Treaties of Westphalia, imposed through the diplomatic genius of Mazarin, extracted Alsace and the Three Bishoprics[10] from the formidable soldiers. Unfortunately, this false peace did not stop the war with Spain, the hemorrhage of the Treasury, and the hostility of the Parliament that accepted with bad grace the compulsory loans to the Superintendent of Finances (another Italian, Particelli d'Emery). In May, the judiciary refused to register an edict freezing the officers' salaries at the sovereign court for four years. Omer Talon[11] resorted to celestial metaphors: "It is a blessing from heaven when the rays of a distant sun penetrate into a room, but it would be a calamity if the burning star penetrated entirely." Patience, Monsieur Advocate General, the Sun King will rise soon. Impinging on the emoluments of the magistrates is an insolence and the judgeship in its Decree of the Union (which bears within it the outline of the government by the judges, the worst of all possible worlds)[12], defied the old monarchy.

June 30. Mazarin pretended to give in, and promised to study a law that would be less sacrilegious. On July 31, at his instigation, the King withdrew his word and "took back" the organization of his authority and his finances that had so imprudently been conceded. His *lit de justice* proceeded amidst a peaceful silence that was disturbed by a new diatribe from Omer Talon. "Formerly, our monarchs' desires were not executed among the people until they were approved by all the Great Ones of the kingdom. Presently, this jurisdiction is reserved to the Parliaments; we enjoy this secondary power that the rules of this era authorize." Just a little less bombastic than Du Sieyès.

But Mazarin was no Dreux-Brézé and, to choke off such anarchistic remarks, he had the big-mouths put away. At the end of the *Te Deum* celebrated in honor of the victory of Lens, he ordered the arrest of three parliamentary agitators: Potier de Blancmesnil, Broussel and Charton (who managed to escape). Barricades went up all over Paris and Paul de Gondi, a dangerous spirit seeking to fool the negotiators between the court and the Courts, nearly got him insulted by the Queen and pilloried by the people. "He is the idol of bad subjects," Chateaubriand would say of him. This dedication justifies my admiration for Cardinal de Retz, whose *Memoirs*, a model, contain not a word of truth. Without decency or measure, he holds his head high and castigates Mazarin, his

twin and his counterpart. His triumphs, falsified accounts of his failures, his successes, inaccurate and flattering outlines of his difficulties,
weave the garlands of a disappointed ambition. "After six days of reflection," he writes, "I chose to do wrong intentionally." He succeeded
in that extremely well — the Cardinal of failure,[13] who throughout the
Fronde was always misled, always mistaken, always wrong. While he
was not an astute politician he was, with Saint-Simon, the acutest
writer of the Great Century and his unpleasant maxims dissimulate the
depth of the moralist: "The greatest misfortune of civil wars is that one
is responsible for an evil that one did not commit," or: "Weak people
never fold when they should." He did not fold or break, he went astray.
When, in his old age, the devil became a hermit, his retirement retreat
would become a test bench where Corneille, Molière, and Boileau
would come to try out their new works. "They try to amuse the good
cardinal," Madame de Sévigné would write.

At the beginning of the uprising, Mazarin was so unpopular that
the Parliament made the use of his name an offence. "His name alone
has become so odious an insult that the judges have given permission to
inform against anyone who uses it against a person," wrote Joly (a renowned jurisconsult). This law[14] left the lawyer speechless. Mazarin,
impassive, had had enough of the factious ones and on January 6, 1649,
during "The Night of the Kings," left the ungrateful capital with Louis
XIV, the regent and the court, for St.-Germain, where he would prepare
to regain legitimacy over the provisional government installed in Town
Hall. While the prince de Conti and the Duke de Beaufort disputed
first place there, Turenne, in Germany, corrupted by his mistress (the
duchess of Longueville, who had become a *frondeuse*), planned to go *nach*
Paris while Condé,[15] in the service of the King, blocked the old city at
the head of his fifteen thousand men.

Condé, an ingenious soldier — Bossuet called his fulgurating ma-
neuvers "illuminations" — was, with the cardinal de Retz and La
Grand Mademoiselle, one of the three legendary characters of the
Fronde. "He was better at winning battles than hearts," the duchess de
Nemours would say of him. To Louis II of Bourbon — Condé's title —
it mattered little under what color standards he was fighting. He
fought the Spaniards, the French, the *frondeurs*, the royalists, all with
the same bravery and even spirits. Devoid of morality, proud, ambitious, miserly about everything but the blood of his soldiers, he
thrashed the rebels at Charenton and, in February 1649, obliged them

to engage in talks with the regent. In the treaty of Rueil, the cardinal, following Concini's method, with an evenhanded prodigality rewarded the faithful for their devotion and the rebels for their allegiance. On a path strewn with gold, the royal carriages re-entered Paris, which enthusiastically greeted the very ones that they had been cursing the day before. On this note, the soap opera of the first Fronde, that anachronistic and futuristic turbulence against absolutism, drew to a close.

When Condé changed camp, the combat changed heart and the second Fronde began. To cool his inopportune and murderous ardors, the Cardinal reacted like Richelieu and the Prince found himself in the Bastille, in the cell formerly occupied by his late father, in the company of Conti and the Duke de Longueville. At this time, the rebellion received an unexpected reinforcement in the person of His Royal Highness, Gaston d'Orléans, the younger brother of Louis XIII.[16] It was said of him that "he had everything that is necessary to a good man, except for courage." The balance was shifted once again in favor of the *frondeurs* and, on June 9, 1651, the Parliament put a price on the head of the cardinal, who was called upon, "with his relatives and his servants, to leave the kingdom of France within fifteen days, [and] forbidding the governors of all the provinces, and the mayors and aldermen of the towns, to receive them and allowing the commoners to run them to ground when the specified time has elapsed." Anne of Austria, hostage of the mutineers, pondered her mortuary; Condé and his brothers found freedom; Mazarin took refuge at the château de Brühl, with the Elector of Cologne. Before taking to the road, he took the precaution of packing up the crown jewels[17] and of commissioning an agent in Paris, by the name of Colbert, to try to save the furniture and, especially, the works in his incomparable library — which was plundered, anyway. It is still shocking to think that these 54,000 rare volumes, having survived intact the ravages of time, were scattered among the unappreciative.

Anne of Austria, in the isolation of the mighty who are fallen, preserved her haughty attitude. However, her demise seemed close at hand and talk began to turn to the idea of entrusting the regency to Gaston d'Orléans, who was always ready to oblige. Only the exile remained faithful to the recluse and, from his refuge, Mazarin advised the Queen, and pulled the strings on a broken power. Paris was not easily deceived and mocked him:

A rumor spreads throughout the city
That the spirit of the Royalist pig from Sicily
Returns to the Court every day.
Still struggling to have his say.
To drive this demon to the great beyond,
We'll use the holy water at the source of the Fronde.

When ambition and love are entwined, prudence and pusillanimity die out. The two lovers came together in February 1652, after the cardinal made a long detour through the countryside, recalling the audacious and perilous return from the island of Elba. He appeared to have little chance against the versatile Condé, who had been promoted general-in-chief of the insurrection. Most fortunately for him and for France, Mazarin recovered Turenne (Henri de La Tour D'Auvergne) from his successive allegiances; wising up, he had returned to the ranks of His Majesty's service. Two of France's greatest soldiers thus clashed under the walls of Paris, in July 1652. Descending from the heights of Charonne, Turenne surprised Condé. He would have captured him if a lady had not miraculously opened the St.-Anthony gate, behind which Monsieur le Prince was engulfed while his battalions were decimated. A Pyrrhic victory.

She could have been Cyrano's sister. She was the daughter of Gaston d'Orléans; she might have become Queen of France. She was the deceived mistress of an unmitigated young scamp. A bit like Madame de La Fayette, more like Madame Bovary, equipped with a ravishing face marred by an aggressive nose, such was Marie-Louise de Montpensier, better known as La Grande Mademoiselle. When Louis XIV forbid her to marry Lauzun (a captain in the King's bodyguard, about whom La Bruyère said: "His life would make a good novel. . . No, it's too unbelievable,") she accepted the whole court in her sad bridal bed. Before taking an edifying retirement, she facilitated that of Condé, by having the batteries of the Bastille fire on the royal troops; she lit the first fuse. "What was lacking in the life of Mademoiselle, in her character as in her spirit, is taste, justice, and grace," Sainte-Beuve would write.

The monarchy restored to its prerogatives, Mazarin's ambition knew no more bounds. France up in arms, the Queen on his own arm, and her nieces manning the armaments, the Cardinal thought for a moment of giving up Paris for Rome. Since he could not be King, he might as well be pope and, if he could not don the Crown of St. Louis, he would readily accept the tiara of St. Peter. While waiting for this improbable designation, the uncle led his family members to the altar and became, with Napoleon Bonaparte, the most famous matchmaker in our history. The Italian with seven nieces, like the Corsican with seven brothers and sisters, used his family to weave a network of alliances, to ensure their fortune and to contribute to the grandeur of a country that they ran without belonging to it. Marriage became an affair of State, a security device as effective as prison — with which it has so many affinities. Through well-conducted nepotism, the Holy Family and the Napoleonides put the bed to the service of France. Conti, that midget *frondeur*, responded aptly enough: "You ask me which niece I would more readily wish as my wife? It doesn't make much difference, since it is Monsieur le Cardinal whom I will be marrying." In the chess game of Europe, the fiancé and fiancée were simple pawns and the unions merely gave weight to state policy.

With their uncle victorious, these budding girls — the "stinking vipers," "mud princesses," — found themselves ethereal goddesses overwhelmed by gifts, graced by heaven and earth. Nobody remembered the treaty of Rueil which had forbidden Mazarin to marry them without the agreement of Condé (now transformed into their guardian), nor the order of expulsion launched against them during the second Fronde. They had not prevented the duke de Mercoeur — elder brother of Beaufort — from marrying Laure Mancini in Brühl, to the great anger of the Parliament: "The aforementioned Mancini is interdicted from entering the kingdom or remaining there, under pretext of this union." When the disturbance was somewhat alleviated and the uncle gave to Conti, brother of the Great Condé, Marie-Anne Martinozzi (the only blonde in this family of prunes), the court swallowed its bile and Madame de Motteville put down her pen. "This alliance did not appear to be appropriate for the grandeur and the importance of the prince; but the grandeur of the cardinal's fortune was so immense that it could, by erasing the lowliness of his race, elevate the family to participate in the most supreme dignities."

The noblest houses were only too happy to participate in his efforts toward social elevation and political consolidation. Laure Martinozzi won the lands of the duke de Modene and France won northern Italy's support against Spain. Their daughter would one day marry

James Stuart II and take the throne of England. Olympus Mancini, as the wife of Eugene-Maurice de Savoie, reinforced the ties between Paris and Turin. They would give birth to Prince Eugene, legendary soldier in the service of Austria, who would demolish the Turks at Zenta and Belgrade. Hortense Mancini, the cardinal's favorite niece, was turned down by England,[18] and was then offered to the son of Charles de La Porte de Meilleraye, Marshal of France, one of the cardinal's few friends. He would become Duke of Mazarin, squander his benefactor's fortune and, through his religious bigotry, lead his wife into regrettable misconduct. After His Eminence's death, the junior, Marie-Anne Mancini, "who is said to be quite divine, having infinite appeal," would marry the Duke de Bouillon. Their younger son would build what has become today's Elysée Palace, an indirect gift from Mazarin to the president of the Republic.

Marie Mancini could have become Queen, but her uncle (who was very eager to play matchmaker but not to be the grave-digger of monarchical aspirations) intervened. The young monarch's matrimonial wishes exasperated Anne of Austria. "I do not believe that the King is capable of such cowardice, but if it possible that he has had such a thought, I can tell you that all of France would revolt against you and him, and that I myself would stand at the head of the rebels and that I would bring my second son into it as well."

The prospect of becoming the King's uncle while attracting the Queen's wrath hardly appealed to the cardinal, who therefore opposed this misalliance that was against the interests of the Crown. He had other plans for his adopted country; he refused a golden Portuguese marriage,[19] and sought to erase the Pyrenees and instigate a union between Marie-Thérèse and Louis XIV. To help his niece to ease her heart, he advised her to read Seneca and to console herself in the arms of Prince Colonna, whose family had employed her father. The day her husband took Marie to visit the modest apartment of "the master of the Chamber," his grandfather, she put him in his place: "Sir, I do not know what my grandfather was, but what I do know extremely well is that, of all my sisters, I am the most badly married." She was right.

"What a novel my life would make," Napoleon would say. That of Mazarin was equally good story material, and his achievements transformed this bird of prey into one of France's greatest statesmen. No fortune was as colossal as his, and it would take all the bailiffs of France to appraise it: abbeys, administrative offices, gold coins, jewels, works of art, rare books, nothing escaped his clutches. Upon his death, his fortune was estimated at between 35 and 40 million livres. Fouquet, who was familiar with some of the Cardinal's accounting stratagems, suggests it was 100 million. These figures make the 20 million left by Richelieu look paltry; they make a mockery of the 15 million that constituted the ancestral patrimony of the Condé family. In contrast to the Great Cardinal his predecessor, buildings were not of great interest to him; nothing was as good as a big trunk filled with ecus, ducats, ingots.

Like all misers, Mazarin was trying to protect himself from fear and death behind the ridiculous fortress of wealth. In his Tubeuf mansion, the two galleries by François Mansart concealed (perhaps not the most apt word, for one cannot be both the robber and receiver of stolen goods) 450 canvases by hacks, minor artists, and by great artists including Da Vinci, Mantegna, Raphaël, Giorgione, Annibale Carracci, Caravaggio, Titian, Veronese. The King's choices? No, the cardinal's. Are we sure? Not at all! "The best mixes with the mediocre, if not the worst," is the assessment of George Bordonove, one of his biographers. Paul Morand is more severe: "He did not understand painting, himself, and he was persuaded to buy some real trash." However, he did not have such bad taste when, in addition to the flowers of the *Cinquecento*, he acquired a Van Dyck representing the family of Charles, the first royal to be decapitated, with the secret intention of handing it over to the Stuarts if by chance they ever attained the throne. He often confided, *sotto voce,* to the happy owner of a coveted prize the emotion that he felt when viewing it. How could anyone refuse such a sensitive man? Fouquet, who would have offered him all of Vaux, parted with two tapestries. Sometimes, the Queen would be used as a front; Francesco Barberini, his old protector, was persuaded to fulfill the desires of Anne of Austria by making her a gift of his Correggio, which was soon found suspended in the cardinal's gothic vaults.

A connoisseur of precious stones, he worshipped them for more than mercantile reasons. He adored his gems, swooning in front of their gleaming light, reveling in their reflections. His passion gave way to neither tragedy nor adversity. From Henriette de France[20] (the hapless Charles I's widow, who was reduced to begging), he acquired for almost nothing the two famous diamonds, the *Sancy*, 54 carats, and *the Mirror of Portugal*, at 26 carats. After Queen Christine of Sweden abdi-

cated, he raided her holdings at warehouse prices and he did even better with the Duchess de Chevreuse, who was ruined by the demon of
gambling.

His salary as chief minister, the income from the lands offered by
the King or confiscated from the over-extended, the benefice of his
twenty abbeys[21] (among most productive in the kingdom), the fruits of
his governorships,[22] the revenues as superintendent of the house and
the buildings of the King and of His education, his brother's house (the
Duke of Anjou), his collections from the domains of the Crown, and the
salt tax, put him far out of reach of any competition. Coeur, Concini,
Richelieu — they were journeymen in the craft of holding multiple offices, but he was the master.

There remains only the accountancy written out in black and
white, the clandestine gold mine that nourished hatred and was nourished by hatred. To measure its full extent, we would need the keen
nose of a tax inspector, the obstinacy of Mrs. Eva Joly,[25] and the means
of Interpol, all supported by international cooperation at the highest
level. Traffic in state offices created just for this purpose, various forms
of speculation, fraudulent benefices, payment of imaginary debts, fictitious credits, fees from State offices, "adjustments" to the "accounting
ordinances,"[24] forgery to the detriment of the Treasury, abuse of public
funds. . . This goes beyond the wheeling and dealing that was generated
and tolerated by the *Ancien Régime*, it is well into the territory of thievery. To top things off, this gambler who could transform brèmes into
assets entered into commercial deals through a squadron of intermediaries. "Mazarin sold everything: the firewood from his forests, the fish
from his ponds, the horses from his stud farms, the pheasants from his
hunts; he made money on the English horses that the ambassador sent
him from England. He sold weapons, regiments, food, and blankets to
the army; he even sold the army its water. He sold government posts,
he sold his nieces (after selling them his old carriages). At night, since
he could no longer sleep, he would weigh his gold coins, and use the
lightest, the least well-formed, for gaming the next day."[25] Even in
Brühl, where carts of ecus still flowed in to him, the Exile continued his
obscure trading.[26] To shelter his indiscreet fortune, he opened accounts in his beloved Italy and, when he felt his end was near, he refused to draw up an inventory of his amazing assets.

At the beginning of March 1661, the cardinal began an interminable period of anguish. His confessor, a théatin monk[27] — virtue in the

face of sin, and death in the face of all audacity, refused him absolution. "You cannot refuse me," the cardinal told him. "All my wealth came from His Majesty." "Distinguish the gifts from the King from that which you have taken yourself," responded the one with no worldly goods. Colbert, a disciple of the Jesuits, came up with a solution. "Donate all your goods to His Majesty. He will return them to you at once." As the ultimate Mazarinery, the first act of cunning on the part of the young monarch, he accepted the offer but was reluctant to restore it. Shylock and Harpagon went into the dying man's room and wept with him over his unhappy family, his poor penniless nieces. Upset by their wailing, Louis XIV put an end to the torment and returned the treasure, purified, to its owner. From that point onward, God could install Mazarin among the elect. When his death was announced, Hortense and Marie both uttered: *"Pure, E crepato! "* ("That's it, he's gone!") Bossuet would have found other words.

Michelet, Lavisse, Paul Morand condemn his demonish memory. However, the "buffoon" saved the throne, subdued the Fronde, and signed (on the little island of Faisan) the definitive peace with Spain. The "parasite" extended France's borders and added Artois, Hainaut, Luxembourg, Alsace, Lorraine, Roussillon, and Casal. With the treaties of Westphalia and of the Pyrenees, the "villain" prepared the European chessboard where France would soon call the tune. Louis XIV knew enough to close his eyes to the weaknesses of his old master. "I liked him and he liked me," he would say to his detractors. The Sun King owed much to the cardinal of the shadows.

Footnotes

1. The Duchesse de Montpensier, a royal princess and extremely wealthy heiress, was prevented by political circumstances from making a suitable match. While Mazarin was in exile in 1651, Montpensier involved her father, Gaston de France, Duke d'Orléans (Louis XIV's uncle), with Condé in the Fronde. In the third war of the Fronde, which Condé launched against the royal government, she commanded the troops occupying Orléans, and saved Condé's army from annihilation in the Battle of the Faubourg Saint-Antoine in 1652) by ordering the Bastille cannon to be fired against the royal troops. When Louis XIV returned to Paris, Montpensier went into exile until 1657; she was exiled again from 1662 to 1664 for refusing to marry Afonso VI of Portugal.
2. 1505 -1570. Italian painter/sculptor who led the School of Fontainebleau.
3. In connection with Savoy and northern Italy.
4. Which allowed foreigners to buy land and offices in France.
5. A council of regency wisely made of the Queen, Gaston d'Orléans, the prince of Condé, Mazarin, Chancellor Séguier and the superintendent of finances, Claude Bouthillier.
6. Second wife of Monsieur, the King's brother, she waited until the death of the concerned parties to write, in 1717, that, "The late Queen did far worse than love Cardinal Mazarin; she married him."
7. (*L'Envoi de Mazarin a mont Gibet, Vertus de sa Faquinance, Lettre de Polichinelle a Jules Mazarini, Gueuserie de la Cour, Le Dereglement de l'etat, Le mauvais usage de la politique...*)
8. *Letter of advice to Messrs of the Parliament, written by a provincial*, March 4 1649.
9. *Catechism of the courtiers to the court of Mazarin.*
10. Metz, Toul and Verdun, *inter alia*. These two treaties reflect the end of the Thirty Year War, modified the European order by breaking apart Germany and by reducing Austria, in accordance with Mazarin's wishes, giving France the dominating role on the continent.
11. A prominent magistrate in the Fronde.
12. The *Arret d'union* prescribed the meeting of the Parliament, the Great Council, the Court of Auditors, the Court of the Assistance to deliberate on affairs of State.
13. According to Andre Suarès.
14. It would be taken up again during the Stavisky affair, where a taxi driver had one of his colleagues condemned who had called him a deputy.
15. 1621-1686.
16. Son of a King, brother of a King and uncle of a King.
17. That the Queen would have considerable difficulty in getting back, during better times.

18. Charles II of England, having taken refuge in France, wanted to marry Hortense. Mazarin, at this time the ally of Cromwell, refused. When Charles attained the throne upon the death of the Lord Protector, the cardinal organized a marriage between Henriette Stuart, his sister, and the brother of Louis XIV.

19. Portugal, enemy of Spain and combined France, wanted to marry the girl of the King with Louis XIV and offered to Mazarin a fatty reward to conclude this union.

20. Daughter of Henri IV and sister of Louis XIII.

21. He did better than Richelieu, who only accumulated about fifteen of them.

22. La Fère, La Rochelle, Dunkirk, Brouage, Toulon, Antibes.

23. A famous examining magistrate.

24. Slush funds.

25. Paul Morand, *Fouquet oule soleil offusque*, Gallimard, 1961.

26. He even managed to sell to the duke of Vieuville the Superintendence of Finances, which provided an income of 400,000 livres.

27. An Order that he had brought up from Rome as a countervailing power to the Jesuits and which he had installed opposite the Louvre, on left bank of the Seine.

Chapter 6

FOUQUET

Nicolas Fouquet, 1615-1680, supported Cardinal Mazarin and Louis XIV during the Fronde. He was appointed Finance Minister in 1653, a position that enabled him to extend his wealth and, coincidentally, to extend considerable loans to the royal treasury.

> "If you leave aside his taste in buildings and in women, Monsieur le Surintendant would be a great man."
>
> Mazarin

"O mankind, make no mistake! The future holds too many bizarre twists of fate, and loss and ruin seep into men's lives by far too many chinks and crevices to be stopped entirely. . . . So much sweat, so much work, so many crimes, and so much injustice — and you will never extract from destiny, no matter how hard you try, anything more than a wretched 'maybe.' Understand that nothing is guaranteed to you, not even a tomb upon which to engrave your superb titles, the only remains of your demolished grandeur." In his first sermon before the court, on the fourth Sunday of Lent, (March 19, 1662), Bossuet the golden-tongued flattered the king, stoked the fire that would burn Fouquet while sparing Mazarin, and castigated the high and mighty in their declining glory.

While the walls of the Louvre were quaking under the echoes of Bossuet, a young moralizer in a long robe, the superintendent was cooling his heels in his cell in the Bastille. Since his arrest in Nantes, September 5, 1661,[1] he had been under provisional detention. His long, rich brown hair (reflections of autumn, said his lady admirers), bleached by anguish and melancholy, rendered France's premier dandy unrecognizable. He was completely cut off from outsiders. The recluse, whom the magistrates were considering "to try as a deaf-mute," had, indeed, become three-quarters dumb. His wife was exiled far from the capital and his children, with no fixed residence, had to beg for alms.

When Richelieu (the chief minister) died, followed by Louis XIII, his king, the country was thrown into the abyss of interregnums. Released from the dictatorship of the red robe, the Great Ones and the Parliament gave themselves up to the puerile orgies of the Fronde, declined the supervision of Anne of Austria (the regent) and of Mazarin (the favorite, the lover, or the morganatic husband — or perhaps all three). Fouquet did not take the revolt seriously; hebecame the right-hand man of a cardinal who was a bit short of loyal supporters. In November 1651, he was offered the position of Attorney General in the rebellious Parliament; he skillfully corrected its erring ways, thus preventing the kingdom from falling into the pernicious trap of allowing the judiciary to have the upper hand.

To get his century finally get underway, Louis XIV needed an expiatory victim who could exorcize the sins of His late Eminence. Egged on by Colbert, who had sworn to get the better of a man whom he hated (for being all that he could not be), the autocrat chose Fouquet. The scapegoat would be undone by that which he loved most: wealth, ostentation, women.

The party he gave at Vaux-le-Vicomte, on August 17, 1661, was unequaled in legend. Intended to dazzle the King with its display of fine taste and stunning effects, in fact it fed his envy and aggravated his hatred. "Mr. Fouquet, these vermeil forks and spoons are splendid." "That's not vermeil, Sire, it is gold." Fouquet would have been wiser to keep the comment to himself. But his beautiful face lacked a perceptive nose, and he did not realize that he had just humiliated Louis XIV. The festival of the century would be fatal to him. There were fireworks, an artificial lake, swings, games, carriage rides, fountains fed by streams channeled through pipes of lead (taken from the royal artillery), and landscapes that imposed French rationality where disorder had once reigned. And this mad residence that cast Fontainebleau into the shade became obsolete overnight, along with the ornaments, tapestries, tableaux and sculptures celebrating the glory of the owner (disguised as Hercules, Jupiter, and haloed Phebus). Mlle de Scudéry would write in her *Clelia*: "This new star (?) at Heaven's zenith (*sic*) showed that there was nothing higher than the glory of Cléonime."[2] Buffets were arranged in the gardens by Vatel (famed director of kitchens and special events), where the *précieuses* could eat their fill and recline on *chaises longues*; the sky was intermittently brightened by the rosettes of the fireworks. "An enchanted place," the Palatine princess would say (the one from the Fronde, not the big one). Enchanted? Louis was not enchanted, and La Fontaine tried in vain to salve his wounded pride. "Everything competed at Vaux to please the King: the music and water, the lights, the stars." When Molière's *Les Fâcheux* (*The Annoying Ones*) began, with the lines, "Under what star, dear Lord, must I have been born / to be constantly vexed by annoying people?" the monarch could barely disguise his exasperation. "We will get back at these people," he said to his mother in the carriage that whisked them away, in the middle of the night, from the château of maladroit entertainment and corruption. But, in the space of one evening, in the shade of this patron who harbored the incipient germs of genius, he had found the direction for his reign. Without La Fontaine, Molière, Madame de Sévigné, Racine and Le Brun, deprived of the creative flesh that nourished his symbol, Louis XIV would have been recognized as the cruel sovereign of a country decried for its plunders and its arbitrary persecution. Providence — God was on their side — did not allow that, and transformed this imperfect mortal into a demiurge, the only conqueror since Alexander to defy the sun. He carried the French — i.e. France — into the fullness of its glory.

Louis' hatred reaches its zenith when Fouquet compromised Louise de Vallière, his hapless mistress. Fouquet had a go-between deliver the tempting sum of 20,000 pistoles to the King's favorite, seeking to trip her up in her steady virtue. In love, the young woman reacted like Andromache mortified: "Even 250,000 livres would not tempt me." Nicolas tried to recover, and forced an occasion to praise the king's merits to Louise. However, such intimate talk was a state secret (the relationship was kept quiet, to avoid offending Anne of Austria, the King's mama), and Louis XIV did not forgive these gossipy remarks made by a man who had treated his mistress like a strumpet.[3]

That was the last straw; Fouquet was lost. His trial was an offended sovereign's revenge. Louis used his judges to settles his domestic accounts. This tale is one of many in which justice is called in to arbitrate on moral matters. These extraordinary jurisdictions, made up of ordinary magistrates, were charged with pursuing speculators, embezzlers and other nouveau riches usurers who had achieved their success to the detriment of a Crown that was in a state of near bankruptcy. The superintendent was not the only one to be hauled in. Turenne, the Duke de Richelieu, the Cardinal de La Rochefoucauld and many others would experience the rigors of the law during the reign of Louis XIV, which was marked, like François Mitterrand's two terms, by scandals. In total,[4] 251 of the biggest tradesmen of the kingdom were invited to restore, through the payment of fines, 160 million livres (twice the annual receipts). But this gold mine was not enough to cover the expenses of the gluttonous war. To do that — and, if possible, to win it — three things were needed, as observed Turenne's old adversary Montecuccoli[5]: "money, money, money." Destitute like the son of Harpagon (hero of Molière's comedy, The Miser), the son of Saint Louis had a hard time making ends meet and had to pay hyperbolic interest rates to the money-lenders.[6] Fouquet was thought to be fabulously rich and the financiers competed to bring their gold to him, a borrower who seemed to be dripping with resources. To further the illusion of unequalled opulence, his domains were the most imposing,[7] his debtors (virtuous ladies of the impoverished nobility) were the most tempting, his collections the rarest, his stables, rich with the most beautiful Andalusians, his offices, the most prestigious. He bought everything, even hearts; he gave stipends to artists, writers, and poets; secured for himself the services of the ruling class (and of the lower classes), the Church and the Parliament; he entertained spies among the servants of His Majesty and the Queen Mother herself became his agent, thanks to a pension of 500,000 livres. Bussy-Rabutin, a good observer and a bad scandalmonger, jealous of this rival's tender friendship with his cousin, the inextinguishable Marquise de Sévigné, would say: "She received a stipend as soon as she wanted."

Throughout all his service as superintendent, from 1653 to 1661, Fouquet used appearances to serve solvency and he placed the illusion of solvency at the foundation of the State. Only he was lent to, and as Minister of Finance to an insolvent throne he never hesitated to reach into his own pockets when those of the bankers remained closed. He spent the last cent of his illicit fortune in the service of his dreams and those of France. Illicit? The confusion between the sums that he advanced, the appropriations that were authorized by others, the collateral that was distributed, the shell-games he played in paying his troop of intermediaries, the dubious deals intended to bring in some money, all this shady world blurs the line between the superintendent's financial delinquency and his responsibility. The confusion between his patrimony and that of the State was hardly in his own favor. Little by little, Fouquet was ruined by paying notes that came due and by trying to get the most advantageous rates.

In 1656, the Great Condé went over to the ranks of the Spanish enemy and inflicted a bloody setback on the French. Mazarin, on the point of succumbing, called on the clergy to come to the rescue: 1,800,000 livres in the name of Heaven. The Church ignored his pleas and the Italian, unable to tap into the church-offerings, turned toward civil society. Colbert, a petit-bourgeois man, regretfully gave him 300,000 livres, his wife's entire dowry. Fouquet, a great lord, pulled together in four days, on his signature alone, 900,000 livres and saved the French army from a rout. The Cardinal wrote him a syrupy letter: "I know that you raised this sum on your own personal obligations, and that you have committed all that you have in this world to assist us in the present economic situation. . . I recognize that I am deeply in-debted to you and I am touched beyond everything by the way in which you have responded. I have told Their Majesties all about it, and they agree that your zeal and support are impressive, and that one must set great store by such a friend as you. They have charged me with thank-ing you on their behalf, and with ensuring you that they cherish the memory." "They" would soon forget. When Nicolas produced that mis-sive during his inquest, the judges, however accustomed they may have been to the ingratitude of the powerful, could not remain indifferent.

In connection with Mazarin and Fouquet, Michelet (the great rhetorician of oneiric history) speaks of "the exploitation of France by a rascal, for a rascal." This characterization is contestable, and there is no similarity between the two. All his life the Cardinal, that cunning devil, socked it away, hoarded, dissimulated. Wealth was his lover. He enjoyed it without touching it, for fear of wearing out its charms. "Will he never be sated with gold?" asked Anne of Austria, exasperated by his rapacity. Fouquet, a spendthrift, let the ecus slip between his fingers to entertain young ladies, duchesses, men of letters and of wit, in luxury and joy. Having become the man with the golden mind, he holds a unique place in the history of corruption. Jacques Coeur was a traf-ficker, Concini, a procurer; the Superintendent was a casual lover of glory. The Cardinal recognized this assistant's qualities — he did not covet money, but despoiled himself to make everyone believe that he had more. He associated him with Colbert, his clerk for base deeds, who would gather up for his master vacant benefices and alienated grounds; he would adulterate the offices; hold the farmer generals for ransom; and compete with the well-fed ammunition dealers who were bleeding the armies. A snoop and a spy, he grew rich in secret while disseminating lessons of virtue. Fouquet, in broad daylight, seemed to be the only accomplice of the great director of French thievery; he exposed himself to the dissatisfaction of a country squeezed between high taxes and the Cardinal's abuse. Gourville reveals each one's role, in his *Memoirs*. When he bought the big farm of Guyenne,[8] he ran into opposition from Fouquet, on the pretext that he did not have enough money to take on such a burden. "The Cardinal retorted that he was owed 2,700,000 livres for advances that he had paid for the service of the King, and that Mr. Fouquet would have to pay over to him the assigns, and that he would be satisfied if he signed an agreement that he should be repaid." Fouquet pretended to believe this fairytale and the prelate was able to reimburse himself for money that had never been spent.

On October 1, 1659, Colbert forwarded to Mazarin (who was negotiating the peace with Spain, at St.-Jean-de-Luz), a 22-page report wherein the snake[9] transformed himself into a cockroach. He denounced Fouquet, accused him of all sorts of misdeeds, criticized his disorganization and the time wasted at Vaux, and deplored the state of the balance sheet. "I cannot admire this man whom I have seen grabbing, squandering, corrupting. We should make him cover all these expenditures, himself." He then suggested hauling him before a tribunal headed by Nesmond and Talon, whose biddableness he could guarantee. This memorandum was addressed "without desire to harm nor with any other secondary agenda," but it did not prevent this by no means disinterested man from presenting his candidature to replace his rival. Fouquet got wind of it and dashed off to St.-Jean-de-Luz. Without making reference to the intercepted report, he denounced the plot being hatched against him. He proposed to give up the superintendence and to withdraw from all such matters. Of course, the Cardinal kept him on. The Treasury needed 30 million livres, the price of peace with Spain, and Fouquet alone could provide such a sum. Mazarin, an expert in duplicity, wrote the very same day to Colbert. "The information your letter provided has given me great comfort and I will take as much advantage of it as the present situation allows."

This syrup of honey and gall would end up catching Fouquet the day that Mazarin departed this world, finally giving up to Louis XIV the reins of the power. "The face of the theatre is changing," he declared to his Council. "I will be applying different principles in the

Government of my States and my finances." Fouquet, persuaded (like Anne of Austria) that "he will soon tire of taking care of everything," did not fully appreciate the scope of the warning. Colbert, being far craftier, set out to make sure that the young monarch would not ask to see an accounting from the accomplices of the financial *Mazarinades*. To save his own hide and to further his career, he would have to sacrifice Fouquet. Never mind choosing between men, the King was forced to make a choice between two world views: either his reign could bring about the reconciliation of the French and cauterize the after-effects of the Fronde (in which case, Nicolas would become chief minister); or he could build up the Absolute State, Richelieu's heritage, and Colbert would be the chief servant. How can an aesthete compete with an accountant?

From Day One, His Majesty made his choice clear. "And you, Monsieur le Surintendant, I have explained to you my wishes. Please make good use of Colbert, whom the late Monsieur le Cardinal recommended to me." Fouquet's friends called upon him to be prudent, urged him to be discreet, sought to kindle his mistrust. Nothing helped. Certain that he would receive the dividends of his devotion and his prodigality, he believed he had made himself indispensable to a sovereign who, in fact, despised him. "He took charge of everything, and pretended he was Chief Minister," wrote the abbot of Choisy (a man whose morals were unmentionable — allowing Christian charity to spill into his own baptismal font). To dupe him all the more surely, Louis XIV favored Nicolas with his royal friendship, summoned him to his High Council, listened to his confessions,[10] gave him absolution, and approved his plan for economic reform (which Colbert would take over a few months later). Behind a gracious mask, the King and his devoted henchman, the "two furies of absolute power,"[11] were preparing his demise, plotting to strip him of all his supports and even, with the complicity of that old cat Chevreuse, to alienate Anne of Austria from him.

In spite of his new isolation, Fouquet remained beyond the reach of the secular arm: as Attorney General of the Parliament of Paris, only his peers could judge him. Unable to force him to resign, Louis XIV convinced him to give up the robe in order to devote himself fully to the matters of State. "The young King had already learned that hereditary dissimulation, that life-saving and fertile art of deception that is one of the most important royal virtues."[12] Fouquet ignored Turenne's wise council: "You need to be more concerned for your safety." On August 12,

1661, he sold his commission to Achille de Harlay for 1,400,000 livres and, the height of obtuseness, rejected the honorary membership and the letters that would have preserved his privilege of jurisdiction. He would never see an ecu of this fortune: 400,000 livres went to his brother, the abbot Basile, a simpleton with a revealing first name; and Fouquet offered the million that remained to the King who, embarrassed by such generosity and frankness, confided to Colbert: "Everthing is fine. He is going to shoot himself. He came to tell me that he was sending us the money from his commission." The treasure chest would soon be found in the monarch's cellars, in Vincennes, where Mazarin had tucked away his own.

On August 26, 1661, right after Saint Louis Day, Louis XIV borrowed 20,000 pistoles from his superintendent (the same sum that Louise de Vallière had turned down). Then, under the pretext of going to seek additional subsidies from Brittany, he took the court to Nantes, where the tragedy would unfold.

After the party at Vaux, Madame de La Fayette, a modest writer, expressed her impressions with one astonishing sentence: "The King was astonished and Fouquet was astonished that the King was." Fouquet would soon know a crueler astonishment. He was suffering from quartan fever (a form of malaria) and his usual effervescence was weighed down with fatigue, when the King summoned him, on the evening of September 3, to attend his Council the following day. At five o'clock in the morning, His Majesty opened the meeting. It had hardly begun when the hounds and the horns were heard. Nothing could delay the hour of hunting and Tellier, Lyonne and Colbert asked permission to withdraw. Fouquet, shivering, was right behind them; but Louis held him back, asking him to help him "find a mislaid document." This gave the musketeers time to array themselves outside the walls and to intercept the superintendent without violating the laws of hospitality. "The King is indeed master, but I would have preferred, for his glory, that he had acted more openly with me," Fouquet commented, broken, when one of the d'Artagnans apprehended him. Not a word of anger. The tightrope walker had fallen.

In "the close-walled room, the cramped place,"[13] Fouquet had the bad taste to survive both prison and disease. Louis, finding that God would not take him off his hands, decided to rely on his judges. Thus on December 3, 1661, before the Palace of Justice (witness to so many injustices), the crowd gathered under a thin winter sun turned pink with shame. The curious, behind their masks of decency, were swooning at the prospect of contemplating the misfortune of such a man, constrained to expose himself. This was a political case, and the Court was there to punish someone who had presumed to cast a shadow over the Sun. The Fouquet scandal was the first financial case in modern times. The defendant was no longer threatened with torture, like Jacques Coeur; and he was not charged with sorcery, like Galigaï. Only to strengthen a weak case, the crime of lese-majesty was added to the charges of financial irregularities; this had the merit of entailing the death penalty.

With no lawyer and no files to consult, Fouquet had to answer questions starting on March 4, 1662. The two magistrates, Poncet and Renard, were flanked by Foucauld, the clerk vetted by Colbert. From the first day, the prisoner refused to take an oath, citing his former positions of superintendent and Attorney General. Today the oath is required only from the witnesses. At the time, the defendants were supposed to swear it in order to dissuade them from lying to God (like a certain United States president). Fouquet, who knew how to marry the joys of earthly life with the imperatives of a profound faith, sought to spare Heaven. However, a few days later, not wishing to defy the King any longer, he agreed to raise his hand, and went on raising the tone of the proceedings.

The case against him is quite in line with the legal customs of the day, when absolutism gave the superintendent as few guarantees as Jacobinism would grant to Louis XVI. With admirable courage and nobility, he faced his accusers and conducted, on his own, a compelling defense. But it was a losing game. Even a consummate lawyer cannot serve as his own advocate for long. Pleading a case requires an attentive detachment and the most lucid man will deviate fatally, since even partial subjectivity will influence his behavior. Fouquet was not long in making some major errors that would weigh heavily during the interminable audiences. Instead of flattering the commissioners in order to seem more appealing, he spoke about the incompetence of the Court, and questioned its powers. Then, he took refuge behind the need for secrecy. "I implore you," he said to the magistrates, "to advise the King that I have many secret things to make clear to His Majesty, whom I entreat to send me a person he trusts so that I can explain them — Mr. de Colbert, if he likes." Another great lost soul, the duke d'Enghien, eager to have himself heard by Bonaparte, would make a similar petition to the military commission. In vain. Torturers are reluctant to face their victims and I have known a president of the court of appeals and an attorney general who blanched the day a young man was executed whom they had abominably and wrongfully condemned.

Legal instruction has its own logic: it revives a past that is illuminated by its light alone. With each action, each gesture, it furthers a cause whose objective is to facilitate the achievement of the charge pursued by the judge. Fouquet was reproached, one after the other, for "agreements" charging overhead on tithes, taxes on sugar and wax, for trading in official positions and commissions, and for privileges. All the charges against him were sustained. With no documents, he could refute nothing. "I beg you," he wrote to the commissioners, "to be given the receipts, the letters from the Cardinal, from Mr. Tellier, from the King, and all the papers that can be used for my defense, for it is not right that these papers can be used against me and that I do not have the freedom to use them for my defense." Request denied, and ridiculed; exhibits were purloined, his homes were searched, seals were posted everywhere. With the passing days, the questions became more incisive. "Explain the real estate acquisitions made since you were commissioned as Superintendent." The answer betrayed an unusual embarrassment: "It is difficult for me to give you the proper details about *small* acquisitions that I made. I can only remember the *largest*. The more so as, by my nature, I do not get involved (or only superficially) in domestic matters." Roland Dumas, again, would say almost the same thing, and neither one of them was lying. Then they came to Vaux-le-Vicomte. "I cannot say to how much the property of Vaux returned, for I have been working on the property since 1640. It is true that these last few years, I made large expenditures there, for the house was not yet as I wished it to be, and no one would have agreed to buy it."

In spite of the prosecution's zeal, the King fulminated and Colbert insisted that "the Chamber's work be accelerated." Accelerated? Only victims have the right to complain about the slow pace of justice. Fouquet was a victim indeed, and instead of allowing himself to be worn down by time, fatigue and partiality, he strove to disentangle the knots of one catch-all charge that deeply disturbed him: poor administration of the royal finances, extortion and graft, of buying at discounted prices the domains belonging to the Crown, expenditures that were disproportionate to his means. There were 97 counts in all. "My fortune? Alright, let's talk about my fortune. I have nine million, but I owe twelve;

and these twelve, I spent in the service of the King." After pleading a lack of organization, now he was pleading the thesis of prodigality. He needed a curator, not a judge; and the only court whose jurisdiction he could not have disputed would be the court that assigns guardians and supervisors.

In Paris, rumors were rife and the broadsides distributed by his friends flooded the streets of the capital. The prisoner was gaining ground and was on the verge of smashing a case built of cards. But the commissioners were still holding the decisive card up their sleeves. During a search at St.-Mandé, Colbert had discovered six small pages hidden behind a mirror, on which Fouquet had outlined a plan to spare himself the ingratitude and ill humors of the Cardinal, in 1657. Persuaded that this was proof of another intended Fronde, the magistrates baited him. "Didn't you fortify Belle-Isle in order to maintain yourself there as superintendent and minister against the State, to the detriment of the public well-being? Didn't you write a far-sighted memorandum describing what was to be done if you should be arrested and tried?" The defendant, who thought he had destroyed those accursed papers, could not lie anymore and was powerless in the face of the obvious. "I beg you to consider that the paper that is being shown to me is only a draft and the expression of a thought that came to my mind a very long time ago, the kind of notion that often occurs to men who are in affliction and the greatest displeasure, as was my case. For the eight or nine years during which I was superintendent, I was always in despair of the treatment that I received from Monsieur le Cardinal Mazarin. . . And the King forgave me, besides. There were amnesties." This answer marked a turning point in the lawsuit. Fouquet stumbled for the first time and conceded some partial culpability.

He caught his balance again soon, and for four hours, he tried to convince the judges of his good faith, entreating them to give him "councilors that are above suspicion, to be able to act freely in this business." After interminable excuses, he was given two: L'Hoste and Ozanet, seventy years old, in the twilight stage where honorary positions are more attractive to lawyers than the perilous honors of the bar. They acted like Malesherbes[14] and, in the tradition of the bar, became hindrances to circular arguments. They gamely denounced the arbitrary charges of which their client was the victim: distorted quotes, missing correspondence with Mazarin and Colbert. This series of breaches, intended to sink Fouquet, would end up exasperating the "decent people" who made up the Chamber of Justice and spared him from death. The powers that be are always wrong to play with the judges' pride.

Three years, nine months and nine days after his arrest, the investigation came to a close and on November 14, 1664, the trial finally began. In his *Instructions to the Dauphin*, the old monarch would aptly note: "Of all the scandals I had to contend with, the Fouquet affair is the one that gave me the most pain and caused the most embarrassment." However, he did not miss any opportunity in orchestrating his vindication and in rounding up magistrates who were respected for their docility. On the bench were Colbert's men: Ste-Hélène, Poncet, Voisin, Berryer, and Pussort (his uncle); representing the prosecutor were Talon and Chamillard, famous for feeding the scaffold. The clerk, the ubiquitous Foucauld, was nothing but an indentured servant. The King and Colbert calmly awaited the expected verdict. But they had underestimated how tired the court had become, since Richelieu, of executing the whims of the reigning power; the arbitrary charges pained their consciences. Colbert himself would be upbraided by Lamoignon: "I do not have to give you my opinion as to the fate of the defendant. A magistrate gives his opinion just once, on the *fleurs de lis*."[15] He would be replaced as president by Séguier, a man loyal to the house.

The audience was closed to the public — *in camera* being the equivalent of *in a trap*. The defendant, dressed in a simple cloth suit, was invited to take a seat on the commoners' bolster. He agreed to sit on this humiliating seat, but, faithful to himself, again refused to give his oath. The following day he stood, the better to dispute the Court's legitimacy. Séguier asked that he "be treated like a mute, and be judged *in absentia*." D'Ormesson opposed this iniquity and the Court ignored the request. Indeed, the chancellor had pressed the defendant hard, since the first count of indictment (the pension derived from the salt tax). Fouquet retorted that "It was Cardinal Mazarin who granted me this pension, as reimbursement for a loan of equal value that I had had the honor to grant to the King." When he was reproached for dubious relations with intermediaries and accomplices, he still held his ground. "I am told to defend myself. But I am hamstrung, my hands are tied. I am asked about fictitious people. These matters of adjudication are never conducted otherwise than under the names of servants, to protect the interested parties from the unpleasantness of traipsing from office to office, and to avoid the arbitrary dangers of taxation. There is nothing, in all that, that is not innocent. I have never placed my own interests before those of the King." This condescension worried Madame de Sévigné, who had been promoted to legal chronicler. "He became impatient about certain objections that were being made about him and that appeared ridiculous to him. He showed it, a little, and answered with an attitude and a disdain that were displeasing. He would correct himself, for this approach is not helpful, but in truth, he was out of patience. . . It seems to me that in his place, I would have done just the same."[16] Renard, a member of the Court, vouchsafed to the Marquise, "I have to admit that this man is incomparable. He never spoke so well in the Parliament."

I was just finishing this chapter when I met Councilor Fabre, a long time president of the (Parisian) correctional court, in front of the statue of Verlaine in Luxembourg. As I was asking him about his retirement, he confided to me, "I am getting used to it. . . I only miss my little nap at the beginning of the audience. It was very restorative." He had a famous predecessor in Séguier, and the sleep into which he sank made the defendant smile, the guard laugh, and the Court worry; and it obliged Talon to maintain the continuity of the proceedings. On December 3, the sleeper, shaken by Colbert, suddenly awoke. "Monsieur le superintendent, explain your personal expenditures. According to the dossier, from 1653 to 1656, they exceeded 23 million livres for your three domains of St.-Mandé, Vaux and Belle-Isle. The Court notes with interest that, according to Vatel's accounts, your expenses for meals alone added up to more than 400,000 livres." Fouquet maneuvered away from the direct threat by making fun of Colbert's legendary avarice, and he curtly concluded: "It is only my own money that was used, and not that of the State."

The following day, at the beginning of the audience, Séguier held up the document from St.-Mandé. "This paper is significant in all its aspects and it would be appropriate to remind the defendant of its content. Clerk, take the document and read it." Fouquet did not capitulate. "My misfortune is in not having burned this wretched paper, which was so far gone out of my memory that for two years I never thought of it, and did not think that I still had it. . . In any event, I repudiate it and beg you to believe that my devotion to the person and the service of the King has never been dissimulated."

Then the defendant took the offensive. He did not spare even Mazarin. "One of the things that pains me most, before this assembly, is that I cannot defend myself without mentioning the Cardinal, to whom many seem to believe that I owe everything, without knowing how much he owes to my services," nor Séguier: "Dear Sir, at all times, even at danger to my own life, I never abandoned the person of the King. But what *is* an attack on the Crown, is to be at the head of the Council of the Prince's enemies; it is to grant passage to the Spaniards via one's son-in-law and thus allow them to penetrate to the heart of the Kingdom. *That* is a crime of State."[17] And Colbert: "It is he, through his calumnies, who impels the King to this end. The way I am being hounded, you would think that it is in the State's interest to give up everything in order to get rid of an enemy of Colbert." This former parliamentarian then waxed poetic and sublime. In a broken, agonized voice, he addressed himself to the Divine, "Our Lord Jesus, I ask you to bear witness to the truth of my responses."

When everything seems to be lost, the heartless dialectical counts for less than the eloquence of the heart. It undoubtedly saved Fouquet from death. He also owed his preservation to the determination and tenacity of d'Ormesson, who saved the Court from dishonor. Out of twenty-two judges, nine voted for the death penalty, and thirteen for banishment; the Monarch had to miscarry justice in order to inflict life imprisonment upon this generous and disinterested reprobate. D'Artagnan refused to be appointed his guard for life, saying, "I would rather be a common soldier than a jailer." Understandable.

Was Fouquet guilty? His confession to the King, his memoirs, the admirable pleas made by his wife, the stunning petition from his mother, his admissions to the audience, hardly leave room for doubt. Guilty he was, like Concini, Richelieu and Mazarin, the leading lights of a regime that encouraged not very scrupulous practices to ensure its supremacy. Fouquet, that poetic and ardent emblem of corruption, found a sweet revenge in friendship. Along with L'Hoste and Ozanet, his defenders were innumerable. And such defenders: Patin, Mme de Sévigné, Mlle de Scudéry, Pellisson, La Rochefoucauld, Condé, Turenne and, later, Madame de Maintenon, who, in remembrance of the superintendent's kindnesses towards Scarron's wife who was always short of cash, brought some humanity to the prisoner's last years. And let us not forget the best, the greatest of his advocates, La Fontaine.

He is punished enough by the rigors of fate;
To be innocent is already unfortunate.[18]

Councilors and readers all, lend an ear — La Fontaine is still pleading.

Footnotes

1. Colbert had recently come begging, at Fouquet's sick bed, for funds in the name of the king, for his Navy. . .
2. The rather ridiculous name given by this scholar to the character of the superintendent in his novel.
3. The king's mistress would soon be promoted to Duchesse de Vallière, a brief moment of glory before she found her life made miserable by a rival, the Marquise de Montspan.
4. *Fouquet*, Daniel Dessert, Fayard, 1987.
5. 1609-1680: Italian marshal in the service of the Empire, author of several treatises on the art of war.
6. The interest rate, in theory, was limited to 5.5% and any excess became usury. To circumvent this regulation, lenders disbursed only part of the funds and charged interest on the totality of the sum theoretically advanced. Thus one could arrive at rates higher than 25%.
7. Morand named Vaux the temple of public relations, a concept invented by the superintendent.
8. For this reason, he had to pay to the Treasury a contractual sum each year and the difference between the aforementioned sum and the amount of the recovered taxes represented the benefice of the "tax collector."
9. The grass snake is displayed on Colbert's arms.
10. Fouquet thought he was clever in revealing to the King the turpitudes of the Mazarin system.
11. Paul Morand's felicitous phrase.
12. *Louis XIV*, Louis Bertand, Librairie Arthème Fayard, 1923.
13. La Fontaine decried his friend's incarceration, after a visit to the château d'Angers where the prisoner had fought for his life.
14. Malesherbes, in spite of his advanced age, courageously agreed to defend Louis XVI, sacrificing to his king the little life that remained to him. An honor that Target, his fellow-member, had shamefully refused.
15. The bench of the judges was upholstered with a fleur-de-lis tapestry.
16. D'Ormesson reported the ins and outs of the trial to the Marquise, who reported them in her letters to Arnauld de Pomponne, son of the Jansenist Arnauld d'Andilly. Pomponne, because of his friendship for Fouquet, had been exiled in Verdun, by order of Colbert.
17. Fouquet refers here to the factious role of the Séguier family during the Fronde, which had taken up the rebels' causes.
18. Inscription on the nymphs at Vaux.

Chapter 7

MIRABEAU

Honoré-Gabriel Riqueti, comte de Mirabeau (1749-1791, was the most influential figure in the first two years of the French Revolution. A moderate and an advocate of a constitutional monarchy, he was distrusted by the royalists and revolutionaries alike.

> "Mirabeau: the most glorious political genius this country has had since the incomparable Cardinal Richelieu."
>
> Gambetta

> "In the midst of the appalling disorder of a session, I saw him on the tribune, somber, ugly and immobile: he recalled Milton's chaos, impassive and without form in the center of its confusion."
>
> Chateaubriand

"Mirabeau shouted so loud that Versailles was shaken. No such tempest had crashed down on men's heads since the fall of the Roman Empire, and passions mounted in terrifying waves surging ever higher." Thus opens Louis-Ferdinand Céline's doctoral thesis in medicine,[1] defended in 1924 and focusing on Philippe-Ignace Semmelweis. This epic evocation of the French Revolution, of its turbulence, torments and torrents, this depiction of Mirabeau's tirades had little to do with the work of the Hungarian hygienist. However, Céline made good use of it, undoubtedly because the formidable and title-bearing orator from the third estate was "a vociferator," to borrow the qualifier that Leon Bloy applied to his own person. In his unexpected analysis, the author of *The Voyage* retained nothing of Gabriel-Honoré de Riqueti but his ardor, his deep deafening voice, his furious and impassioned eloquence. The portrait stops at the surface: Céline was not studying giants but microbes.

Never was the demiurge of Revolution — which began with the occupation of the Jeu de Paume and ended with the sacking of the Tuileries — burdened with so much faith, distrust, honor and indignity. What a mixture of perseverance, talent, bombast, and confusion in his intrigues and his efforts to rescue an imperiled masterpiece: the monarchy. He was condemned to the firing squad at the Champs-de-Mars on

July 17, 1791. That day, the police force, as we say today, under the command of the astronomer-mayor Bailly[2] and the brilliant La Fayette — "Gilles Caesar" — shot at the petitioners who were calling for murder in the name of philosophy. Among those sacrificed were Diderot, Voltaire, the abbot Raynal and, especially, the King, who was struck with a knife in the back — a Swiss knife. He did not recover, and from that point onward would lose first his crown and then his head.

Honor and indignity. The great Corneille comes to mind in connection with the difficult relations between Mirabeau and nothingness. "Let us impose order on the funereal ceremonies, / Commensurate with our famous name"[3] and his successive and highly contrasting funerals? On April 4, 1791, after the great orator had, in the inept words of Talleyrand, "dramatized his death," an interminable cortege headed out from the Chaussée d'Antin, passed through Saint-Eustache, and reached the Pantheon, lulled — dragged would be more precise — by fitting music written by Gossec, the lyric propagandist of the Revolution. The army, the clergy, the whole Assembly (or almost), the ministers, the sans-culottes, the penniless, accompanied the scruple-less to his final residence. At ten o'clock in the evening, they had not yet arrived at the old Sainte-Geneviève church,[4] transformed into a lay repository intended to receive the great men of "the era of French liberty." Mirabeau was "deemed worthy." More than 300,000 people mourned one of the least virtuous but most lucid heroes of a history that was finding, after its last sigh, a second breath.

The most appalling, disastrous day (in parodying the speeches, we are not making fun of the dead) was in fact the one in November 1792, when Gamain, the metalworker, revealed the existence of a certain iron cabinet. It was built and installed in a secret place in the Tuileries on order of the King, he told the Convention (which was just preparing its regicide). The hiding place was said to hold devastating documents.

Roland, Interior Minister, spelled out the implications. "This discovery will compromise several of our fellow-members who have sat in the Constituent and Legislative Assemblies." Then, he mentioned "original letters from the above-mentioned King." These remarks by "the evil old man" (to use Jaurès' unpleasant expression) revealed how vulnerable was our hero, whom Manuel, a deputy of Paris, proposed should be tried postmortem. "There are no great men without virtue." His statue was covered with canvas, his bust was smashed, his correspondence with Louis XVI was made public.[5] Marat triumphed. Since

1790, he had been denouncing "Mirabeau's dreadful secrets" in his newspaper, *L'Ami du people [The Friend of the People]*. Suddenly, an odd document appeared, *Le Livre rouge*, laisting him among the pensioners of the court and ascribing to him an annual stipend of 195,000 livres. "People, give thanks to the gods! Your worst enemy has just fallen under the scythe of the Parcae. . . ," he exulted, before spitting out: "Mirabeau in the Pantheon! Oh rage, oh derision!" On September 21, 1793, Marie-Joseph Chénier, a mediocre writer whose tragedy *Charles IX* had just become a hit, got the Convention to approve a punishment beyond the tomb: the hide of the Inhabitant of Aix was thrown out of the worthy crypt and his remains, piled into a pine box, were dumped in a common grave.

But one corpse would drive out another, and the pox of the cast-down idol would give way to the pustules of "the Friend of the people," who was de-pantheonized in his turn, in February 1795, when the Thermidor bandaged the Terror's wounds and stripped the survivors. France was sucking its own blood during a long night watered by an interminable river glinting with vermilion reflections. Only Mirabeau's genius could have avoided the bloodshed that still compromises liberty, with all due respect to those who were eternal lovers of the *Louison*,[6] who were so complacent about political assassination. Paradox and irony: the same people eagerly signed, without the least risk, the abolitionist proclamations. From Mathiez to Soboul, they cursed him. Counter-revolutionary historians, heirs to Bonald and Maistre, cannot find harsh enough words for him: traitor to the cause of the people, stoolpigeon for the King.

Such pettiness is dwarfed by Mirabeau's stature. His errors in 1789, his maladroitness, opened the way for the parliamentary tyranny of "the Incorruptible" but, to an enlightened conscience, he remains the only man who was capable of marrying absolutism with tolerance, of reconciling equality and the hereditary transmission of power. "I want a constitution that is free, but monarchical," he would repeat, in the face of incomprehension and ill will. This slandered slanderer would howl, impotent and premonitory, against the incompetents who were leading the country at so crucial a moment. "If Monsieur Necker had an ounce of character, he would become Cardinal Richelieu in the Court and would regenerate us; if the government had the least skill, the King would declare himself a populist and, in truth, we would be in a position to write the second volume of Denmark."[7]

But there was something rotten in the kingdom of France, and Death, bloodthirsty, would not allow him to take it under control. It was immense. Already, in 1790, he prophesied: "The King has the support of only one person, the Queen. I tend to believe that she would not enjoy her life without her crown, and I am quite certain that she will not preserve her life if she does not preserve her crown." Why, Your Majesties, did you not listen to Riqueti? What torments he would have spared you.

His father, Victor, Marquis de Mirabeau, certainly did not spare him any. A paranoiac, he persecuted himself and others; he was dogmatic, a reactionary who has ahead of his time. He was a worthy son of Jean-Antoine de Mirabeau who, crowned in glory on the battlefield, answered sharply a banal compliment of Louis XIV: "If I had spent less time in battle and more time at court currying favor, I would have had more promotions and fewer wounds." Victor was not very different. He pilloried "the philosophical dirt, the encyclopedic scribbling hack," while dreaming of the laurels of Fontenelle, d'Alembert and others; then he took up with physiocracy, the favorite trend among "thinkers" and fools.[8] This doctrine preached laws (that were not as "natural" as we were told they were), a return to the land and an economy based on agriculture, the principal source of wealth — at the very moment when the industrial revolution was in full swing in England and had begun to make inroads on the continent. Victor, imperturbable in the face of the world's evolution, set out a whole jumble of generous and anachronistic ideas in a book published in 1756, *L'Ami des hommes* (*The Friend of Man*). This title would become his sobriquet and would ensure him, finally, of a brief celebrity that would cauterize his morbid jealousy with regard to a son whose genius irritated him until the end. He considered himself a luminary in a century that had to grope its way along in the dark, and he proved Montesquieu right for saying (having met him in his youth), "What genius is in that head, and what a pity that we all we can get from it is noise."

Unfortunately, the Friend of Man was not that of his wife or his children. When Gabriel was born, he refused even to glance at the mini-monster whose disgrace clashed with his Platonic love of beauty. His resentment was constant toward the "complete scoundrel that should be effaced from the memory of mankind." The *lettres de cachet* followed one after another, and "the little monster," having become big, began a despairing tour of the prisons of France. The first stop was a form of house arrest in Manosque, calculated to calm a delinquent minor; and the shy one did not want to leave. The second stage: the château d'If, where myth blends with the imaginary and the dungeon of Mirabeau merges with that of Edmond Dantès. The third stage: the fort of Joux, where Toussaint Louverture would die of cold and of murderous nostalgia. Not far from there, in Pontarlier, Gabriel fell in love with Sophie de Ruffey, whose husband, the worthy Marquis de Monnier, leavened the weight of his years with the lightness of his wife.

This adventure, in an era when deception had the impertinent blessing of Beaumarchais and Marivaux, had an unsuspected political impact. Mirabeau, indeed, had married Emilie de Marignane a few years before; her dowry, inversely proportional to her virtue, had attracted him. His misstep brought upon him a lawsuit instigated by his father (of course), and a death sentence. (Pontarlier at that time followed the custom of today's Teheran; illegitimately ruffled clothing was transformed into a shroud.) For want of any better alternative the culprit was executed in effigy, for the two lovers, tipped off by Malesherbes, had fled to Amsterdam. Later, from his prison, Gabriel would write admirable, encyclopedic and salacious letters to his mistress, where his love, his culture, his precious eroticism and his unhampered pornography would startle Victor Hugo (who, in *Littérature et philosophie melées,* would admire "the pure passion" that burned in certain pages, but would draw "the appropriate veil" over others.) Mirabeau, endowed with the skepticism of Laclos, wrote: "Love, which we take for the cause of our pleasures, is at most only the pretext." When he tired of this liaison, Sophie, dethroned from the Venusian heights, fat and forsaken, put an end to her days that had been stripped of their delicious nights.

In 1777, the Friend of Man, tireless and ornery as ever,[9] obtained a new *lettre de cachet* against his son. Shut up at Vincennes for more than three years, he wrote a scathing attack against the abuses of absolutism, *Les Lettres de cachet et des prisons d'Etat,*[10] and the bulk of his erotic-political work that was so lovingly exhumed by Apollinaire. This work explores the relations between libertinage and liberty. Mirabeau, in whom both were indissolubly joined, felt that together they could break the yoke of superstitions denounced by the Enlightenment. His amorality, his atheism, made him appear abominable to more timid consciences. Madame de Staël, filled with aversion, described him walking with the deputies of the three estates on May 4, 1789. "The Count de Mirabeau was especially notable. No name, except his, was yet famous among the six hundred deputies of the third estate. One's opinion of his mind was singularly increased by one's fear of his immorality."

Necker's daughter was mistaken. Mirabeau's license was not an endorsement of anarchy — the confusion and lack of discipline among the third estate made him indignant — but a search for a new order through pleasure, as a way to deliver the being from its chains. The "irregular power" that terrified Germaine de Staël is that of creation itself and, during the turbulent days of June 1789, Mirabeau endeavored to impose his truth on the representatives of the people: "You started with chaos; and did the world start with anything else?" He was faithful to Diderot, who had exhumed sexuality from its convent, to enable it to take part (like philosophy and politics), in the development of a better world where man would finally find his place. In *Erotika Biblion*, based on exhaustive biblical and traditional scholarship, Mirabeau denounces the arbitrary nature of the coercive laws invented by the Church to rein in the body's explosive energy. Mirabeau is the Voltaire of the flesh.

The black did not excite the count the way it obsessed the divine Marquis de Sade, his detested jail mate,[11] and, if sometimes Mirabeau seems to imitate Valmont, he never becomes Bandole or Bressac, the boring and libidinous tormentors of Justine. After the critique of privileges, *Le Rideau levé, ou l'Education de Laure* (*The Raised Curtain, or the Education of Laura*)[12] defends enlightened absolutism through the image of the good father, philosophical and clear-sighted, who pushes his philosophy and his clear-sightedness to the point of sexually initiating his daughter. This licentiousness derives its energy from a searing reaction to the lack of affection and the abuse of power to which he had been victim since his youth. All prisons revolt Mirabeau, who gives this wrenching report: "I saw that I was always wrong, because I was never loved." This great man speaks the language of the Small Thing; there is no break between his political thought, his lack of love, his naughtiness. For this philosopher juggler, imposed virtue is the *lettre de cachet* of the heart.

When Louis the Well-Beloved rendered up his soul,[13] Louis XVI began the long and wavering walk toward the scaffold. His first wrong move was to dismiss Maupeou, who wanted to set the Parliaments straight. This need ran up against the King's suicidal blindness, who hastened to restore its old prerogatives to the judiciary. Unhappy is the monarch who does not understand that by cherishing the legal, the executive disarms itself. The chancellor was right: "The King is done for . . . I had him win a trial that was going on for three hundred years. He wanted to lose it. Well, he is the master." This trial, the Fifth Republic, won by the judges, was lost by them in turn.

Mirabeau, who had a presentiment of the inevitable crisis, thrashed about like a raging bull, preached in the desert, prophesied in the wilderness of indifference. In 1785, after his legal failure in Aix,[14] which prevented him from recovering Emilie and her riches, he made a short visit to London where, not finding a situation worthy of his talents, he was fascinated by the debates of the two Chambers where the eloquence of Pitt and the philosophy of Burke were outstanding. Back in Paris, he was constrained once again to find a way to make a living and, banned from politics, he offered his services to Clavière, a Geneva banker. This high level money-launderer would educate him on the nebulous subtleties of black money; he was an apt pupil.

That year, the Treasury was bone dry. Rebuilding the fleet (which ensured Beaumarchais many comfortable commissions), and the war in America, had dried up all the reserves. How to stave off bankruptcy? The generalized tax did not belong to that century. Calonne, Controller General of Finance, chose government loans, always a favorite among financiers of the second zone. Three stocks, the Caisse d'escompte (forebear of the Bank of France), the Saint-Charles Bank and La Compagnie des Eaux de Paris (the Paris water company), of which Beaumarchais (him again!) was a shareholder, exploded and speculation went wild. To allow for the penalty of eviction, so dear to economists, Calonne recruited Mirabeau to his battalion of quill-wielding serfs mobilized to cause a drop in the exchanges and to attract investors to the loans. The *Mirabelles*[15] became more and more harsh, until the day when a lampoonist suspected the minister of being "initiated" (in the Mitterrandian sense of the term). Mirabeau, shameless, changed his tune: "I have opposed speculation in all its forms, speculation that has sucked the cash out of the kingdom." Rivarol was not easily deceived:

Oh mighty Mirabeau, may your spiel
Bludgeon the bums who block our deals.
A reformed thief must decide others' fates
And preach from the ladder while hanging his mates.

Calonne was furious and Talleyrand, virtuoso of the oath (the only politician that Mirabeau considered his equal), dispatched this unlikely preacher to the court of the aging Frederic II in Berlin to spare him from the vindictive minister's rage. (This exile would lead him to decide in favor of the emancipation of the Jews, after having contemplated the message of Haskalah, the Judaism of the Enlightenment theorized by Moses Mendelssohn. He even wrote a work on that philosopher, and on December 24, 1789 he had these lessons on equality in mind when he intervened at the Assembly in favor of extending to the Israelites and to comedians the rights of citizenship.[16]) A few days later, he again took inspiration from Mendelssohn in his famous diatribe against the Treaty of the Blacks. Most particularly, his sojourn in the German capital enabled him to look further into and to refine his constitutional vision:[17] the sovereign must be the premier magistrate of his kingdom, privileges must be removed, and privileged people must be resisted. The constitution that he drafted went beyond the Voltairian concept of enlightened despotism, but did not go as far as Condorcet's republicanism. As a promoter of a popular monarchy that would, perhaps, have spared France a liberating and disastrous revolution, he was a royalist and would remain so all his life.

1789. The country, with the Estates General, traversed a century in twenty-four hours. "The day has come when talent will also be a power," commented Mirabeau who, true to form, supported "the conspiracy of the decent people" and the Society of the Thirty, founded in April 1788, where the men of liberty congregated: Lameth, La Fayette, La Rochefoucauld-Liancourt, Sieyès, Duport, Talleyrand, Condorcet... Misjudging their contempt for him, he dreamed of becoming principal minister and piloting the ship of State that was soon to sail off the end of the Earth.[18] While waiting for this fantasy promotion, lacking his father's authorization and lacking money, he could not take a seat among the nobility. He tried in vain to mend relations with the Friend of Man, dedicating to him his work *De la Monarchie prussienne*; the avaricious old coot remained indifferent and refused to loosen the cords securing the purse that was, it is true, none too well-rounded. In despair of cause, the son tried to buy a fief in Dauphiné, a province that was open to progressive ideas, but he did not have the resources to pay for the rights of succession. In order to mitigate his penury, he offered his services to the Crown via Montmorin:[19] "Is the minister concerned with ensuring that there will be no reason to fear the control of the Estates General? . . . Without the secret support of the government, I could not be present at these Estates." Then, he cried misery to Biron: "Why is it that we, who are better than the ministers, are fated to be lacking the one decisive power at this moment, money." Money? All his short life would be marked by a double urgency: to get his hands on money at any cost, and to spend it as fast as he could.

To keep pace with the changing times, he turned toward the third estate and the aristocrat became a displaced person; his blue blood was changed to red. On April 6, 1789, he was elected deputy of Aix. While Provence was up in arms once again, he ignored the paternal ire, faced down the peasants and calmed the riots in the city of seven fountains and at Vieux-Port. "Woe to the privileged orders. . . ," he hammered, "for the privileges will come to an end; but the people are eternal." This prophetic rhetoric startled Louis XVI, who was incapable of interpreting these locutions which, to spare the furniture, broke everything. He thought Mirabeau was conspiring with Laclos (the future Philippe-Égalité's right-hand man) and Camille Desmoulins (his mouthpiece), to hoist the future regicide onto the throne. When, on April 27, 1789, Orleans fomented the riot in Saint-Anthony, Mirabeau crystallized in his person the hatred of the court, which accused him of causing all its troubles. He was unfazed, and ranted unstintingly in his *Newspaper of the Estates General.* Soon banned, the broadsheet changed its name but not its style and *The Letter from the Count de Mirabeau to His Principals* defied his impotent critics. Doesn't every deputy have the right and the duty to report to his constituency?

And one historic day followed another, while equally historic words were being forged. Bailly advanced to center stage, glorious and timid. "The Nation, assembled, cannot receive orders." Granted. When Mirabeau returned the Marquis de Dreux-Brézé's bow, the swords remained sheathed. But wait. After the aversion came adulation and Louis XVI, before becoming Hugh Capet, was promoted as the "new Henri IV," "the Father of the people." Against a backdrop of small talk, conquests and generosity, the orator was leading the ball at the wedding of the people with the King: "I have managed more than any other mortal, perhaps, in conducting, enhancing, and extending a revolution, that will advance mankind more than any other." It is a great wrong to be right too early; and his contradictors overpowered him. The Right treated him like a Catiline avid for power, sowing chaos in the furious crowd. The Left, without realizing that, with his slogan "the Law and the King" he embodied the innovative spirit that had fed hope since Pierre Bayle, reproached him for playing a double game.

Throughout this period, the monarch, whose only absolute quality was his hesitation, allowed the Revolution to pick up speed and wielded the stick and the carrot alternately, without realizing that the root was still being held to his throat while the branch was breaking his back. The Count of Provence deplored "the King's weakness and indecision, [that are] beyond all description. To give you an idea of his character, imagine greased marbles that you are vainly striving to hold together." The Empress Marie-Thérèse was no more tender towards her daughter, Marie-Antoinette. "I know her insolence and her indolent mind, together with the usual dissipations of her age. As soon as any serious topic comes up that she believes may cause some difficulty, she avoids reflecting and acting appropriately." When La Marck spoke of a providential man, the Queen shut him up, saying, "I doubt that we will ever be in such sad condition as to be reduced to relying on Mirabeau." Poor woman. She did not realize that between monarchy and anarchy only one obstacle remained: the object of her dislike.

The royal couple's blindness dismayed the powerful orator and he begged Malouet and La Marck to inform them of his true intentions. "Let the Château know that I am for them, more than against them." Unable to make himself heard, he tried to make them listen, he stirred up more fire while trying to keep it under control. He was already envisioning himself masterminding the affairs of France, when it might have become a monarchy in the English style, when the Assembly, at Lanjuinais's instigation, gave the extremists a boost by voting in favor of an insipid text forbidding a deputy to become minister. "Reduced to an advisory role, never being able to act, I will probably have the fate of Cassandra: My predictions will always be true and I will never be believed." Maupeou was right, the King was indeed done for. Prohibiting office plurality alone cannot save a regime.

While Marat, visionary of misfortune, was claiming ten thousand heads ("within a few months, perhaps, you will cut down a hundred thousand of them, and you will have created a wonder"), the one whom Goethe called the Hercules of the French people, a giant now in chains, with no real hold on events, saw his destiny slip through his fingers. A Don Quixote with the physique of a Sancho Panza, he was fighting against windmills whose vanes were accelerated by the winds of history, and soon by its tornado. The greatest defender of the Throne, appointed to this position by destiny and by himself, he was seen as its worst adversary and, instead of thanks, he reaped only incomprehension and ingratitude. If the King and the Queen were unable to appreciate his disinterested — for the moment — assistance, some their close relations were more lucid. Through La Marck and the Austrian ambassador Mercy d'Argenteau, negotiations finally took place. While the former, an old friend, was playing an appropriate role in bringing the genius closer to misfortune, the latter, a diplomat, was guilty of interference in the affairs of France. His mediation cast a shadow on Mirabeau's shaky reputation and lent weight to Barnave's scandalmongering and Marat's wild imaginings, who would accuse him of joining the Austrian committee and of being the agent of a foreign power.

From that moment onward, everyone hid his motives; and Louis XVI told La Marck that "Everything that Mirabeau does must remain a deep secret from my ministers. I count on you for that." He played the presidents of the Fifth Republic against each other in a period of cohabitation, and they, instead of conducting one policy, were constrained to conduct two of them. This duality transformed the chief of the executive into a leader of the opposition. In such an absurd context, it is difficult to be a Richelieu, and Mirabeau was reduced to playing Father Joseph, even if it only meant throwing his homespun cloak over the nettles as fast as possible. When La Marck asked him how much he owed, he was unable to answer. He made his calculations, went back twenty years and arrived at a dismaying total: 208,000 livres. Never would the Château agree to wipe that slate clean. Mercy d'Argenteau eased his fears: "Since it's not more, the King would do well to pay." After the Man from Aix signed a letter of allegiance to the sovereign, on May 10, 1790, an agreement was concluded: the debt would be erased; a monthly allowance of 6,000 livres would be granted; and a reward of a million livres would be given at the end of the session of the Assembly ("if he serves me well," specified the King, who gave La Marck four receipts for 250,000 livres. This war chest, enough to pollute many consciences, left Mirabeau's intact; according to La Fayette's (intelligent, for once) assessment, he only betrayed in the sense of his convictions. He became the King's employee, not his servant. In his speech on the clergy,[20] he already justified his role. "Dear Sirs, in this Revolution that is giving birth to such righteous and generous feelings, it is time to abjure the prejudices of proud ignorance that make us scorn the words 'wages' and 'paid.' I know of only three ways of getting by in society: one must be a beggar, a thief or on someone's payroll."

A thief he never was — or if so, only a little; a beggar, he no longer was; and this relieved debtor, having concluded the agreements with the King, allowed himself a burst a puerile joy: here he was, influential, powerful and rich, rich like he had never been. He enjoyed the whole panoply of the new opulence: a house at Antin, sumptuous dining, well-furnished rooms. Suddenly becoming a bibliophile, he even allowed himself Buffon's valuable collection of books. The good La Marck regretted this imprudence. "He wanted to promote both pleasure and business, and though he often spoke about his reputation and the glory to which he aspired vis-a-vis posterity, he was not a man to sacrifice the present entirely to the future."

On July 3, 1790, he met Marie-Antoinette at the château of Saint-Cloud. He treated her like Fersen. She treated him like Rohan. Contempt generated spite. "You will see, the rabble will tear apart their corpses." Politics abhors a vacuum and, when Necker departed on September 4, the unofficial adviser to the King suggested giving the Jacobin ministers the position, an infallible means — he thought — of neutralizing them. This idea disconcerted the King, who was unable to understand the message that was constantly being embellished around one and the same theme: "I am a man to re-establish order, not to re-establish the old order." Until the very end, Louis XVI preferred courtiers to prophets. Jaurès was right: "Louis XVI's greatest crime is to have failed to understand Mirabeau, it is to have scorned him, it is to have seen the admirable political advice by which he tried to render the Revolution comprehensible to him as nothing more than the miserable work of an adventurer at his last resort."

Mirabeau — son of the Encyclopedia, a libertine, a partisan of the middle way, sanctified, demonized, unbending adversary of the "formidable forces" referred to by Céline — should he have a place in the black Pantheon of corruption? If being corrupt means being paid to act, to write, to speak against one's conscience in favor of a foreign party, Mirabeau was not that. Admittedly, he pocketed considerable sums, but at no time did he give up defending his ideas which, if they had triumphed, would have averted the bloodshed of the Terror and the hemorrhage of the Empire. Mirabeau was not bought; he was disinterested. During his transitory and futile cohabitation with the court, he acted as a man of the *Ancien Régime* (which he never ceased being), as a visionary who remained that all his life, as the lawyer that he dreamed of becoming. That was no under-handed pact that he signed with the King; it was a schedule of fees. Today, the Bar, as finicky as ever, would find this just remuneration absolutely normal for the inhuman labor provided by this incomparable defender. Countless astute and far-sighted analyses and syntheses, strikingly subtle comments, irreplaceable councils, moving petitions, and firm and respectful injunctions fill the forty principal memoranda he submitted to the King — always pertinent, yet never heeded by Louis XVI. Once he took up his pen, the counselor-at-law transmuted into Cicero... and with such a voice, such verve and such flair. Only one of these services would have been worth the sums that were grudgingly and stingily given to him. Proudhon, not known for his indulgence, spoke aptly enough: "He was a consulting lawyer whose talent, days, nights, secretaries and servants were exploited, whose life and courage were consumed." There is nothing amoral in this diligence or, rather, the amorality pertains to the court which, to further its own interests, had made a pact with that which it found repulsive. Chimerical and profound, Mirabeau sacrificed his last energies in defense of a utopian transfiguration of absolutism into a parliamentary monarchy governed from the center — i.e., by him — with no Bastille and no *lettres de cachet*, where the King and the people, reconciled, would sing a royalist song in unison to the tune of the Marseillaise.

Mirabeau was a trader, not of favors but of genius. He agreed to be paid for an invaluable talent, at a time when the cruelty of September had not yet dissipated the hopes of July. He proved the axiom of great lawyers: the enemy is the client. And such enemies they were, the King balking before the hurricane that he mistook for a north wind, the Queen, saved from a stupid life by a sublime end. Faced with so much weakness, he defended a powerful executive. "I believe the King's veto so necessary that I would rather live in Constantinople that in France if it did not allow it;"[21] and he won the battle against Barnave when the Assembly adopted his amendment: "War may be declared only by decree of the legislative body rendered upon a formal proposal from the King." The Jacobins were indignant; she who was yet their muse, Mme. Roland, stamped her feet: "A hateful, purely illusory and entirely royalist text."

Mirabeau, leaving the Left to its rage and the Right to its suspicions, continued to outline the contours of his ideal constitution that would never see the light of day. He fought State religion, responsible for so much butchery, the revocation of the Edict of Nantes, and the French Inquisition that was already turning Voltaire's stomach and fanning the flames of Casanova's libido.[22]

When the deputies quarreled over the colors to be flown by the Brest navy, he stood for the Tricolor: "Our colors will sail on the national seas, and will gain the respect of every region, not as the sign of combat and victory but as that of the holy confraternity of the friends of liberty all around the globe and as the terror of conspirators and tyrants." Such eloquence was not found again until Lamartine: "The Tricolor has been around the world with the Republic and the Empire, with your freedoms and your glories, while the red flag only went around the Field-of-Mars, trailed in the blood of the people."

And the chasm went on expanding between the defender and his underwriters. Each one dug his own tomb in his own way: Mirabeau, by the weight of his task and the ardor of his excesses; the King and Queen, by their stubborn refusal to see what was coming and to focus only on mirages. Until the final moment, the great orator strove to convince them. It was no good. Instead of becoming discouraged, he insisted, he tried from every angle, in fact he tried too hard. Incorrigible and ever willing, he even found time, on March 20, 1791, with death waiting in the wings, to support the dubious cause of his friend La Marck in the sinister affair of the mining concession. On April 2, when the buds of springs, tiny and trembling, adorned the still fragile trees of freedom, Mirabeau, exhausted, gave up his soul. To God? Perhaps. To the devil? Why not. He was the apostle of an impossible cohabitation — which, as France knows, is the only kind.

Footnotes

1. A French physician and writer whose stark, bleak novels in the 1930's were well-received; his reputation diminished during and after World War II as he became more bitter and disenchanted.
2. Curiously forsaken by the French, this pacifist scientist was closely studied by the Anglo-Saxon historians.
3. *Sertorius*, Act V, Scene VIII.
4. Started by Soufflot in 1764, completed by Rondelet in 1789 and modified by Quatremère de Quincy.
5. Under the title of *Items printed in accordance with the decree of the national Convention of December 5, 1792 (Year II of the Republic)*.
6. Nickname given to the guillotine.
7. After the revolution of 1660, Denmark was ruled by a King who relied on the will of the people.
8. Physiocracy, dubious ancestor of liberalism, was founded by Quesnay, a doctor and economist.
9. The marquis de Mirabeau would fire off no fewer than 44 *lettres de cachet* against his wife, his daughter Louise and his elder son.
10. *Les lettres de cachet*, read throughout Europe, would incite the King to close the Vincennes dungeon in1784. In anticipation of the Bastille.
11. Mirabeau and de Sade were held in the same prison starting in January 14, 1780.
12. Published anonymously in 1788.
13. Louis XV died on May 10, 1774 at Versailles.
14. A trial during which Mirabeau was his own lawyer. Although the verdict was unfavorable, he won several points (thanks to the genius of his elocution) against the petty and limited Marignane clan, who had the support of the Attorney General, all the Aix nobility and, naturally, the Friend of Man.
15. The term used by Beaumarchais, a savage adversary of Mirabeau, to designate his orations.
16. An eloquence whose fruits he would not live to see, for the Jews were emancipated in two stages: in January 1790, then in September of the following year.
17. Meditations that would lead to two works: *The Prussian Monarchy under Frederic the Great*, published in 1788, and *Secret History of the Court of Berlin*, which was published a year later, anonymously, causing a scandal.
18. As the celebrated Henri Monnier said.
19. The Minister for Foreign Affairs, whom Mirabeau approached several times to solicit, in vain, an ambassadorial appointment and advances. When Armand de Montmorin finally agreed to work with the great rheto-

rician to save the monarchy, it was too late; he would perish during the troubled days of September (See the chapter on Danton).

20. The Assembly debated making the clergy subservient to the nation.
21. On September 11, 1789, the Assembly granted the King a right of suspensive and non-absolute veto, as Mirabeau desired.
22. Casanova and Tireta, his companion in vice, rented a window from which they could witness the execution of the chevalier La Barre, during which they indulged in "indecent pleasures."

Chapter 8

DANTON

Georges-Jacques Danton, 1750-1794, was a leader of the French Revolution and particularly of the extremist Jacobins, whose goal was to ensure national unity and a stable republican government. He gradually emerged as a voice of moderation, and was overthrown by Robespierre.

> "Nature gave me an athletic form and the rough physiognomy of liberty, in equal parts."
>
> Danton

At the exit of the Odéon subway station in Paris, not far from boulevard Saint-Germain where romantic couples meet for their first dates, the statue of George-Jacques Danton has been making the same gesture since 1891. The monument was erected in his honor during the Third Republic[1]; three years before, a first mausoleum had been dedicated in his honor at Arcis, while Alphonse Aulard, who held the "History of the Revolution" chair at the Sorbonne, had been spreading the Gospel according to Danton and preparing his sanctification. After Saint Mirabeau, Saint Danton? Why not. The grateful Republic sublimated his memory, worshipped his legendary personality, glossed over the details.

Aulard's beatific work dispelled the suspicious aura of shady influences that fluttered around his mutilated hide. Aulard's successor, Albert Mathiez, a member of the French section of the Communist *Internationale* and an adherent of straightforward Jacobinism, pursued a campaign to demolish that which had been erected by his predecessor. Historians, except for the rare survivors of the cult of Aulard, acknowledge the great speaker's corrupt practices and accept the theses of Mathiez who, otherwise, they despise.

These contradictions are explained by the duality of his character.

Under his boxer's physique, Danton hid the subtlety of Ulysses, an un-principled cunning, and a choleric self-control. What were his political ideas, he who, according to Gaxotte, "threw himself into the Revolu-tion the way a mower attacks a field"? Did he really have any? Was he a friend of the humble or a pragmatic man guided solely by his own in-terest? The shady character or the public figure, which should we be-lieve? An ingenius propagandist, whenever he addressed the Corde-liers, the Convention or the Jacobins, he galvanized his audience. Whether he was weaving his intrigues with Orleans, Dumouriez, for-eign agents or the court, this parricide sought to smother the red infant and to steal its burial funds.

His charisma was so spellbinding that it is impossible to speak of Danton without looking for some extenuating circumstances. How about revolutionary corruption? From the Girondins to the entourage of the Incorruptible,[2] the Pure Ones were far from perfect and they were as sophisticated in their creative accounting as today's officials are![3] In 1798, Joseph Fiévée (the King's agent, and Bonaparte's, and various others', happy prefect of Nievre — a very flourishing depart-ment — and an open homosexual), published the novel, *La Dot de Suzette* (*Suzette's Dowry*), in which he denounced the men of liberty. Along with the giants, how many stunted, pretentious and mediocre individuals were to be found, who were not satisfied with the meager provisions of the Convention. Eighteen livres per month, per deputy. Misery! So some boasted of their poverty while others found a way to grow rich and, in contrast to purification through virtue, practiced accumulation through vice, to the detriment of implacable and lethal morality. Tal-lien, Barbaroux, Barras, Fréron made a fortune in the name of equality; Chabot, d'Espagnac, Delaunay, Fabre d'Eglantine, Basire, Lacroix made the best of the tight circumstances in the name of fraternity; and Dan-ton, with a completely free hand, dipped into every till. Now it was no longer the king who was being cheated, but the nation, and the Masters of the moment proved Montesquieu right when he wrote in *The Spirit of Laws*: "When the public treasury becomes the patrimony of private in-dividuals, the Republic is a shell and its strength is but the power of a few citizens and the license of all."

In 1759, in the writings of Jacques Danton and his wife Marie-Madeleine Camus a little monster was born, as repellent as Mirabeau. It wasn't easy being from the provinces in the 18th century. Scorned like

Jacob, the main character in *Le Paysan parvenu*,[4] these migrant workers were destined to become lackeys in the capital, where they were persecuted and mocked for their regional accent. They pronounced "King" (roi) "roua," whereas people of quality said "rouay," never suspecting these louts' pronunciation would prevail. (Now we all sound like dishwashers from the countryside.) However, Danton's father was not a domestic but a bailiff, a condition that was lower still. He would end up becoming prosecutor for the bailiwick. Prosecutor? Is that a step up? There is no happy childhood and the son is often father of the man who brought him into this world. The Rousseauian early years of our hero, entrusted to nature's care, should have made him a philosopher of the rear-guard and not the inspiring orator of the masses. Since his youth, he was fascinated by power and guided by license and, after his father's death in 1767, he was abandoned by a mother with too many children. Danton wandered across the fields (which he would later buy in a frenzy[5]), tested his mettle with the bulls that twice disfigured him (those of the Convention would decapitate him), barely missed losing his ample virility between the teeth of a pig (the teeth of the speculators would later tear it to shreds), contracted smallpox and became uglier still. In school, he met Thuriot (whose name Cadoudal distorted, during his trial, so that it came out "King-killer" ["Tue-roi"][6] In 1775, he was present in Rheims for the coronation of his future employer, Louis XVI, who would also become his victim. In the shadow of the cathedral, he received his law diploma, at a nice university comparable to that of Corsica during my adolescence, where a sheepskin could be had for about 500 livres. This dubious market became a meeting ground for dubious pupils: Couthon, Brissot, Chabot, Pétion, Louvet, Buzot, Saint-Just. They would not be repeating history.

Biographers are still divided as to Danton's culture and intelligence. According to Aulard, this saint had no flaws. "No one was more moral, better informed, more humane, cleaner in his dealings with money and freer of hatred. To an oratorical genius that was more original and more French than that of Robespierre and Vergniaud, Danton added the genius that his famous rivals lacked." Roederer takes a different view: "He had no education, no political or moral principles; no logic, and no dialectic ability; such was Danton." Must one be brilliant to become a lawyer? A robust constitution, a good memory, infinite patience, the art of never looking back are enough and Danton, who had these qualities, moved to Paris in 1787 and settled on the rue des

Mauvaises-Paroles ("Bad-Words Street"), a suitable site for this exceptionally gifted speaker.[7]

The Law courts always prefer attractive names, so as soon as Danton was registered at the bar, he embellished his patronym and made it d'Anton. The particle was the badge of honor in the *Ancien Régime* and the young lawyer strutted it with puerile pride. He would soon remove it again under the new regime, thus imitating Fleurville who, hauled before the Revolutionary Tribunal, was called de Fleurville by the president. "Citizen," he retorted, "I did not come here to lengthen my name but to shorten it." He saved his neck. Danton was not so lucky.

The first years at the bar are always hard and clients are scarce in the neophyte's waiting room. Mme. Roland describes the man who succumbed neither to her charms nor to her spirit as "a poor wretch of a lawyer, with more debts than responsibilities." One can hardly contradict the charge given that, since he took oath until 1791, he pled only twenty-two cases. This modest performance, reinforced by a lazy nonchalance, left him plenty of spare time. He haunted the Café Parnassus, fell in love with Gabrielle, the daughter of its rich owner, and married her. The 20,000 livre dowry enabled the couple to settle on rue des Cordeliers, at the Commercial Court, and to visit the royal palace, domain of the future Philippe-Egalité where the outcasts, misfits and marginal figures congregated who, soon enough, would be leading the charge.

The Revolution, of which Danton is both the shame and the glory, often took its relentless course in his absence. "He preferred giving orders to the masses than to merge with them. Like most of the revolutionary leaders, he was irremediably bouregois," wrote a contemporary. However, the 1790 idol of Paris became that of France in 1999, when the movies, theatre, television and other factories of simplistic legends transformed this debatable character into a paragon of virtue. Nobody remembers his singular and convenient disappearances during the great revolutionary days. He did not take part in the storming of the Bastille, but came out of refuge the following day to seize the Cordeliers Club, catalyst of effervescence. When, on October 5 and 6, 1789, responding to the call of the clubists, the rabble led by Maillard and miserably followed by La Fayette, captured the King at Versailles and brought him back to Paris, Master d'Anton was at the Palace. The Palace of Justice, that is. On July 17, 1790, he took an excursion in the countryside while the insurrection, of which he was one of the instigators, raged and left fifty dead on the cobblestones. He missed his appointment with History, but made a success of his love affair with Legend.

When he was present, it was worse yet. He was splattered by the blood of September, but not soiled by it. However, since August 17, 1792, he had been warning, "I have reason to believe that these outraged people whose indignation is sustained against those who have attempted to limit their freedom . . . will not be reduced to taking justice into their own hands, but will obtain it via their representatives and their magistrates." As Minister of Justice,[8] he did nothing to prevent the slaughter and allowed the assassins to sharpen their spades on the prisoners of Orleans. To those who begged him to intervene, he nonchalantly responded, "I don't give a damn about the prisoners: let them do whatever they can." A few months later, he took the future Louis-Philippe by the sleeve and, teasing, whispered to him: "Listen, these September massacres that you keep going on about, do you want to know who made them happen?" — Then, after a dramatic pause, "It was me." This conversation, reported in the bourgeois King's memoirs, sheds a sinister light on the scene that took place upon his return from Belgium where, on a mission, he missed Gabrielle's funeral. Upon his arrival in Paris a few days later, he had his beloved — one of the most deceived women in France — dug up, embraced her corpse, and had a mold of her face taken by Deseine, a deaf and dumb sculptor who would exhibit his malevolent work at the undistinguished salon of 1793. This devotee of mad love, this desperate depressive, married again four months later the young girl who was governess to his children.

We will not desecrate Danton's grave with a post mortem lawsuit. Only one question remains: was the great conventioneer corrupt? Historians are neither prosecutors nor lawyers, but clerks. If they want to become judges (in Danton's case, the temptation is severe), they must consider all the evidence before coming to a verdict, erase all bias, and set aside the inclinations of the heart. Louis Madelin[9] himself would fall victim to the charm of this masterful scoundrel. He looked at the facts from every direction, reconsidered every document, weighed every scrap of testimony. In vain. The truth will out: the Drum of the Revolution pounded out the general cause with one hand and extended the other toward Orleans, toward England, the people in power, the court, all the wheeler-dealers, thieves and crooks. "Unfortunately, there are facts that per force leave one perplexed," concludes the most scrupulous of his biographers.

In the course of my lifetime, I have defended some appalling causes, without any particular anguish or self-doubt. This time, I have to lay down my arms and agree: the letter addressed by Lucerne, French ambassador in London, to the Minister for Foreign Affairs (on November 29, 1789) was overpowering. "I am told that there are two British individuals in Paris, one named Danton and the other, Paré, whom some people suspect of being very special agents of the English government . . . I do not know if anyone has looked into this matter to find out whether they really exist." Alas, they did exist, and the second was none other than the Secretary of the first. Not satisfied with being an agent of His Gracious Majesty, he was also in the pay of the future Philippe-Egalité. Choderlos de Laclos and Camille Desmoulins, the most eloquent hack of the time (whom Michelet, who was often more inspired, called "the Voltaire of the Revolution,"), served as intermediaries, as they had done with Mirabeau. Easy work for Orleans, Grand Master of the corrupt practice as well as of the Grand Orient (a Masonic organization), the richest man in France and England (where he had placed his fortune to shelter it from the disorders that he was fomenting). When the prospect of a change in dynasty, that had once seemed imminent, receded, the orator abandoned Orleans and accepted an offer from the court, without, however, breaking with his former employers. He became a multifaceted representative of duplicity, and joined the Revolution through the safe-deposit room.

All men of justice know that there are three kinds of witnesses: true, false, and true-false — honest servants of the miscarriage of justice, who lie in all good faith, misled by faulty and selective memory. In Danton's trial, their misrepresentations leave my inward conviction intact. Even while I challenge Duquesnoy, who was too deeply committed to be impartial, and La Fayette, too thoughtless to be credible, the charges are substantiated and leave no room for doubt. Starting at least in 1790, Danton was in the pay of La Marck, Talon, Molleville and Montmorin, great distributors of slush funds from the civil lists, who used venality to try to divert the course of destiny.

On March 10, 1791, Mirabeau reproached La Marck for wasting the king's money. "Yesterday Danton received 30,000 livres and I have proof that it was he who, yesterday, passed it on to Camille Desmoulins. . ."[10] Having delivered this sermon, unexpected from such a man, Mirabeau then took the occasion to request, in disarming terms, a monthly stipend of 6,000 livres. "It is possible that I might squander them, but at least they would be more innocently spent than Danton's 30,000 livres. . . It is a great mistake in this base world not to be not rascal." Mirabeau knew what he was talking about.

The relationship between Danton and Montmorin[11] was more disconcerting still. On November 10, 1790, shortly after the unrest in Nancy, the thundering spokesman of the Cordeliers nailed the king's Ministers to the cross with a philippic that was comparable, according to Desmoulins, "to the most beautiful monuments of Antiquity." However, he did not mention the name of Armand de Montmorin, and demanded the departure of his colleagues but not his own. Danton's portfolio had a short memory, as Luce de Montmorin (a relative of Armand) learned to his dismay. The populace was indignant that he was acquitted by the "Tribunal of August 17,"[12] and Georges decided to howl with the wolves — the following day, he ordered the arrest of the one declared innocent the day before. Armand de Montmorin would be slain in the September disturbances and Danton, who was so much indebted to him, made not the slightest gesture to help. For a corrupt figure whose appetite has been quenched, the only good corrupter is a dead one.

How much money did he receive from the court? By definition, clandestine funds are unaccountable and only rumor can give an approximate idea of their scale. 300,000 livres is the figure advanced by Bertrand de Molleville in his *Memoires.* Brissot "studied a receipt for 100,000 livres signed by Danton to Molleville," and Mallet du Pan[13] said "The sums Danton received on the civil list are indisputable" Lessart speaks in the same vein; and then there were the five "modest citizens" who affirmed, according to Louis Madelin, having heard "from a certain Philippe, of Arcis-sur-l'Aube, a cousin of Danton, that he had received 150,000 livres in *assignats* (Revolutionary scrip) from the Lameth brothers, who had been agents of the court since 1791."[14] When Talon was hauled into court upon his return to France, he revealed to the judges that he had gotten into England, just like Talleyrand, using a counterfeit passport provided by Danton himself. And he added, "I had relations with him and these relations were of the nature to conceive that which could touch upon the personal safety of Louis XVI." Furthermore, Pellenc, another of the king's spies, had indicated to Mercy d'Argenteau in 1792 that "Talon, *who is of the same party,* owes his salvation to Danton most of all."

Was it permissible to rob the Republic? He did not hold back, and even boasted about it. "The kings," he said one day, "enriched the nobles. The Revolution must enrich the patriots." The day came when the Convention demanded accounts from the ministers. Roland provided his receipts with all the meticulousness of an expert; Danton, who was unable to do so, pitifully looked for loopholes. "We were leaders of liberty. . . I don't believe I deserve to be reproached for my political conduct." On the ropes, he had to admit that he could not provide any justification. "For most of these expenditures, I acknowledge that I do not have any legal receipt." No receipts at all, in fact. He added, "I spent money without restraint, in order to build public confidence and to give impetus to all of France." He barely avoided the charge of wasting public finances. France's envoy to Belgium was not guilty of plundering the enemy but of pillage at home. In contrast to Bonaparte, he scarcely benefited France with his indelicacies and kept his plunder for himself. On two occasions, at least, mysterious carts bearing chests inscribed with his name or that of Lacroix, his accomplice, would be intercepted at the border under the impassive gaze of the guards.

The trial of Louis XVI is the first republican example of "retained justice"[15] and the new sovereign, the people, demanded an accounting from old sovereign, the King. No magistrates are needed to do the dirty work of the State; it was the State itself that judges and kills. In a paradox of these outrageous hearings, the defendant failed to save his skin, thanks to his defenders and to certain bold conventioneers like Lanjuinais; and thanks, especially, to the corruption that marred the hearings from the first day. Every faction was fed by a morbid distrust. Everyone suspected everyone: the Girondins, of having allowed themselves to be bought; Mailhe, of having allowed himself to be circumvented; Danton, of having allowed things to run their course after having allowed himself to be bribed. The English Prime Minister declared in full Parliament, "The Chamber may be convinced that every conceivable means has been employed to preserve the head of Louis XVI from the dreadful fate that hangs over him and his family alike . . . ; but in the Assembly there are cruel and inflexible men. . ."

Danton did not share this support; European public opinion did him in. Bertrand de Molleville denounced him in his "*Dénonciations des prévarications commises dans le procès de Louis XVI*" (A Denunciation of the corrupts practices committed in Louis XVI's trial), and stripped him of any hope in a letter dated January 2, 1792 "I do not believe I should leave you unaware of the fact," he wrote to Danton, "that the late Monsieur de Montmorin gave into my keeping, toward the end of last June, a bundle of papers that I keep it with me. I have found therein a note that indicates, date by date, *the various sums that you pocketed out of the secret expense funds for Foreign Affairs.*" After this reminder, the threat became specific. "I have never made any use of these documents until the present; but I warn you that I am enclosing them in a letter that I am writing to the president of the National Convention, which I am sending to a trustworthy person with orders to deliver it and to have it printed and posted on every street corner if you do not act in the King's case *as a man who was so well paid must do.*" Then, unctuously, he concluded: "I have not confided to anybody about the letter that I am writing to you, therefore you should have no concern in this respect. . . " Later, the master storyteller would set the record straight. "The truth is that Montmorin had really shown me these documents a year before, but he had never entrusted them to me; they were by no means in my power, though I swore the opposite. . . " For a royalist, a lie to a *sans-culotte* was no lie at all, and the blow struck home. Danton was delayed in Belgium and arrived in Paris on January 15, 1793, to dig up his wife and to bury the King.

This shameless man, organizer of the resistance, could not be absent during the third roll-call where the fate of God's secular representative was decided. However, he never considered Capet's death necessary to the salvation of the Republic. "A nation saves itself, it does not take revenge," he pleaded before his faithful Cordeliers. A king without a crown can be used as a hostage, a king without a head is transfigured, he becomes a martyr. Thus it was in all good faith that he asked Pitt for four million in fees and a modest provision of two million to save the prisoner of the Temple. Then, he negotiated with Ocariz, Spanish *chargé d'affaires* in Paris, to grant a measly two million more to assure his diligence.[16] At the same time, he confided to Lameth (who, in the face of danger, had returned to Paris), "Without being convinced that the King is irreproachable, I find it just, I believe it useful to get him out of the situation he is in. I will do as much as I can, with prudence and boldness. . . "[17] and — Danton exhibits his entire essence in these few lines — he concluded: "*I will expose myself, if I see a chance of success but, if I lose all hope, I can tell you now, I do not want to have my head fall with his and I will be among those who will condemn him.*" When his interlocutor protested such cynicism ("Why do you add these last words?"), he retorted, "To be sincere, as you asked me to be."

Lameth would give him absolution in his *Notes et souvenirs.* "As long as he had any hope of success, Danton did all that he could to save the King. Abandoned, if not betrayed, by the foreign courts, more than abandoned by Pitt and by everyone outside of France who should have helped, he gave up." The Englishman, indeed, refused Talon, the man with the counterfeit passport, the additional two million sought by the man from Champagne. The blood of a prince is not to be sold. Danton was defeated by the inexorable — British tight-fistedness, its insatiable thirst for money. Upon his return to Paris, not being able to dull the national razor, he sharpened it. He began by berating the Convention for quibbling at such a serious hour over the fate of *the Friend of laws.* "I will acknowledge, Citizens, . . . that I thought we should be engaged in something other than comedy. . . . It is tragedy that you must give to the nations. You must make the tyrant's head fall, under the axe of the law." When the deputies, returned to their duty, debated what majority must vote on the sentence, he stood up again. "I ask why no one thought of raising this question when it came to abolishing the royalty; the fate of a whole nation was pronounced by a simple majority." Constrained, the deputies decided that "All decrees must be made by absolute majority." When his turn came to decide what sentence to impose on the monarch, he gave the death blow. "I do not compromise with tyrants . . . Kings must be struck in the head. I vote for death." However, the sentence was very nearly put to a second ballot, and only won on Champigny-Clément's reversed vote.[18]

The Revolution, having become cultural, struck, struck more and more cruelly, striking down its own after having struck all the others.[19] On March 31, 1793, Danton went further. "One can only represent the nation when one has had the courage to say, 'The king must be killed.'" He might have added, "Especially when one sold oneself to save him." This swaggering would not spare his life and, soon, he would mount the fatal cart and follow the route marked out by the corpses of the Girondins, Mme. Roland and d'Hébert, the route that Robespierre and Saint-Just would take soon enough as well.

In the most tightly constructed indictments, only the cold poetry of the statistics does not lie. At his death, the visible fortune of "the lawyer without a brief" amounted to more than 200,000 livres, not counting purchases made under assumed names and the commissions paid off the books, like the 300,000 livres shared with the Baron de Staël, the Swedish ambassador to Paris (Germaine's husband), in order to improve maritime cooperation with France.

For a man who began life with a few thousands livres, this disturbing affluence explains Robespierre's and Saint-Just's choice in instigating his downfall. They would inform against him in a trial for corrupt practice. To strengthen the case, the duettists of death lined the stands, alongside politicians like Philippeaux and Camille Desmoulins, with all the lace-cuffed scoundrels: Fabre, d'Espagnac, Chabot and Delaunay, both compromised in the Compagnie des Indes scandal. This was more than a taxi to the guillotine, it was a vendetta, an attack against defense. Nothing was missing: the retroactive application of laws, bias, allowing other powers to influence the application of justice. The better to shut the defendants' eyes, their mouths were shut and the courtroom door was shut. When ignominy combines with baseness, their victims seem noble by contrast. The moment he was expelled from the courtroom, Danton entered French mythology. Losing his head, he retrieved his honor — and his humor. "I offer my b. . . s to Robespierre." The Incorruptible would have been well-advised to accept this legacy.

Danton is often compared to Mirabeau. They resembled each other physically, but their weaknesses were not the same. Danton allowed himself to be bought to defend ideas contrary to his own; Mirabeau, to support his own principles. Mirabeau made money while doing what he would have attempted in any event and for free. Danton dipped into the till but did not commit any action against the Republic. Garat, his faithful successor at the Ministry of Justice, was correct in writing, "It is possible that he received something. It is certain that if there was a market for something, he did not give it away." The two men debased themselves but did not dishonor themselves; they betrayed everyone, but their convictions remained intact; they abused the confidence of their backers, but remained faithful to France.

Writing this on a Sunday in November, I contemplate Danton's bust in the dusty maze of the Carnavalet museum. Fascinated by this giant round-faced man, his massive neck set on shoulders built like Les Halles, with the thick, sensual lips that kissed with just a few months' interval the putrescent remains of Gabrielle and the breasts of a sixteen-year-old Louise, I cannot tear my eyes from his Tartar gaze. Was he the executioner of September, the beggar of slush funds, or the colossus of the upheaval? He was all that and more. "Better to be guillotined than to be the guillotiner." This ultimate bravado clarifies the memory of the man who dreamed of reconciling freedom and equality, forgetting that freedom is a disloyal, equality is lethal, and that they almost never find a way to get along.

No matter. Tomorrow I will deposit a bouquet of forgets-me-nots at the foot of his statue. I will go and drink a cup of coffee to the health of the Corrupt, so much more appealing than the Incorruptible.

Footnotes

1. The Third Republic was constituted in the 1870's, in the wake of a defeat by Prussia and the repression of the Paris Commune; in the wake of another successful attack by the Germans, it voted itself out of existence in 1940, under the Vichy regime headed by Petain and Laval.

2. *The Incorruptible* was a name for Robespierre; now, the *Inrockuptibles* is the name of a rock group, among other things.

3. See the iconoclastic work of White Olivier, *Corruption under Terror.*

4. An admirable and too often forgotten novel by Marivaux.

5. During his short life, he went to the notary no fewer than 37 times, accumulating land the better to dig in his roots.

6. Thuriot, the regicide, was one of the judges of the trial of the chouan.

7. It was also Richelieu's first Parisian address.

8. A function which he occupied August 10-October 10, 1792.

9. *Danton*, Librairie Hachette, 1914.

10. Desmoulins opposed the King's aunts attempted trip to Rome: "No, Lord, your aunts do not have the right to go and eat up our millions on papal territory." Desmoulins' stammer impeded his career as a lawyer, but in 1789 he suddenly emerged as an effective soap-box orator, helping to instigate the storming of the Bastille. He published a pamphlet, *La France Libre,* summarizing the principal charges against the rapidly crumbling *ancien régime.*

11. Armand-Marc of Montmorin-Saint-Hérem succeeds Vergennes as Minister for the Foreign Affairs (1787 to 1791). Intermediary between the court and Mirabeau, he will be accused of having formed part of the Austrian committee and will die in the prisons of September.

12. Authority founded by the Commune to judge the crimes of the anti-revolutionaries on August 10, 1792.

13. Spokesman of the French royalists abroad, Charge de mission to the sovereigns of Europe.

14. Louis Madelin exhumes this testimony from the Public Records.

15. Under the Ancien Régime, there were two forms of justice: the deputy justice pronounced by the magistrates in the name of the king, and restrained justice, rendered directly by the king himself.

16. See A. Mathiez, "Danton, agent of the civil list," in *Historical Annals of the French Revolution,* 1914, p. 98; "Danton and the Death of the King," according to a new document, *ibid,* 1922, p. 336; "Danton, Talon, Pitt and the Death of Louis XVI," *Studies robespierrists,* Paris, 1918, T II, p. 104.

17. Cited by Frederic Bluche, *Danton,* Perrin Editeur, 1984.

18.   Paul Lombard, *the Trial of the King*, Grasset, 1993.
19.   Pierre Jean Jouve.

Chapter 9

TALLEYRAND

Talleyrand (1754-1838) began a career in the priesthood in 1775 and moved up the Church hierarchy until he was excommunicated in 1791; he went on to become a statesman and diplomat, alternately serving Napoleon, the Bourbons, and whoever else might have had the upper hand.

> "He would sell his soul for silver, for he traded his manure for gold."
>
> Mirabeau

> "When Mr. de Talleyrand is not weaving intrigues, he is trafficking in one thing or another."
>
> Chateaubriand

> "In politics as in everything else, it is better not to engage with all one's heart, not too become too attached; that makes a mess of things."
>
> Talleyrand

Having traversed an interminable eighty four years, in spite of a limp that was transformed into elegance, through the *Ancien Régime*, the Revolution, the Directoire, the Consulate, the Empire, the first and then the second Restoration and the monarchy of Louis-Philippe, Talleyrand earned his title as a peerless marathon-runner of successive allegiances.

In his *Dictionnaire des idées reçues*, the *Dictionary of Generally Accepted Ideas* (which Bouvard and Pecuchet could have written), Gustave Flaubert sides with those who have already judged him. "Prince de Talleyrand = Oppose." However the French, attracted by this aristocratic rascal, are not opposed to him; in their amused admiration, they scarcely tease him. Napoleon himself would often forgive the fluctuations of his Minister for External Relations, on the pretext that "he was from a great family and that erases everything else." And for other less admissible reasons.

He has been compared to Judas Iscariot — an unjust and insufficient analogy. He did not betray only the Son of Man, but the whole world. Drunk on gold like Concini, relentless like Richelieu, a trickster like Mazarin, prodigal like Fouquet, libertine like Mirabeau, unscrupled like Danton, more diplomatic than anybody before or since, his words (like those of Clemenceau) still sparkle. To his grandson

Morny — twice a bastard — he would bequeath his penchant for ostentation, arrogance, and the insolence of a premature dandyism. This amiable and lethal man, with the features of a blond cherub engraved in a soft frame, a beardless Don Juan of dubious sexual proclivities, kept the volatile equilibrium of his multiple personalities in check by two principles: money, and France. All his life, he would drag one foot, and his right hand would be unaware of the gifts he received with his left.

When Charles-Maurice was struggling to be born, in 1754, Louis XV was on the throne and the monarchy was living in a complacent twilight. A privileged existence, very much in the tradition of the *Ancien Régime*, seemed to await this eldest son of one of France's noblest houses. Destiny decided otherwise when his nurse dropped him on the floor. His club-foot would exclude him from a military career and would throw him into the arms of the Church, of which he would become the prodigal and faithless son. Like Mirabeau, from his earliest years he was deprived of parental tenderness. "I am perhaps the only man belonging to a great and highly esteemed family, who has not had for one week in his life the sweet experience of living under the paternal roof." His youth unfolded within the confines of the religious section of the Left Bank, between rue Garancière where he was born, the College of Harcourt on rue de la Harpe where he studied, and the seminary of Saint-Sulpice, founded under the reign of the Sun King by the great mystic Jean-Jacques Olier, where he stagnated.

The young cripple made his first misstep one day during Lent when his parents, believing they were eating a permissible plate of fish, found that they had, in fact, consumed prohibited pork. Horrified, they tasked their son to consult his superior on this dire problem of conscience and dietetics. To encourage the monk to be lenient — an unintended sin is not a sin— they entrusted to the child a donation for the poor. Charles-Maurice pocketed it, spared himself the trouble of visiting the monk, and assured his father and mother: thanks to their good offices, they were absolved.

While awaiting Divine judgment, the seminarian led a life of dissolution, he lied, gambled, and cheated, and showed a preference not for the *viaticum* but for earthly foods, and not for cassocks but for skirts. A child of God, a child of the chorus, and above all a child of his own creation, he became a sub-deacon in 1775; four years later, he was ordained. "They wanted to make me a priest; they will regret it!" His prophecy would be fulfilled. Religion and freemasonry are not incompatible. Talleyrand thus became a child of the Widow[1] as well, where he met up with Provence, Artois, the Duke of Orleans and most of the nobility. When the recluse of Ferney went to Paris in 1778 for his apotheosis, organized by the [Masons'] Lodge of the Nine Sisters, he knighted Périgord. Was he a believer, like Pascal? Not necessarily. Was he a deist like Voltaire? Not likely.

His loathing for the ecclesiastical state by no means kept him from seeking the relevant emoluments. In 1775, his uncle, co-adjutant of the archbishop's palace in Rheims, obtained for him the title of *abbot-commanditaire* of Saint-Denis de Rheims, with a comfortable revenue — "a very sweet moment," he would write in his *Mémoires*. In 1780, he became general agent of the clergy, the true Minister of Finance, manager of the holy gold mine. This new function put him in contact with Calonne, who taught him political economics, the subtleties of business and the advantages of speculation.

In 1785, at the Assembly of the Clergy, he wrote a memorandum supporting the inalienable rights of the Church, whose secular opulence he defended, the counterpart of its tireless charitable action throughout the kingdom. His arguments won him the congratulations of his superiors, who gratified "this monument of talent and zeal" with a reward of 24,000 livres, and then a little supplement of 7,000 livres more.

In 1788, with his uncle's and his father's support,[2] he sought the episcopal see of Autun, to the outrage of his devout mother who denounced to the King her son's misconduct and improprieties. Louis XVI, deaf to these not very maternal ravings, hoped that the miter would stiffen the weakened moral fiber of this young man from Périgord; he assigned him the coveted bishopric, adding 22,000 livres to the 18,000 for the abbey of Rheims and the 12,000 for Celle-en-Poitou, another benefice from the sovereign. So here he was with an income of more than 50,000 livres. He waited six months before showing up at his diocese, celebrated a mass there (bungled the ritual for lack of practice), and took confession at very close quarters from the girls in his parish. Monseigneur d'Autun belonged to the new race of ecclesiastics, the monks of the Enlightenment, priests, abbots, bishops, cardinals of the court, the Chamber, and the salon, born with Choisy under Louis XIV, for whom the cardinal de Bernis (an admirer of women and of corrupting philosophy) was the model libertine.

But money is not power. And power was Talleyrand's dream. All his life, he would be fascinated by diplomatic briefs; he would become a great minister and a great rascal. A statesman who never wanted for lucidity, a spirited man adored for his cutting remarks and the charm of his conversation, a tactician with satanic skill, no one carried cynicism and intuition further. To the mercenary income he would add the revenues of felony.

In May 1789, his history really began. France was in a moral, financial, and institutional crisis; it was threatened by bankruptcy caused, in part, by the hemorrhage of the war in America. The confrontation with Parliament turned into a farce, then a tragedy. Mistaking his reign with the regency of Marie de Médicis, thinking he could get away with the same solution used by the old Italian, Louis XVI moved up the date for the 1792 gathering of the nation's deputies and convened the Estates General. Two years before, the bishop of Autun had written to Choiseul-Gouffier, French ambassador in Constantinople, this premonitory letter: "My friend, the people finally will be counted for something." Descending from his observatory, Bailly would say much the same.

When the three bells rang at Versailles, Monsieur de Talleyrand made his entry on the grand stage of history, never to leave it again (except for his ceaseless excursions through the back corridors). He was 35 years old, old enough to remember the delights of the *Ancien Régime*, young enough to hope to lead great changes, gifted enough to succeed in that. When Louis XVI asked Rivarol how to proceed, given this revolt that had become a revolution, "Make him king," answered the insolent polemist of those dark days. Instead of taking this wise advice, he pretended to accept the joint meeting of the three orders (which Talleyrand, a deputy of the clergy thanks to his head office of Autun, attended). He collaborated on the Declaration of the Rights of Man, so often praised, so often trampled. From that moment on, all Frenchmen became active citizens and could freely attain public employment. "Human rights have been ignored, insulted, for centuries," he would say. "They have been restored in this declaration, which will be the eternal war cry against oppressors."

The recall of Necker restored confidence but the Treasury hardly benefited from the dubious genius of the providential man of the moment, whom the French showered with flattery only to cover him with bruises soon after. It would take a grain subsidy to keep the food riots in check. Where could the money be found? Talleyrand, who four years before had declared the assets of the clergy inalienable, preached their nationalization, without worrying about the right of ownership whose constituents claimed were absolute and sacred. Necessity dictates the law, and the Church's patrimony was given to the nation, which gratefully dedicated a hundred million livres to the remuneration of God's shepherds. Abject poverty, compared to yesterday's opulence! The bishop played a leading role and his unselfishness won him widespread admiration. Had he not just sacrificed on the altar of the goddess Equality 50,000 livres annually, the amount of his ecclesiastical benefice? Wasn't that altruism? No. It was profit, achieved through shameless speculation on interest rates, which shot upward the day after the confiscation. He made a half-million livres on this insider trading, which more than made up for the lost benefices.

"The most astute man of his era"[3] always needs an accomplice. Soon, it would be Fouché; for now, it was with Mirabeau that he formed a stormy and intermittent couple. The lame one leaned on the hail, trying to save the crippled monarchy. On July 14, 1790, the festival of the Federation was underway during a downpour, no doubt expressing God's spite. Yielding to the King's request, the bishop of Autun celebrated mass with an iconoclastic humor: a shaking pyramid was used as the altar; La Fayette mimicked the vergers; and Mirabeau, as he had done the day before during a salacious evening, played with the children in the chorus. Before four hundred thousand drenched faithful, the celebrant stumbled again during the liturgy, misreading the Gospels. At the beginning of the service, he had begged La Fayette not to make him laugh. Alright, the mass was said and the bishop *cum* bourgeois gentleman ended this edifying day in a gambling party at the Palais Royal, where he broke the bank.

In autumn 1790, the Gallic Assembly voted to nationalize the clergy. Talleyrand was the first prelate to give his allegiance to the Civil Constitution, provoking the resentment of the priests of his diocese. They sent their pastor a scandalized letter: "You have given an oath in betrayal." Why complain? That was his only vocation. Anathematized, he assuaged his sorrows with his friend Lauzun. "You know the news, excommunication. Come comfort me and have supper with me. Everyone will refuse me heat and water; therefore this evening we will have only cold meats and we will drink only ice wine."

"I am not afraid to admit the part I played in this business; the Civil Constitution of the clergy was the Assembly's greatest political mistake," he would write in his *Mémoires*. While waiting for this belated contrition, haunted by the prophecy of Choiseul (who declared the era of Richelieus, Mazarins and such, prelates and political wheeler-dealers, to have ended), the bishop discarded his cumbersome surplice. He took Adélaïde de Flahaut as mistress and soon made her pregnant. (Charles, their hybrid son, would become the lover of Queen Hortense and the father of the duke de Morny.) It was Adélaïde (or one of her many rivals) that count de Montrond had in mind when Talleyrand launched this barb at him, "I was just thinking of you, and wondering whether you will die of hanging or of syphilis." "That depends, Monseigneur," he retorted, "on whether I take up your ideas or your mistress."

With Mirabeau scarcely ensconced in the Pantheon, he approached the court with offers of service (for pay); two of his letters would later be found in the iron chest. He sought to gain the King's confidence in 1791, but in vain — a new "purity" was already coming into vogue and Camille Desmoulins played the role of a professor of morals before the Assembly. "How can we rail against gaming, when the pillars of the club include three presidents of the National Assembly:[4] Beaumetz, Le Chapelier and the bishop of Autun? It is true that the 500,000 francs that the bishop made off with just the other day were won, not in a gambling den, but at the home of Mme. Montesson."[5]

Alas, the cardsharps turned out to be disloyal and Talleyrand, deep in debt, sought stipends from foreign courts. Moscow was the first object of his assiduous attentions. Monsieur de Simonin, Catherine II's agent in Paris, wrote to the Tsarina, "Monseigneur d'Autun has replaced Monsieur de Mirabeau in the diplomatic committee." Madrid, to secure the Constituent Assembly's renewal of the alliance with Paris and to get the funding approved for outfitting twenty-seven Spanish ships, gave the bishop 500,000 livres.

And France? Talleyrand never forgot it. With Condorcet and Monge, he began constructing a law on education that he pursued for many years and which Jules Ferry would implement in 1882 with the advent of state education, secular and compulsory. This brilliant and egalitarian plan must be credited to this swindler who was ahead of even Danton in calling for education as a basic right of every person.

When Napoleon offered him the principality of Bénévent (stolen from the pope) in reward for his good and loyal (?) services, he would become the only sovereign of Europe to ensure boys and — a still more enlightened idea — girls, free schooling.

The Legislature, with bellicose egalitarianism, set loose the storm of fraternity across the continent. In order to impose liberty on the world, it declared a new and merry war with all of Europe, and the situation continued to deteriorate. In 1792, Talleyrand, who detested bloodshed almost as much as lost causes, was sent on a mission to England, to seek to negotiate its neutrality. He left for London in January and returned to Paris in time to witness, on August 10, the royalty's descent into indecision and anarchy. Not very eager to play the role of a martyr, he got a passport from Danton and on September 9, set out again for London where he learned that he had just been registered on the list of emigrants to be arrested on sight, now that the iron chest had been opened. Pitt, who saw him as "a spy from the Terror," was not deceived when the good apostle donned mourning clothes in honor of the execution of Louis XVI (an occasion that allowed France to join England in the club of regicides); he expelled him. Germaine de Staël, his former mistress, tried to get him into Switzerland; in vain. One after the other, each canton refused the renegade the right of asylum.

In summer 1794, he disembarked in New York, where he speculated in real estate, often with good results, and champed at the bit while waiting for better days. They came with the month of Thermidor, when the upstarts seized power — with Barras, the man who had boasted that he had never given in to tyrants, at their head. They pulled France out of the Terror; and the thirteen directors[6], due to the licentiousness of some of them, ensured the reign of indecency. However, let's not forget that they saved the republic from invasion and counterrevolution.

Talleyrand — who "changes principles more often than underwear" (to quote Carnot) — wanted at any cost to get back to this pragmatic and impure France where, he thought, a man like him could develop his full potential. "In critical circumstances, you have to mobilize the women." Faithful to his maxim, he called Germaine de Staël to the rescue once again and, this time, successfully. In July 1797, with the help of Benjamin Constant (her lover) and Marie-Joseph Chénier, he got the Assembly's permission to go back. Through intrigue, from blackmail to suicide threats, begging and prostrations, he persuaded

Germaine to convince the Directoire to appoint him Minister for Foreign Relations, in the place of Delacroix (whose position and whose wife he coveted). Their adulterous love would give birth to Eugene Delacroix, one of the greatest painters of all times, who would make color serve movement, and who would be overcome by his genius, a romantic and cruel beauty.

When Talleyrand first crossed the threshold of his Ministry, located in the hotel on rue de Grenelle where the Italian cultural center is housed today, he was giddy with joy. Many witnesses heard him say, "I'm going to make a fortune, an immense fortune." He kept his promise. Every diplomatic initiative taken by a foreign government was taxed by the minister, either directly or indirectly, through intermediaries. Barras, in his *Mémoires,* affirms that during the Directoire alone, Talleyrand pocketed 13,500,000 francs, including one million from Spain, one million from Prussia and 150,000 from the Pope. Only the puritan United States resisted his conniving demands when, after the French corsairs had seized American ships heading for England, he asked their representative to send Paris 50,000 livres sterling in fees. They refused, in stinging terms. "We know how to deal with pirates. Our government would have thought that to anticipate such a proposal from France would be an insult." The minister did not stumble before this rebuff but he was tripped up the day when President John Adams exposed this sordid matter in a message to Congress.[7] He defended himself by blaming the accomplices behind whom he had had prudence to hide.

Talleyrand first met Bonaparte at the end of 1797, and this would turn out to be the best day in his life, to use the expression that Mr. Prudhomme borrowed from Henri Monnier. On January 3, 1798, the Minister greeted the General as if he were already the French Premier, with an imposing reception at rue du Bac — reminiscences of the *Ancien Régime.* This sealed Talleyrand's future, as the party at Vaux had sealed that of Fouquet, but in the opposite sense. After the Egyptian disaster that was transformed into victory, and the return of the deserter metamorphosed into savior of the fatherland, came the 18th of Brumaire. The trusted advisors decided to bribe Barras to leave, he who could not resist temptation. Ouvrard, the crooked banker, provided the necessary funds, a bill of exchange for three million francs. Talleyrand was charged with giving it to the director, and with convincing him to exit gracefully. Walking into the Tuileries, where his former benefactor resided, he gently took him by the arm and walked him over to a window, where he showed him the agitated crowd at the gates of the palace and the guards ready to intervene. Barras, who had no desire to undergo the fate of Capet, signed the letter of resignation without waiting to be begged. This precipitous acquiescence allowed the messenger to overlook the other side of the deal and to pocket the money. Bonaparte was free to establish his dictatorship and Talleyrand became the Consulate's Minister for Foreign Relations and, soon, the Empire's.

The two men were complementary and their relationship was one of mutual fascination. The General was charmed by the diplomat. The prelate was entranced by the Corsican's romantic *furia*. The parvenu and the aristocrat formed a unique political couple. Bonaparte closed his eyes to his minister's peccadillos. Talleyrand sought to delay the inevitable end of the honeymoon, then to control its disastrous scope. Bonaparte wanted to make him knuckle under, and Talleyrand gave in.

Defrocked, having given up the miter in 1791 (without Rome's approval), he allowed Napoleon to dictate his private life. He put up no resistance when the despot told him to regularize his situation with Mme. Grand, of the checkered past. Without the blessing of the Pope (who refused it), he placed a notice in *The Monitor* — the official journal of the time — announcing "the return of the ex-bishop of Autun to the lay state." This event did not open the doors of Notre-Dame to him but it did allow him to betray the confidence of the priest at Epinay-sur-Seine, who, believing he was acting in agreement with the Holy See, in September 1802 consecrated his union with a hussy who was tired of his wayfaring habits. Only the Restoration would enable him to get rid of this cumbersome wife, when — as a joke of history — Chateaubriand would be constrained to take back his.

The marriage did not temper his passions. "It doesn't take *esprit* to make a fortune," he said, "it takes a lack of delicacy." One could hardly have been more delicate than he; and to draw up an inventory of his indelicacies would be a more delicate matter still.

In 1800, he negotiated a commercial treaty with Livingstone, the United States' ambassador. This time, America turned out to be less virtuous and made a covert payment of two million francs. Monsieur de Talleyrand became guilty of passive corruption.

Pursuant to the treaty of Basle, Spain had been paying France an

annual fee of five million francs since 1795. In 1800 again, the first consul was considering letting it drop. Upon the advice of his top diplomat, he split his generous gesture in two. Everyone knew about it except the King of Spain who, for more than a year, continued to pay off
the debt. The good apostle and the Spanish minister Godoy (the
Queen's lover), shared two and half million francs. Monsieur de Talleyrand became guilty of active corruption.

In 1801, the treaty of Lunéville forced Austria to pay off the loans
contracted by the former Netherlands, then under its dominion. The
former bishop started a rumor that these funds were lost, and he
bought up the titles for the price of the paper they were written on.
When this issue became public, the exchanges skyrocketed. His
profit — seven million francs. Monsieur de Talleyrand made himself
guilty, once again, of the crime of insider trading.

In 1802 and 1803 came the re-division of Germany. The number of
States fell from 360 to 82; that of the free cities, from 51 to 6. In order to
avoid disappearing (or to annex neighboring territories), the princes
were ready to sacrifice everything. The French representative auctioned off Germany and removed from the sale those portions fetching
the lowest offers. Thirty to forty million in profits. Monsieur de
Talleyrand was guilty of abuse of power.

1803, the first consul — the Francophone world would never recover from this discount sale — gave Louisiana to the United States.
Starting price, 80 million. The deal was done at 54 million. Into whose
pocket might the difference have gone? Don't even ask. Monsieur de
Talleyrand was guilty of breach of trust.

In 1805, shortly after Austerlitz, Austria signed the peace of Pres-
bourg. Napoleon established the penalty at 100 million. His minister
convinced him to reduce it to 85, not without some difficulty. Thus he
pocketed a comfortable commission. Monsieur de Talleyrand was
guilty of embezzling public funds.

In 1806, the German Holy Roman Empire was conquered by the
sublime child of Ajaccio. The King of Saxony paid a million and the
town of Hamburg, four, to avoid being annexed by France. In vain.
Four years later, Hamburg would become the prefecture of Bouches-de-
l'Elbe. Napoleon, having been made aware of the maneuver, would
oblige the fundraiser to restore a few hundred thousand francs. An ordinary work-related accident. Monsieur de Talleyrand was guilty of
swindling.

When the emperor questioned him about how he paid for his opulent lifestyle, he answered, "I bought investments on the 17th of Brumaire and I sold them on the 19th." Corsica pretended to believe him, and when he cried poverty, he helped him to acquire the château of Valençay, a domain worthy of a monarch, which brought in 140,000 francs per annum. As great men often do, Napoleon gave the impression of not noticing anything and allowed his entourage to grow shamelessly rich. In a weak position to play critic, he showered his indispensable factotum with favors. In 1804, Talleyrand became grand chamberlain, and thus took part in the masquerade of the consecration; in 1806, he became Prince de Bénévent; in 1807, vice-grand elector. Fouché made the pun, "That is the only vice that he was lacking." This vice brought him 330,000 francs per annum.

The emperor's indulgence was not based on blindness but on a tacit agreement concluded with the great master of foreign relations on March 21, 1804, in the dungeons of Vincennes. The executioner of the Duc d'Enghien was from now on bound to his assistant; Talleyrand had a hold over Bonaparte. He knew that, in executing a prince of the blood, the first consul had carried out a premeditated political action. It opened the way of the Empire to him, enabled him to join the club of regicides, to reconcile with the Left and to terrify the Right (before rallying it to his cause, in turn). To exculpate himself in the eyes of Europe, right up until his departure for St. Helena, the Emperor would accuse bad luck, fate, and secondary figures such as Caulaincourt and Savary. He fooled everyone, except for his accomplice who considered the execution neither a crime nor a fault but one of those cruel constraints of which history is so replete.

Omnipresent during the days preceding "the catastrophe,"[8] serving as a diplomatic lightning rod to protect the future emperor from the electrical storm of Europe, it was Talleyrand who persuaded Bonaparte of the need to get rid of d'Enghien. To achieve this end, ignoring the scant regard they had for each other, he made an alliance with Fouché (head of the police). The executioner of Lyon proclaimed that "the air is full of daggers," and prophesied the assassination of Bonaparte by the monarchists. The bishop diverted attention to the duchy of Bade, where a minor duke was mistaken for the Great Condé. Talleyrand's role in the kidnapping, then in the murder, forever bound his destiny to that of the future emperor who, to ascend the throne, stepped on a corpse.

The facts leave no room for doubt, everything and everyone point to Talleyrand. Credible witnesses accused him. The count de Molé said, "The duke of Enghien perished as the result of an intrigue by Talleyrand and Fouché, who wanted to inveigle Napoleon and put him in their power, by putting him in complicity with them so that afterward he would not be able to reproach them for any aspect of their revolutionary life." According to the baron de Vitrolles, "It is Talleyrand who is guilty of the duke of Enghien's murder, by justifying it, if it not by advising it. The voices that have accused him of being the first to have caused this violation of all human and divine rights, his position as Minister of Foreign Relations and the letters that he wrote in this capacity to justify the horrible assassination, are sufficient proof of his participation in this crime." In the words of Queen Hortense, "Murat accepted orders from Mr. de Talleyrand, who lingered at his place until 4:00 in the morning. All was forgiven him. He had absolution. Thus, he would never reproach him for the death of the duke of Enghien, *of which he was one of the principal authors*." Chancellor Pasquier said, "The very same day that the news of the kidnapping came in, there was a ball at the hotel de Luynes. Mr. de Talleyrand was there. Someone asked him quietly, "But what will you do with the Duke of Enghien?" He answered, "He will be shot."

One piece of evidence made trouble. When Talleyrand burned some compromising papers in 1814, a letter dated March 8, 1804 escaped the auto-da-fé. Chateaubriand took great joy in revealing its contents: "The First Consul must prevail against his enemies . . . As justice obliges him to punish rigorously, politics requires him to punish without exception."[9]

In 1809, he showed it to the Emperor. "And this man, this poor man — who alerted me that he was staying at Ettenheim? Who urged me to move against him?"

Talleyrand's own attitude condemns him. The night of the execution, he did not recite the prayer for the dying but played craps with the duchess of Luynes. At two o'clock in the morning, he uttered these words: "The last of the Condés has ceased to exist," then picked up his cards again. When *The Monitor* announced the shooting, one of his aides, d'Hauterives, allowed his distress to show. The head of French diplomacy said,

"Why are you standing there with your eyes popping out of your head?"

"Why? For the same reason that you would be, if you had read the papers. What a horror!"

He received this paternal admonition, "Well, well. . . are you mad? Is there any reason to make such a fuss? A conspirator is seized near the border, he is brought to Paris, and he is shot. What is extraordinary in that? Come on, d'Hauterives, *that's business!*"

Three days later, he was leading the diplomatic corps in a great ball. Their Excellencies, under the wand of the lame ballet master, danced the minuet of a choreographed death.

When everything was consummated, Talleyrand displayed, in the continental arena, the full scope of his talent. He began by putting the teary-eyed monarchs in their places. To Tsar Alexander, he applied the knout. "The claim that Russia raises makes me wonder whether, when England was contemplating the assassination of Paul I, if the plotters had been found within a mile of the border, the emperor would not have not hastened to have them seized." In *The Monitor,* he took a swipe at Gustave Adolphe of Sweden. "You are still young. . . France is quite indifferent to all your initiatives. . . She will not confound a brave and honest nation . . . with a young man who is led astray by false causes and who is unenlightened by the exercise of reflection." Then, to give Napoleon time to be proclaimed emperor, on May 29, 1804, he deferred from May 7 to June 18, 1804 Russia's request before the Diet.[10] Not particularly anxious to anger the crowned despot, the Diet soon withdrew the matter from its docket, reserving its rigor for less dangerous causes. The international jurisdictions took a lesson from that. Lastly, as Talleyrand's crowning achievement, he obliged Perfidious Albion to admit its criminal interference in French affairs. "If His Majesty's government," conceded Prime Minister Pitt, "neglected to regard the sentiments of those among the inhabitants of France who are, rightly, dissatisfied with the current government of that country, if it refused to lend an ear to the plans that they have been forming to deliver their fatherland from the shameful yoke and corrosive slavery under which it is presently groaning, it would not be fulfilling its duties." This admission, extracted by Talleyrand, justified Bonaparte's severity and enabled him to take advantage of the all-absolving excuse of self-defense. At St. Helena, the Emperor would say, "He always served as a faithful minister."

In 1807, the official diplomatic career of the Prince de Bénévent came to an end and, replaced by Champagny, he left his ministry. Of his own volition? Out of indolence, as Metternich thought? Driven out by the Emperor, tired of his whims and caprices? Out of a desire to break with the dictator's frenzy of conquest? "At a considerable price, I swore to myself to stop, being his minister," he would write in his *Mémoires*, one of most beautiful webs of lies to be found in a literary genre where, in any event, they abound. Bonaparte was not, in any case, deprived of his enlightened and, of course, well-remunerated councils. On September 1808, he accompanied him to Erfurt, where the Corsican was to meet the Tsar, with whom the diplomat entertained good relations. Instead of winning him over to the imperial cause, he encouraged him to resistance, "Rein Napoleon in. This man has lost his mind." He used similar language in addressing Metternich, in a correspondence where, seeking to cover his bets, he provided the chancellor with covert civil and military information, including, as one would say today, defense secrets. Thus he made the leap from corruption to high treason. With all the perspicacity of a nonchalant cat, he watched, impassive and greedy, as Europe sharpened its bayonets and Germany fell into the Prussian nationalism crystallized by Fichte and the romantic philosophers. While the Grand Empire was crumbling into 130 departments, its last incarnation, Napoleon was being courted by Goya. In Paris, Fouché and Talleyrand were preparing his downfall and planned to replace him with Murat. Tipped off by his all-powerful police, the Emperor crossed the Pyrenees, made it to the Tuileries and, in front of his reduced Council, hurled insults at the conspirator, creating a scene where suddenly everything came out on the carpet.[11] He relieved his grand chamberlain of his charge and withdrew his intimacy but, oddly, spared him and soon missed him. Exasperated, he blurted out to the poor Champagny (who was dragging out the negotiations with Austria), "You have stipulated 100 million in indemnities for France; I know that all of it will go into the Treasury. In Talleyrand's time, we would have gotten perhaps 60, and he would have gotten at least 10. But it would all have been concluded in fifteen days. Wrap it up."

In 1811, Talleyrand, a little short of cash, tried to tap the Tsar for 1,500,000 francs in exchange for new responsibilities. Alexander brushed him off politely, but preserved his imprudent correspondence. In 1813, the defeat of Leipzig opened the borders to the coalition. The lame Devil saved the Emperor from an unquestionable capture by informing him of the Bavarian troop movements, which were on the brink of cutting off his retreat. One last time, Napoleon tried to rehabilitate this so valuable man and proposed to him to take up his portfolio again and conduct, single-handedly, the negotiations with Europe. Not very keen to play Good Samaritan for a false and wayward god, the Prince de Bénévent refused. Unable to induce him, the bald one once again gave vent to his rage, and threatened him with the fate of the duke of Enghien. Talleyrand, that courageous coward, stood up to the fury of the murderous despot. "It takes vice to practice virtue," he later conceded.

In January 1814, Napoleon set out on his penultimate and disastrous campaign. He would never again see the traitor who had served him so well. Through the baron de Vitrolles and his friend Dalberg, he encouraged the allies to march on the capital. At the end of March, the coalition troops seized Meaux and crossed the Marne at the bridge of Triport. The road to Paris was open.

In the capital, which was ready to fall, King Joseph called a catastrophic special session of the Regency Council (appointed by his brother) whose duplicity was renowned.[12] Cambacérès took the podium. "Should the Empress and the King of Rome retire to Blois?" Talleyrand responded, "Her Majesty the Empress would not run the least danger, and it is impossible that she would not obtain better conditions from the Emperor, her father, and the allied sovereigns, than those which they would grant if she were fifty leagues outside of Paris." This advice might have saved the Bonaparte dynasty, but the Council ignored it; and Marie-Louise and the Little Eagle packed their trunks. Later, when Louis XVIII filled the vacancy, he justified himself with an extraordinary coolness. "If I advised the Empress to remain in Paris, it is because no one trusts me. I knew that if I advised her to go, the Empress would stay; I insisted that she stay, only with the intention of encouraging her departure for Blois." While waiting, he proclaimed himself president of the provisional government, convoked the Senate and had it pronounce Buonaparte's forfeiture. On March 31, the Tsar dined with his agent. Warmed by the reception, seduced by this evening that reflected the end of one reign and heralded the advent of a new one, Alexander promised to protect a "great and powerful France," and toasted his host's health.

On April 3, Louis XVIII named Talleyrand Minister for Foreign Affairs. His first concern was to justify the return of the Bourbons. "It is a principle, all the rest is just an intrigue." "Why didn't I have him shot?" murmured Bonaparte, as he signed his letter of abdication.

For the zealous servant of His potbellied Majesty, the hardest task had still to be tackled: to negotiate an honorable peace with the allies. This adjective sat poorly with him, although he managed well enough. On May 1814, the Treaty of Paris conferred upon France its 1792 borders; the invaders evacuated its territory; and the majority of Bonaparte's stolen goods remained at the Louvre. There was only one shadow in the picture. Once the talks were over, the French Minister for Foreign Affairs was awarded the Austrian Golden Fleece. With Talleyrand, nothing is ever clear; when somebody thanked him, one ought to wonder why.

On September 1814, he left Paris for Vienna, where the Congress would redraw the map of Europe. He was accompanied by Dorothée, future duchess of Dino, his mistress and his niece (through marriage, it is true). In the Austrian capital, to avoid having his fatherland playing defendant against the four victorious powers, Austria, England, Prussia, Russia, he persuaded them to include Sweden, Spain, Portugal and. . . France. What an exploit. The vanquished took a seat among the winners. In spite of his efforts, the rationalization of Europe obliterated Poland, brought Prussia to the Rhine, and ensured the expansion of Austria and of Russia; but, thanks to the genius — no other word will do — of its representative, France preserved its territorial integrity and most of its influence. Aggravated by Metternich's conduct, the prince of Ligne, on his deathbed, uttered the witticism, "The Congress is not moving forward, it is dancing." And dancing on a powder keg, for yesterday's alliances were on the point of exploding. Talleyrand cooled things down and raided the token box. Murat offered him 800,000 francs to preserve his throne in Naples; Ferdinand de Bourbon, five times more. Talleyrand even tried to make money on his principality of Bénévent.

In March 1815, Napoleon was setting out from the Var coast, sowing consternation on the Prater. Talleyrand, to avoid losing face, made all the powers sign a non-appealable judgment of "criminal delusion" against him. Non-appealable but not non-repealable, for once again France fell into his hands. One hundred days later, Waterloo. Blücher was early, Grouchy late; and Parques was on time. In the vans from abroad, the very catholic Louis XVIII, flanked by the de-mitered prelate, made it back to his fickle capital. He named Talleyrand head of the government and Fouché prime minister, eliciting the terrible diatribe from Chateaubriand: "Suddenly, the door opened; silently, Vice entered, on the arm of Crime, Mr. de Talleyrand supported by Mr. Fouché; the infernal vision passed slowly before me, penetrated the office of the King and disappeared . . . Fouché had just sworn faith and homage to his lord; the trusty regicide, on his knees, had placed the hands that took the head off of Louis XVI between the hands of the brother of the martyr King; the bishop apostate was guarantor of the oath." Vice and Crime would not remain long at their posts. Fouché, struck by the anti-regicide law, would die in exile. Talleyrand, draped with honors — duke and peer, knight of the Holy Spirit, grand chamberlain — would have no role to play under Louis XVIII and Charles X. Deprived of influence, he could no longer peddle it. Excluded from the game of politics, he engaged in word play. When Richelieu became Prime Minister in his place, he punned, "He is an excellent choice; he is the man who knows *Crimea* best."[13] The day the duke was replaced by Villèle, Talleyrand passed the two men in the staircase leading to the King's office and reminded them to "not trust appearances, Messrs; that which goes down goes up, and that which goes up, goes down." After Charles X abdicated in favor of the duke of Bordeaux, the miracle child (who hoped to reign under the name of Henri V), he took to reading omens. "He doesn't have a chance. Henri IV did him too much harm," and Louis-Philippe ascended the throne.

He called upon Talleyrand when the situation called for the ultimate craftsman: the English feared that France would annex Belgium, which was in revolt. The old diplomat crossed the English Channel one last time, with all his former ambition, to seal the *Entente Cordiale* between France and England. During his embassy, from 1830 to 1834, he negotiated the borders of the new Belgian state, avoided a rift between London and Paris and, at eighty years of age, presented his resignation.

To avoid the affront of a civil burial, he began one last negotiation with God, through His Holiness the Pope. On the verge of death, he signed his last pact, an act of contrition as crooked as his limbs, as questionable as immortality.

"I want people to discuss what I was, what I thought, what I wanted, for centuries." Posterity fulfilled that dream and, of all the characters in this book, only François Mitterrand could have made such a wish. Talleyrand shares with him a horror of dogmatism, an absence of prejudices, an irresistible attraction for disorder, a fascination with the double background. For the moment, they are only separated by money. It seduced Talleyrand, but Mitterand appears to have withstood its charms. (Personally, I intend to sound out the rumor mills and I am always on the alert for evidence that he did succumb.)

More than through his venality, Talleyrand sinned by ignorance. He never learned that in creating man, God gave birth to the heart. In love, Talleyrand replaced it with sex; in politics, with the stomach; in society, with *esprit*. Three components of superficiality. Which did he do more: betray or serve? This question will never be answered. Diplomats are like lawyers. The treaties signed, the verdicts pronounced, the negotiations and the pleadings turn to dust, dispersed by the vicissitudes of memory. This curse no doubt explains why there is neither a square nor a street named after Talleyrand in Paris. Perhaps one could take the rue de la Santé and name it after him, to rectify this injustice.

Footnotes

1. A nickname of the freemasons.
2. His father had carried the holy orb during the Louis XVI's coronation.
3. According to Sainte-Beuve, who, however, was hardly a fan.
4. He had had the revolving presidency of the Assembly in February 1791.
5. That is, Madame de Montesson, the morganatic bride of the duke of Orleans.
6. Including Barras, Carnot, Letourneur, Rewbell, Révellière-Lépeaux, Barthélemy, Treilhard, Merlin, Sieyès. . .
7. In April 1798.
8. This is how people referred to the assassination of the last of the Condés.
9. Meneval, Napoleon's Secretary, confirms the accusations of the great, rancorous poet.
10. The Assemblies of the Holy Roman Empire, made up of three colleges (that of the Electors, the princes and the cities) which, since the Middle Ages had deliberated on war, taxes, and laws. The decisions taken were then ratified by the emperor. The Diet disappeared in 1806 with the Empire but the Congress of Vienna restored it.
11. This memorable rage, which made the imperial court tremble, took place on January 28, 1809.
12. This assembly of 17 members, the Empress included, was made up of imperial notables including Cambacérès, Lebrun, Savary and Talleyrand.
13. Armand Emmanuel du Plessis had emigrated to Russia where he became governor of Odessa, thanks to the favors of Tsar Alexander. He returned to France with the Restoration and replaced Talleyrand as Prime Minister.

Chapter 10

THE NAPOLEONIDES

Napoleon I [Napoleon Bonaparte]
Joseph
Lucien — Louis [King of Holland 1806-1810] — Charles-Louis Napoleon [Napoleon III]
Elisa, etc.

> "I am destined to be grist for writers, but I am not afraid that I will become their victim. However hard they try, they will never amount to more than powder puffing at granite. . . And, when they want to be noble, they will praise me."
>
> *St. Helena Memorial*

> Hudson Lowe to Bonaparte: "Why do the Frenchmen always fight for money, and Englishmen, for honor?"
> Bonaparte: "One always fights for that which one does not have."

What a combination of glory and misery! Such legends, of black and gold. What deaths — and so many deaths. Napoleone Buonaparte (Chateaubriand called him by his real name, thinking it would humiliate him) was born in 1769 in Corsica, and should have died several times in the course of his extraordinary existence: of the plague in Jaffa in 1799, of the *pronunciamiento* of the 18th of Brumaire, of sunstroke in Austerlitz and of frost in Moscow, of the Spanish influenza, of drowning at the island of Elba and then at St. Helena. He is the most alive of the living dead.

Which Napoleon Bonaparte shall we consider? The child, called Nabou by his mother, who became French due to a blunder by Louis the Well-Loved who, by 1768, was hardly French any more himself? The man who wrote the French Civil Code, a priceless gift despite its militarism and its misogyny; a dictator of democracy? The poet of action who loved power as much as Ingres loved his violin? Or the ogre who swallowed up, without managing to digest them, both Europe and freedom?

Napoleon the parvenu denounced by Fichte, the usurper vitriolized by the Viscount? The boor who kept bumping into Germaine de Staël as they both traversed the continent? Or Tolstoy's, in *War and*

Peace? Napoleon has been glorified and damned in countless classics of literature.

None of these Napoleons will be my hero; nor that "Robespierre on horseback" who so impressed Hegel ("I saw the Emperor, the Spirit of the World," he wrote on October 13, 1806, "leaving the city to go on reconnaissance. It is indeed a marvelous feeling to see such an individual, who extends across the whole world and dominates it, concentrated in one point, seated upon a horse." His exaltation was tempered somewhat when the *grognards* (Napoleon's soldiers) raided the philosopher's cellar and his schnapps supply. The author of *The Phenomenology of the Spirit*, no longer mindful of his past effusions, would usher in that Prussia that the century would hear so much about. No, here we will not be considering an exceptionally gifted man nor a Consul — albeit the First — nor a great General nor a small corporal, but rather the head of a clan whose most astute panegyrist was Al Capone. "I take my hat off to Napoleon," this rascal would say, "for he was the greatest racketeer in the history of world."[1] This homage from a man whose Berezina was the IRS, to the man for whom the Continental Blockade was as helpful as Prohibition, is unfortunately not included in most textbooks.

It was in Corsica, side by side with Pascal Paoli (and later in opposition to him), that Napoleon learned the art of clan behavior that is so cherished by the inhabitants of the Isle of Beauty. On August 10, 1792, he learned the lesson of wanton destruction, a discipline in which he would soon excel in a Europe that put up little resistance, in the face of the capture of the Tuileries by the savage and braying battalions from Marseilles.

Napoleon's successive deaths should not make us forget his many births and resurrections. They were innumerable but, to avoid tiring the reader who must be filled with awe by so many wonders, we will mention only three of them: in 1773, the publication of the *General Essays on Tactics*, the basis of his military genius; in 1775, the earthly arrival of Lucien, who served as midwife to his political victory; and in 1802 — when the century was but two years old — the advent of Victor Hugo himself, who would adorn, forever, his immense forehead with the winner's laurels.

The man who opened the doors of Italy to Bonaparte was named François Apollini de Guibert. This military man was born in 1743 to a family of the impoverished old nobility; he died in the United States, where he had taken refuge after his failure at the Estates General. An arm-chair strategist, he authored a prophetic and iconoclastic book, *General Essays on Tactics*, wherein he condemns his forbears' conflicts, conducted by heavy and slow-moving armies, encumbered by a superfluity of heavy artillery and the vans of a mercantile and paralyzing supply corps. This character, halfway between General de Gaulle in his writings and General Rommel in his campaigns, became the apostle of a mobile war executed by rapid-deployment units, relieved of their encumbrances, living off the conquered countries and their hard-pressed inhabitants. The buckskin breeches of the General Staff may have been horrified by this audacity, but it impressed Frederic II, and Bonaparte (during the first Italian campaign) made the *Essays* his Bible. "This book is enough to make great men," he said, passing over in silence the vandals and scoundrels. Its reading allowed him to thrash the enemy, to empty the Italian peninsula of its treasures, to enrich France and to build a colossal fortune while joining the ranks of the great predators of Antiquity who were his models. Chateaubriand (him again) wrote, "Taken over by his own existence, Bonaparte reduced everything to his own person; Napoleon had taken over Napoleon. There was nothing left but him and himself." But he was forgetting Napoleon's family, which was endowed with titles, lands and wealth, demonstrating that the Emperor was a follower of Mazarin, ridiculed by this prodigality that was beyond compare in modern history.

When fate struck thrice, the tragicomedy of the 18th Brumaire, or "How to bungle a coup d'etat,"began, and the leading role was suddenly weakened. Lunging at the proponents of the *Ancien Regime*, Bonaparte lost his temper, his voice and almost his party. He blew up, made threats, and his incoherent speech was drowned out by catcalls. The members of Parliament broke loose and one threatened him with a dagger (diverted by the grenadier Thomas Pomies), while his comrades enabled the general to escape from the cursed enclosure, leaving his adversaries frustrated and his friends embarrassed.

What good luck it is to have a brother. Lucien, president of the Council of Fifty-Five, hesitated a moment, then pulled himself together; he threw his toga into the ring and made a theatrical exit in the midst of the brawl. With great aplomb, he seized the moment and harangued the hesitant soldiers: "I declare to you that a small number of furious members are committing a crime by this attack against liberty . . . I confer upon the guards the duty of safe-guarding the majority of the representatives of the people, so that, protected from the stiletto by your bayonets, we can deliberate in peace on the interests of the Republic." In the wee hours of the morning, so favorable for executions and low blows, the regime rocked, the Revolution wavered, Bonaparte died and Napoleon was born from the ashes.

Napoleon's first defeat was his family. Such a man should have been born as a single son, instead of being drowned in a litter of thirteen children. "He had more trouble controlling his family than his empire," Mademoiselle Avillon would sniff. "He would have been better off with no family at all," said Stendhal.[2] "My relatives have done me more harm than I did them good. . . If I had to start over, my brothers and my sisters would get nothing but a few palaces and a few million to spend in idleness," the Emperor confided one day to Metternich. The Bonapartes, hailing from a family of debatable (and much debated) nobility from Geneva, with little means and without a penny once Corsica was delivered to the English, would be impelled toward the Continent 1793 by the waves of fortune. Letizia, future Madame Mother, flanked by her son Lucien and her three daughters, came ashore in Marseilles where the modesty of their lifestyle is explained by their straitened circumstances. To pay their bills, if one believes what forked tongues have to say about them, she transformed their refuge into a house of too easy welcome and put Pauline, a fifteen year old rosebud, into the bed of Fréron, a conventioneer in his forties, all-powerful in the South. He bequeathed to her a sexually transmitted disease and released a nymphomania that would set aquiver for the rest of her life that beautiful body immortalized by Canova.[3]

After Charles, the father, died in 1785 in Montpellier, Letizia was left on her own to raise the eight children who remained to her: Joseph, Napoleon, Lucien, Elisa, Louis, Pauline, Caroline and Jerome. An extraordinary brood: an emperor and a king to boot, a double king and two additional kings, a queen, a prince, a princess, a duchess. Only Hera, the cantankerous wife of Zeus, could claim such shameless, wanton and chaotic offspring; and they ruined the reputation of Olympus.

When he was crowned at Notre-Dame in a memorable display of Capuchin theater, his brothers and his sisters, caught up in the spirit of the game, considered their Italian origins too modest. All the bootlickers and sycophants hastened to fabricate a prestigious heritage for the family, linking them variously to the Comnenes and thus to the Byzantine emperors, or to Henri IV (through the Iron Mask, an anonymous political prisoner who died in the Bastille in 1703). The famous prisoner supposedly married the daughter of jail's governor, Monsieur de Bompart, and their children, impelled by a strange inspiration, Italianized their mother's name to Buonaparte. However, since Alexandre Dumas, everyone knows that the Iron Mask was the eclipsed twin brother of the Sun King. Thus, Napoleon became a Bourbon, the Empire became a Restoration, and the unfortunate Samson who cut down Louis XVI was its blade. When this nonsense was getting a bit tired, the victor of Rivoli, not wishing to be undone by such foolishness, exploded. "This genealogy is asinine and puerile. For anyone who wants to know when the House of Bonaparte began, the answer is quite simple: it dates from the 18th of Brumaire."

The young general who conquered Italy with 45,000 men, a small staff, and 48,000 gold livres (a pittance) had no ancestors and — thank heavens — no successor. In just a few weeks he plucked the Austrian eagle, despite its two heads, and humiliated the bejeweled little princely cowards. Without Italy, Europe — wedged between the heavy dialectics of the Germans and the didactic rationality of the French, would have declined. In the 18th century, its beauty was intact and the splendors that had accumulated since Antiquity made it the promised land for travelers and the delight of aesthetes. The baroque style defied the pure the facades of the first Renaissance, then married them to give birth to the Italian genius, the honor and happiness of mankind, that pokes fun at the whims of fashion and of the times and blossoms in wisdom and folly. Churches, convents, and palaces displayed treasures in which the sacred was a poor mask for the profane pleasures. Altars were covered with fine fabrics from the Orient, with long gold tassels; the jewels embedded in the reliquaries glorified in the kingdom of the living the remains of the dead, a sacred carnal presence in the compost of Casanova. There was no vault, no patrician residence where the masters of the paintbrush and chisel did not leave a trace of their genius. The goldsmithery of the most minor court would have made Louis XIV jealous, if the great king had traveled in the little corporal's retinue. Intact, the statues of Donatello, Cellini, and Verocchio reproached the bums, given to cutting off heads (whether of flesh or of marble), for the excessive sacrilege of their Cultural Revolution.

"I prefer my forefathers' rustic home / To the gilded palaces found in Rome." That was du Bellay's opinion, not Bonaparte's. At the head of children's battalions from a fatherland hauled out of the 18th century by Jacobinism, he seized northern Italy and on May 15, 1796, upon his entry into Milan, he found that the circular from the Directoire ordered him "to seek out, collect and have transported to Paris the most precious objects and to give precise orders for the enlightened (sic) execution of these provisions."[4] All his life would be marked by this republican burglary that equipped France with is fabulous spoils. This 27 year old thief, assisted by a commission of four "experts" from Paris, "to collect monuments of the fine arts," made off with twenty paintings from Parma, fifty from Bologna, and hundreds from Milan and the other subjected cities. Leonardo, Michelangelo, Raphaël, Rubens, Giorgione, Titian, Veronese, Corregio (whose Saint Jerome "is so esteemed in this country that I have been offered a million for it") were piled up in carriages and shipped off to Paris. Other conveyances were filled with precious vases, antique busts, manuscripts by da Vinci and Galileo, and the copy of the Aeneid annotated by Petrarch. The Institute Française, the Botanical Garden, the Polytechnic School and the National Library each received its share of the larceny. Soon, Bonaparte was holding up the pope: 500 manuscripts to be chosen by the French commissioners, 2 million livres (one and a half million in cash and gold ingots, 550,000 pounds of food products, goods, horses and oxen, "to give passage to the Republic's troops anytime a request is made." Bonaparte was the robber, and France was the receiver of stolen goods. Soon he would embody both roles, one after the other, with his brothers, his marshals, and his ministers for accomplices.

The day of the coronation, he crowned himself and Joséphine, elevating his clan and all the leeches who were in his favor, the vampires of fortune. Henri Beyle, with a profundity worthy of Stendhal, would write, "I have reflected a great deal over this obvious alliance of charlatans. Religion crowned tyranny and it was all in the name of the greater happiness of mankind." Then, he added, "I had to wash my mouth afterwards." Adolphe Thiers was no more sympathetic. "This mediocre rabble who give in to the torrent that runs before them, they all give in, especially when they think they will find honors and fortune in its course."

All these "charlatans," this "rabble," fought to find a place worthy of their vanity in the ridiculous procession. When Elisa invoked her seniority rights to get more rewards, Letizia put her back in her place.

"You can only reach the third row here. Madame Joseph (*sic*) and Madame Lucien (*resic*) will be before you. Give up your seat if you do not want the emperor to send his aide-de-camp with orders for you to give it up."[5] While the imperial family was bickering, Joséphine's salon resounded with ridiculous arguments between the new duchesses, of petty extraction and grandiose claims, who extracted the first favors. Admiral Bruix grumbled, "You want to erect a statue to Bonaparte in a Roman toga. Better make him naked; it will be easier for you to kiss his behind." When it became clear that the would not do what George Monk did,[6] Louis XVIII gave him a new nickname, "The Usurper." Napoleon, sorry to tell you, Sire, did not deserve the sobriquet any more than your ancestors and your peers: the Capetians, the Guises, the Valois, Tudors, Stuarts, Hanovers, Orleans, were all usurpers or dreamed of being usurpers, for history keeps serving up the same dishes again and again, whether as tragedy or farce, to parody Marx in connection with Shakespeare. Napoleon's mistake was in being born at the end of the 18th century and reigning at the beginning of the 19th, burdened with the King's errors and the Conventioneers' blunders. He would have done better to wait until the 20th century, so soft on totalitarianism and so favorable to the adventurers of darkness and lies. He wanted to be the successor to Charlemagne and Robespierre — talk about going astray — and he ended up becoming the first dictator of modern times.

Everyone was looking for an award, a medal, a hand-out, and he readily complied, proclaiming his admiration for science, the arts, the humanities. He made Marie-Joseph Chénier a count, when the malingering brother of the great guillotined writer dedicated a tragically bad tragedy[7] to him. The Legion of Honor became an obsession, a temptation. Clemenceau himself succumbed to it. "You call the decorations established by my administration trinkets," Napoleon once commented. "That may be, but it is by trinkets that one leads men." And the trinkets would soon be enhanced with particles to add to one's name.

In creating a new nobility for the Empire, the hero who didn't need anyone's help in making his own name into a legend was playing less to vanity than to political expediency. From the beginning, he was aware of the fragility of his popular monarchy. On one side, the Code, the abolition of serfdom, equality before the law; on the other, perpetual war, the police force, contempt for rights. The Emperor treated men the way the divine marquis did women. To consolidate his achievements he sought, in the absence of a single party, a clique. That gave him the basis he needed to reconcile the achievements of the Revolution and the traditions of the *Ancien Régime*. He cajoled the former: "You should rejoice, for now the old nobility is destroyed;" and, at the same time, he flattered the latter. "Enhanced by new honors, your existing ones shine all the brighter." Then, he reassured his world with the sibylline declaration that, "I am creating a sort of monarchy, because my hereditary titles are like a civic crown, which can be earned through good works." Smoke in the eyes. The imperial nobility was not founded on merit but on the arbitrary whims of a potentate. There were 30 dukes, 450 counts, 1,500 barons, 1,300 knights, not counting the princes and the kings who carved up France, divided Europe and reaped colossal rewards.

Napoleon died again the day Beethoven took his name off the *Third Symphony*.[8] Napoleon set the tune for the waltz of scepters and the saraband of his pals, whom he shuffled from one crown to another the way a middle manager is sent from branch to branch, according to the whims of the head of personnel. Joseph was made King of Naples, then sovereign of Spain before giving up pride and ambition; Elisa, Princess of Piombino and of Lucques; Louis, King of Holland; Caroline, Grand Duchess of Berg and Clèves, then Queen of Naples; Pauline, a Borghese princess through her second marriage,[9] then princess of Guastalla; Jerome, King of Westphalia; Eugene, Joséphine's cherished son, Viceroy of Italy, Duke of Leuchtenberg and Prince of Eichstadt. Everyone found a place, except for Lucien, whose children were, out of meanness, excluded from monarchical claims and successions. Sheridan, contemplating the map of Europe, sighed, "Look. France is everywhere." To tell the truth, it was mostly Corsica that was in evidence.

Inspired by the reverential fear that rendered the Head of the State comparable to Caesar's wife (never tainted by suspicion), I have entitled this chapter "The Napoleonides" and not "Napoleon." Thus, I draw a veil over the acquisition of the house on rue Chantereine, renamed rue des Victoires; on the relations between Bonaparte and Ouvrard, a corrupt military man who was hastily be-knighted by an overwhelmed Joséphine. I have withheld the factotums' speculations about the First Consul; his indulgence towards certain military suppliers who were guilty of fraud, while others, less guilty, paid the penalty. I have ignored his participation, and that of his family, in the capitalization of the Bank of France, where Perrégaux, his principal regent (a follower of Jacques Coeur), secured a monopoly over the emission of banknotes.[10] My discretion conforms with monarchical tradition, where the person of the king was inviolable and sacred, and with Fernch republican law that makes the President a citizen above the others, protected by Article 68 of the Constitution,[11] a legal Maginot line.

"Families, I hate you." That little sentence could have earned a Napoleonic decoration for the author of *Les Caves du Vatican* (*The Vatican Cellars*) that were so often plundered by his armed hordes. His mother, his brothers, his sisters were no paragons. When Caroline and Elisa refused to carry Joséphine's train at her wedding, he blew his stack. His sojourn at St. Helena did nothing to quell his bitterness. "I made myself a King, he believed himself to be one, all at once, by the grace of God . . . He was no longer a lieutenant I could rely upon, but one more enemy that I had to watch out for."

Mama Letizia, avid for money and for honors, called upon her brother, the cardinal — a promotion due to nepotism — Joseph Fesch, for help. The happy owner of a famous collection of primitive art that hardly cost him a penny, contacted his nephew. "Your mother wants a title, a stable position. It bothers her that some people accord her only (*sic*) the title of Imperial Highness, the same as her daughters." Seeking to assuage her, the Emperor revived the pretty Bourbonesque designation of "Madame,"[12] which the countess of Paris had avoided so scrupulously. Letizia balked, then, grudgingly, decided to make do. To comfort herself, she bought Lucien's house on rue Saint-Dominique, and in 1804 received the Grand Trianon,[13] which she soon deserted for the château of Pont , a new gift of filial love. He considered the annual provision of a million francs minimal to enable her to host in a properly "august" manner. When the emperor reproached her "for living like a bourgeois woman from rue de Saint-Denis," she retorted, "You must consider, Lord, if my treatment (*sic*) is sufficient relative to the obligations which my position imposes upon me. I would only spend a million if you gave me two of them." Like Marie de Medicis, she used Italy as a tax haven and socked away the cash.

After the ant, let's consider the grasshopper. Joséphine, a widow before she enters this story, was active in bed and in racking up debts, hoping that the former would put to rest the latter. When charitable destiny enabled this already ripe Creole beauty to allure the young Corsican with the thinning hair, their unexpected union, accompanied by intermittent fidelity, would make her rich beyond measure. She comforted herself for the torments of her husband's absence with Monsieur Charles, a character that Flaubert and Courteline could have fought over, and she dreamed of the return of the warrior, laden with the pharaoh's treasures. She acquired Malmaison without waiting for that dubious event, and established a literary salon where the feeble Legouvé, Beausset and other writers lulled the newly rich to the tune of their soporific works. Her talent for spending knew no bounds. During the coronation, David, his hand forced, painted her with the features of a teenager, and Paris laughed at this miracle of aesthetic sycophantry. The "Inventory of the Empress' Gems and Diamonds,"[14] published simultaneously with this event, takes 30 pages to list her immense fortune: diamonds, antique jewels, garnets, amethysts, topazes, pearls, rubies and other emeralds. There must have been enough in this display case to adorn every one of Bonaparte's many little kitchenmaids.[15] When Bérénice, a little over-ripe, retired among the roses at Malmaison, Napoleon (Titus and Croesus joined together in one person) took as his responsibility and that of France the debts that the abandoned one would rack up until her final moments, stopped only when she drew her last breath.

The day Napoleon offered Joseph the iron crown of Italy in exchange for giving up his rights to the imperial succession, his elder, who did dream of succeeding him, refused (apparently that head-piece was too narrow for his swollen head). In Naples, and then in Spain, he took his role very seriously, refusing the emperor's orders to treat his realms as conquered lands and, as a badly enlightened despot, sought to rule by love. Napoleon curtly recalled him to his duties as an invader: "My brother, it is not by cajoling people that they are won over, and it is not by these measures that you will give yourself the wherewithal to grant your army its just rewards. Impose thirty million in taxes on the Kingdom of Naples. " The message was successfully deciphered and, upon the departure of this good king, the Neapolitans would search, in vain, for 500 million that had disappeared from the public accounts. Sent to Madrid against his will, this son of the Republic addressed a monarchist proclamation to Spain, modestly signed: "Don José, by the grace of God, King of Castille, of Aragon, the Two Sicilies, of Jerusalem, of Navarre. . ." Along the way, he added the titles of archduke of Austria, duke of Burgundy, of the Brabant, and of Milan, and count de Hapsburg. The Spaniards, aware of his immoderate taste for spirits, dubbed him with the less glorious nickname of "Don Pepe Bottela"[16] and transformed his reign into a reign of suffering. When the emperor set out to subdue the insurrection of a whole people, this poor humanist beseeched him, "Lord, I am covered in shame before my alleged subjects . . . I beg Your Majesty to accept my renunciation of all the rights that he has given me to the throne of Spain. I will always prefer honor and probity to power bought so dearly." This honor and this probity by no means prevented him from leaving Spain with a few million more, with select items from the Iberian patrimony, nor, during the Russian debacle, from plotting with Lucien and the English finally to take the place of the vanquished. Retired in Switzerland before the Hundred Days, Joseph would bury his nest egg in a fox burrow, deep in the park of his château. A strange precaution for a philosopher king. . .[17]

Napoleon named Lucien, a skilful political but not a very scrupulous manager, Minister for the Interior — a disappointing reward for the litter-bearer of the 18 Brumaire, who had hoped to become Consul. By way of portfolio, he first of all turned his attention to his own, which was burnished by covert payments, bribes, and under the counter commissions. His venality, denounced publicly, obliged Bonaparte to terminate his services and to dispatch him to Spain, the trash heap of the Empire, far from the hotel of Brienne, jewel of the Grand Siècle, which he had acquired thanks to his embezzlements. In Madrid, Charles IV showered this accommodating plenipotentiary with gifts: money, gold, precious furniture, and canvases by the Masters including one of his portraits wrapped in thick tissue paper. When Lucien tore off the wrappings, a rain of diamonds fell, worth some five million francs, which would soon decorate the pretty throat of Alexandrine de Bleschamp, an opulent widow, with whom he had recently taken up. Napoleon, an expert in misalliances, wanted to force him to divorce in order to marry a misshapen midget with great dynastic hopes. Lucien noted, "You married a widow too, but mine is neither old nor smelly. . . . It is more honorable to marry one's own mistress than someone else's." The two brothers would remain estranged until the Hundred Days when the Prince de Canino (a sacristy title bought from the pope for 500,000 francs) went back to the emperor. Lucien, who had refused to be the slave of glory, would become the free man of misfortune.

Elisa, Grand Duchess of Tuscany, was the ugliest, most intelligent and most pedantic of the three sisters. She was jubilant when her brother granted her the right to call herself "Elisa-Napoleon." "I vow never to forget the duties imposed by a name that will always be the glory of the century and the astonishment of posterity." Chateaubriand, seduced for a moment, dedicated *Le Génie du christianisme* (*The Genius of* Christianity) "To the best of all women, the noblest of protectresses, towards whom my heart is filled with gratitude that nothing will ever diminish." (In his memoirs, he would speak somewhat differently.) An excellent manager, she revived the Carrara marble quarries (so essential to neoclassicism), and, as good blood cannot lie, she herself did not remain as marble before of the pleasures of the flesh. Her house, supported by the civil list — 900,000 francs per annum on top of other advantages — was so starchily ostentatious that it made the sanctimonious members of the imperial court look like libertines. The "Semiramis from Lucques"[18] governed judiciously, fought organized crime, protected the arts and letters, and developed public education. She and Napoleon were the only real men in the family.

Louis, the future King of Holland, elevated to the rank of prince, then of constable — a distinction that had been buried since Luynes, Concini's executioner — benefited more than any other member of the clan from his elder's generosity, who wanted to be forgiven for his arranged marriage with Hortense de Beauharnais, his daughter-in-law and, they say, perhaps something more. Owner of a mansion on the rue des Victoires, and a second one on rue Cerruti, he also acquired the domaine de Saint-Leu, a national asset confiscated from the duke of Orleans.[19] These indulgences did not keep Hortense from despising her husband and from throwing away her crown. From her turbulent love affairs would be born Morny and, apparently, Napoleon III himself, "Queen Hortense's son," as his father called him according to the Civil Code; he refused all his life to meet this innocent proof of his woes. Once seated upon Holland's throne, Louis felt he was sprouting wings and, instead of acting as a mere puppet of the emperor, began to behave like William of Orange's heir. He refused to subject his country to the requirements of the Continental Blockade, made up to the English, and defied Napoleon — who suggested that he "Behave in your domestic affairs in the paternalistic and effeminate way that you demonstrate in government and, when it comes to business, let's have more of the rigor that you show within your household." In 1810, Louis abdicated under the threat of the Grand Army and, as those retiring from fortune so often do, took unhappy refuge in writing.

A woman of domestic inclinations, Pauline, the Princess Borghese, led a hellish lifestyle and her chef alone was paid 12,000 francs per annum (the equivalent of a major general). She aped the luxury of Cleopatra, whose sexual greed she shared (but not her appetite for power). "I leave the taste for crowns to the rest of my family." Indifferent, but capable of serving her own interests, she renounced the principality of Guastalla (which was integrated into the kingdom of Italy) in exchange for an allowance of six million francs and the right to retain her title. She preferred the delights of Parisian life over dreary marital responsibilities. She mocked her unresponsive husband, "I would prefer to be the widow of General Leclerc, with a stipend of 20,000 livres, than to be the wife of a eunuch." This pretty hedonist would turn out to be the only one in the lot to remain loyal to the emperor, her brother (and perhaps her lover, if we take the puritan Madame de Rémusat's word for it). She followed him to the island of Elba, and sold the pearls from the crown that she had spurned.

Caroline — "Cromwell's head on the shoulders of a lovely woman" — also had imperial ambitions. This beautiful conspirator, "lacking both deportment and charm,"[20] had to settle for the Grand Duchies of Berg and Clèves, then the more substantial kingdom of Naples (when the Spanish crown was taken away in favor of Joseph). Murat, her husband, who was so sorely missed at Waterloo,[21] was constrained, poor fellow, to join the army to escape his creditors. His bravery, his alliance with the Emperor, the way his men worshipped him, and his immoderate taste for tinsel, transformed this warrant officer into a legendary marshal. Seated on the throne of Naples, he bedazzled the Italians (who have always appreciated a good farce) with his scintillating appearance at the head of a carnival troupe. The king of operetta, a "Bedouin chief" to Germaine de Staël and a "circus entertainer" according to his brother-in-law, Murat wanted to become a full-fledged monarch and he, too, balked at the imperial diktats; on France's money, he conducted a policy opposing her hegemony. When Napoleon stumbled, Murat shifted his allegiance altogether. "The Emperor only wants war. I would be betraying my former motherland's interests and those of both my estates and yours if I did not immediately separate my armies from his and add them to those of the allied powers, whose magnanimous intentions are to restore the dignity of thrones and the independence of nations." After this manly proclamation, he took his arms, his luggage and his wife over to the enemy. His defection saved neither his crown nor his life. In the moat at the château of Pizzo, instead of the anticipated money, he received twelve bullets, bequeathing to posterity his cranium and his exemplary disloyalty.

Unlike Lucien, Jerome ditched his wife and children to attain the Westphalian throne.[22] St. Peter refusing to annul his marriage, he became a bigamist (what a family!), marrying Catherine of Wurtemberg, a German runt seduced by self-conceit. The luxury of his court, his easy way with money, and his passion for festivities led the kingdom to bankruptcy. Napoleon was exhausted. "It is inconceivable what this young man costs me, while giving me only trouble and being of no use at all within my system . . . His kingdom has no police, no finances, no organization. It is not through unruly luxury that one builds a monarchy." During the Russian campaign he was commander of the French right wing (90,000 men), a "Jerome in petticoats" as his soldiers called him. He caved in before Bagration's cossacks, surrendered his position to Davout, and abandoned his camp; but he rejected the coalition forces' offers. "As a French prince, my first duties are to France and, made a king by his victories, I cannot be king after his defeats. When the trunk is felled, the branches must die." In spite of these powerful words, he remained quite alive, crossed the Rhine and abstained from taking part in the French campaign. After Waterloo, where he finally distinguished himself, Napoleon revised his judgment. "My brother, I came to know you too late." (It would have been better, my lord, not to have known him at all. Then you would have been spared the painful spectacle of the lawsuit he brought in 1820, seeking the restitution of some 1,200,000 francs, the origins of which he had the greatest difficulty to justify.)

Having taken care of his family, Napoleon shared the fruits of his extraordinary expansion with his top officials and his marshals. On March 31, 1806, the Senate ratified the creation of "fifteen duchies as grand fiefs" in the conquered countries: 11 for the Venetian States alone, one in Lombardy, three in Parma and in Plaisance, with the right to be transfer the lands and titles, "from male to male by order of primogeniture," and with the right to a fifteenth of the revenues generated by the fiefs. "When circumstances allow it," the Emperor wrote to Berthier (prince of Neuchâtel),[23] "go to Strasbourg. From there, you will can go on to your principality and make all the arrangements. It provided 50,000 ecus to Prussia, it should give you more."[24]

The other marshals enjoyed identical provisions. Augereau was made duke of Castiglione, Bessières, duke of Istria, Davout, duke of Auerstaedt, Kellermann, duke of Valmy, Lannes, duke of Montebello, Marmont, duke of Raguse, Moncey, duke of Conegliano, Mortier, duke of Trévise, Ney, duke of Elchingen, Soult, duke of Dalmatia, Victor, duke of Bellune, Macdonald, duke of Tarente, Oudinot, duke of Reggio, Suchet, duke of Albufera, Davout and Masséna, prince of Eckmühl and prince of Essling, Ney, prince of Muscovy. They pocketed millions at the expense of the bottomless imperial coffers, of which Talleyrand, Fouché and the civil entourage also took shameless advantage.

When Lefebvre acceded to the duchy of Danzig, Napoleon met with him. "Monsieur Duke, I know that you like chocolates. Please accept this modest gift." Upon his return to his place, the husband of Madame Shameless discovered, in the box of delicacies, three hundred thousand-franc bills: the famous "chocolates of Danzig."

How the little connivances of the Directoire pale by comparison. Instead of becoming the emperor's loyal supporters, the privileged people set about to do everything possible to prolong the pleasure. Some, jealous of Bernadotte's success,[25] felt they had been badly used. Soult wanted to become suzerain of Andalusia, Junot, sovereign of Portugal. Instead of asking "who made you king?," they wanted to know how they could follow suit.

The pillaging of Europe accelerated under the Consulship, the Consulship for life and the Empire. This vast enterprise of appropriation was conducted for and in accordance with the orders of the Emperor by Vivant Denon, who served as his "Minister of Culture." He was Napoleon's Malraux, more or less: the author of *La Condition humaine* was a thief before he reached the national palaces; the author of *Le Point du lendemain* was appointed in order to steal. A one-time gentleman from the king's chamber, spy, diplomat, and orientalist, a mediocre engraver and a pleasing enough draughtsman, Vivant Denon became the master of the haymakers and his harvest is still used to instruct French children in the arts. He brought back from Egypt myriads of pictures and souvenirs (recorded in his *Voyages in Lower and Upper Egypt during General Bonaparte's Campaigns*), a worrisome taste for "the trophies of conquest," and the endearing little foot of a mummified princess that he had taken from the Necropolis of the Hundred Doors at Thèbes. After David and Canova turned him down, Bonaparte called upon Denon to be general manager of the fine arts and the museums and the director of refinements for a court that was sorely in need of them.

Trailing behind the Grand Army, Denon collected scores of paintings and drawings, including a few Rembrandts from the Zanetti collection. "The curator of Europe" had studied a circular from the Directoire that said, "The Republic, due to its strength, the superiority of its scholars and its artists, is the only country in the world that can provide inviolable *(sic)* asylum *(resic)* to these masterpieces." He hid from the Prussians more than 13,000 objects, sacked the royal palace of Warsaw, raided the collections of the old Spanish monarchy, seized the precious paintings from the Belvedere in Vienna, and emptied Italy. Thanks to this official of thievery, Napoleon's museum at the Louvre housed (prior to the Restoration) the Borghese collection, 7 Da Vincis, 9 Correggio's, 15 Veroneses, 24 Titians, 10 Tintorettos, 25 Raphaëls, 24 Poussins and, as gifts from the pagans, the *Venus de Médicis,* the *Belvedere Apollo,* and the *Laocoon. . .* Not to mention the caravans full of objets d'art that were stolen twice — from their owners and then from France, finding their ways to Malmaison, the Tuileries, Saint-Cloud, the châteaux and town houses of the notables. Joséphine auctioned off her treasures to the highest bidders: Tsar Alexandre I bought a few for a million francs. Faithful to my promise not to speak ill of the Emperor himself, I will abstain from pointing out that at the rococo palace of Potsdam, he violated the tomb of Frederick the Great and made off with his sword.

After the Hundred Days, Europe reclaimed its goods in Napoleon's museum, which had been renamed (apparently without the slightest qualm) the Royal Museum. Canova, Commissar of the Italian States, Ribbentrop, in the name of Prussia, Austria, Schleswig and Hesse, and Hamilton, for the English, stripped its walls. "As long as these works remain here, they cannot fail to keep alive in the French nation the memory of its former conquests and to support its military spirit and its vanity," preached the sententious Wellington. "Resist as hard as you can. Only give in if forced," Louis XVIII commanded Denon. He heeded the gouty monarch who believed in inertia, and the Louvre managed to preserve 100 paintings (including *The Wedding at Cana*), 800 drawings from the collection of the duke of Modena, rooms full of antiques, the sublime Albani bas-reliefs, and the astonishing paintings of the Italian primitive school: Giotto, Fra Angelico, Cimabue, Masaccio and Ghirlandaio, in which Canova, blinded by the inept notion of progress in art, was not longer interested.

The Napoleonic system? An imposture and a fantasy. "I am the French Revolution," he liked to say. Which one? That of human rights, which he exported? Or of the terror that he imposed? He is an ensemble that incorporates opposite qualities. Apostle of freedom, he held the continent in slavery; cheerleader for equality, he adorned the new adventurers with old privileges. He fought corruption but, a corrupter himself, he surrounded himself by the corrupt. He detested money, but allowed the golden calf to graze in his mass graves. His intention, to build a Europe that would be absorbed by France, would never see the light of day; but, for the first time since Charlemagne, a man strove to reunify the old continent. This ambition would outlive him. Without this lover of war, Briand, Robert Schuman, Adenauer, the apostles of peace, would have never dared to set their plan in motion. How obsolete Charles Joseph de Ligne now seems, who lamented, "Europe is a coquette who has lost sight of the rules." You are mistaken, my prince, it is finding a new youth.

Footnotes

1. In John Kobler, *Capone and the Gulf War in Chicago*.
2. *Life of Napoleon*.
3. When one of her ladies-in-waiting, shocked that she had posed nude for the sculptor, told her that she should not have done it, Pauline was surprised and answered, "Why? It wasn't cold, there was a fireplace in the studio."
4. Circular dated May 7, 1796.
5. According to *Memoires d'une femme de qualite sur le Consulat et l'Empire*, Mercure de France, 1987.
6. George Monk, duke of Abermarle, at one time a supporter and a lieutenant of Cromwell, later helped to restore Charles II to the throne of England.
7. *Le Couronnement de Cyrus*.
8. Bonaparte's name had appeared alongside the title of this symphony (the Heroic one), when the General of the Revolution still represented to Beethoven the heroes fighting for the liberation of the people. The typesetter removed the name when he understood Napoleon's ambition to become emperor.
9. Celebrated after the disappearance of the good General Leclerc, who so feared the "heat and the negroes."
10. After the 18 Brumaire, the Consulate wanted to have its own bank. The Bonaparte family, the consuls and the ministers were the principal shareholders. They received interests of about 10%.
11. "The president of the Republic is not responsible for the acts committed in the performance of his duties except in the event of high treason. He can be indicted only by the two assemblies ruling by an identical vote, open to the public, and in the absolute majority of the component members; he is judged by the High Court of Justice."
12. Her official title was "Her Imperial Highness, Madame the Mother of the Emperor." She preferred Impératrice Mère and not this "Madame" which, under the Bourbons, had been reserved for the sister-in-law of the king.
13. Pauline would receive the Petit Trianon.
14. Frederic Masson, of the French Academy, *Mme Bonaparte*, Albin Michel, 1927.
15. Thus one called the women of the imperial court.
16. In one night, he and his officers emptied one of the most famous cellars of Spain. Thus, the inhabitants of Madrid depicted him as a big, staggering bottle.
17. Self-proclaimed.
18. Thus her fans obligingly called her.
19. With the Restoration, Louis XVIII would make Hortense, a royalist, the

duchess of Saint-Leu.

20. According to Laure d'Abrantès, jealous of Caroline's sleeping with her husband, Marshal Junot.

21. The emperor would say, at St. Helena: "Murat's presence at Waterloo would have given us the victory."

22. Jerome, coming from America with his family, disembarked in Lisbon in 1805. On order of Napoleon, his wife was refused a passport for France. While Jerome prostrated himself before his brother's wishes, his young wife was dying in Dover where she was in confinement with their second child. She never saw Jerome again.

23. He would later become prince de Wagram.

24. Berthier was not satisfied with so little: 100,000 francs of annual rent on Westphalia, 141,000 on Hanover, 300,000 on the departments of the Saar and Roër, 100,000 on Mount-of-Milan, 200,000 on the Rhine, 250,000 on the château of Chambord.

25. Napoleon's former marshal, Jean-Baptiste Bernadotte, was elected heir to the Swedish throne in 1810.

Chapter 11

MORNY

Half-brother of Napoleon III, Morny (1811-1865), was instrumental in the successful coup d'etat in 1851. He served as Interior Minister and President of the Corps Législatif.

> "It is time to give liberty, before it is taken by force."
>
> Morny

On the evening of December 1, 1851, a few hours before the coup d'etat that he had instigated, Morny was attending a performance at the opera. A lady with a seemingly detached air, pinched by her crinoline, approached his box. A good fairy? No, a busy-body. She asked him, "What will you do, Sir, if they try to sweep away the National Assembly?" — "In such a case, you may be sure, Madame, that I will strive to be on the side of the handle." Edgar Faure would say almost the same thing. "If you want to be faithful to your ideas, you often have to change parties." And he added, "It is not the weather vane that turns, it is the wind." Morny was not a weather vane but a spinning top. This voluptuary embodied polymorphic lying, self-interest, and good management, and he almost always won.

A photograph taken in 1858, when he was 47 years old, shows his scornful gaze, majestic nose, and curved face sweeping up to a bald pate, with a goatee and a handlebar moustache. Who was this child, born on October 22, 1811 and registered at a town hall in Paris? Officially, Charles, Auguste, Louis, Joseph Demorny was the legitimate son of a certain Demorny. The happy father, after having settled up with the registry bureau, dashed over to Notre-Dame-des-Victoires to have the brat baptized. As the first lie, the name was split to allow for a fake particle to adorn the newborn baby, and he found himself ennobled: de

Morny. For the good Demorny, whose assistance was purchased by a life-long stipend, was only a fake father. Morny was a corrupter from birth.

Charles was the illegitimate fruit of Queen Hortense, the dissatisfied wife of Louis Bonaparte (brother of Napoleon and illegitimate King of Holland) whose virtue had yielded to a cavalry officer from the Grand Army, Charles de Flahaut, himself a natural son of Talleyrand. Morny tried to have himself recognized until 1837, when the dethroned sovereign disappeared. The favor was refused and this woman, so emotional in her memoirs, never showed Charles the maternal love that Rostand would say is divided yet remains whole.[1] For lack of recognition, he invented a count's title, added a hydrangea to his coat of arms, pinned this flower to the lapel of his frock coat, and adopted the Latin motto, "*Tace sed memento,*" ("Say nothing, and remember"). Hortense was also the mother of Napoleon III; he was known as "Hortense's pale son."

In the totalitarian State of Corsica, this pregnancy and childbirth were kept under wraps. Apparently, it was a matter of the security of the Empire and the interests of France. The kid was shuttled from nurse to grandmother — far from his father, who was fighting a war, and from his mother, who was simpering with her admirers. When Napoleon precipitated France into the Hundred Days catastrophe, Flahaut (Talleyrand's putative son, as we have said, a French general and diplomat, lover of Napoleon's sister Caroline and then of Hortense) rejoined the service and attracted the rage of the extremists. Talleyrand, not very eager to see his son suffer the same fate as his own victim, the duke of Enghien, intervened with Louis XVIII to save him from the firing squad during the White Terror. Morny's dubious heredity is quite in line with the cynicism and the feigned ease displayed in the salons of the Second Empire: "I call my father *Mister*, my daughter *Miss*, my brother *Lord*, and that is all considered natural!" Morny might have added, "In my family, almost all the children are natural."

What opportunities could the ambitious find during the Louis-Philippe monarchy? Arms? Business? Politics? Morny started with the flag, a service that was pure façade, far from military conditions and constraints. This led him to Fontainebleau, a gloomy village where he was appointed thanks to his father, who had become the pear-shaped King's[2] general. From 1831 to 1833, all braid and epaulettes, he danced the polka and his grand uniform won him many hearts. When Paris, nostalgic for laurels, sought to conquer Algiers, Morny embarked for Africa. He distinguished himself during the siege of Constantine where he saved the life of General Trezel. This exploit, much publicized, did not convert him but made him General Oudinot's aide-de-camp. After a foray into the Jebel mountains of Algeria, he was struck by a fever. Shivering in the sun, he was lying at the edge of a river when an unknown officer approached him. "Monsieur de Morny, you are quite ill; would you allow me to offer you an orange?" — "Thank God! I will never forget your gesture, comrade. What is your name?" — "I am Captain Changarnier." He remembered his benefactor well, and had him thrown into a cell in Mazas shortly after the coup d'etat.

Turning in his uniform in 1837, he resigned from the army to devote himself to his true vocations, politics and business. Or business and politics, to be precise. He was constrained to give up his ruinous adolescent conduct, for Flahaut could no longer pay his debts. The nobility of sufficiency and that of the usurpation, since the Restoration, had given up on the interdict on labor; blue blood and tricolor blood could now grow rich any way they could find. But where to start? Morny knew Count Walewski, owner of *The Messenger*, natural son (of course) of the Ogre and of Marie Walewska. He chose the press abused by Balzac, and, like Bel-Ami (who would resemble him) leased out his talent. In one of his articles, he took the side of the beet growers against the importers of sugarcane, and became their scribe. As bees prefer sugar to gall, Morny soon became the owner of a refinery near Clermont-Ferrand; here he forged his first weapons in the industry where he would soon become one of the great captains.

Business isn't much fun without women. Building on the motto of *The Sylph* (by Crébillon, Jr.), "Having fun while making a profit," the count was a ladies' man, whose love affairs were never disassociated from money. He made good use of the ladies, and chose as his mistress Fanny Le Hon, the beautiful wife of the ambassador of Belgium and the cherished daughter of Mosselmann (the fabulously rich banker from Antwerp). Charles made her blossom; Fanny spoiled him; and the money pump worked overtime. Morny used his adulterous finances to invest in the Vieille-Montagne mines, where Mosselmann was majority shareholder. Louis-Napoleon ("the emperor of the demi-monde"), would do the same with his political muse, Madame Howard.

Morny allied himself with the July Monarchy and tried his

chances in the 1842 elections in Clermont-Ferrand. The prefect, knowing his ties with Louis-Philippe's entourage, did not think the young *arriviste* had a chance, and withheld his support. However, Morny put on a dazzling campaign and came out the winner.

In the Chamber, the new deputy was hardly outstanding; he only took initiative when it came to the legality of the futures markets, which stood to make him a substantial profit. He finally found a cause worthy of himself, where the public interest coincided with his personal interests: railroads. Arago was horrified by the railway, the peasants were afraid of the embers that ignited their harvests, and the fatal accident in 1842 stood in the way of the railroad's triumph. Morny had confidence in these new forms of transport so essential to the first industrial revolution. However, although he was certainly on the gravy train himself, he did not own any engines or cars. An unforgivable lacuna. To fill it, he proposed to build a line between Moulins and Clermont, using Mosselmann's money and the profit derived from some remote-controlled lucky strikes on the stock exchange. (Those windfalls made him a new convert to the crime of insider trading, a family custom, and promising a brilliant future.) The cosseted bourgeois was transformed into a great lord, owner of a sumptuous house at the Champs-Elysée circle, a collection of fine furniture and masterpieces worthy of his grandfather, Talleyrand, along with a stable of racehorses with glowing and profitable colors.[3]

This brilliant and sudden fortune made tongues wag, and disturbing rumors reached the Assembly. But the voters, who readily transform candidates' flaws into so many qualities, remained faithful to the corrupt official. In 1848, that fatal year for Orléans, Marx wrote his *Manifesto*, and "class struggle," the bogeyman of the conservatives, shook the old continent. In Paris, Frankfurt, Vienna, and Prague, not to mention Buda and Pest, the treasure chests trembled. The hand gun and the firing squad were called in to restore order. In France, Victor Schoelcher released the slaves but a graver danger laid in wait for the right-thinking people — the hardened masses, bereft of moral values, bloodthirsty through hereditary transmission. In spite of the literary idealism of the time, social Darwinism was in full play. While the notion of the evolution of the species was not new,[4] the 19th century drew from it conclusions of a terrible determinism, which Zola would echo. By a wild and idiotic dialectic, the Lantiers were condemned to forfeiture and the Vandals were at the gates. For Ernest Coeurduay, the anarchist (author of *Hurrah! Ou la Révolution par les cosaques*, in 1854), the saber-wielding primitives who had camped on the Champs-Elysées after Napoleon's collapse, bore the flame of Redemption. In 1832, after the silk workers' revolt in Lyon was bloodily suppressed, *Le Journal débates* measured the danger. "The barbarians who threaten society are not in the Caucasus nor in the steppes of Tartary, they are at our city limits."[5] After the radical uprising of February 1848 and its repression, Morny hyperbolized, "If you look closely enough at a Socialist, you will find that you prefer the cossacks."

Cut out of the political game, ruined by the days of 1848 (together with Fanny, whose fortune was washed away by the democratic tide), Charles was in poor shape. When the populist Right took in hand the Second Republic, the two lovers were able to return to business. Relieved of a cumbersome Orleanism, Morny approached his half-brother (who, by default, had become champion of the order). This weak and intelligent autocrat, whose real defeat was not Sedan but Victor Hugo, had a conflicted democratic vocation that would push him, too late, toward a liberal empire. As Prince-President, he forgot Prudhomme's wise council to his son. "Dear Sir, be wary of ambition. It has been fatal to the greatest. If Napoleon Bonaparte had remained an artillery lieutenant, he would be still on the throne." December 2 would be his 18th Brumaire and Charles, his Lucien.

The speculator and the conspirator were made for each other. Louis-Napoleon was by no means an "easily led cretin," but a political ambiguity and a pragmatist in search of his Talleyrand. He chose his half-brother for accomplice. When the regime was embroiled in crisis, the Assembly entered into conflict with the executive, and Morny declared himself in favor of a *pronunciamiento*, of which he became both the angel and the demon.

Of course, it all started with a lie. At the Opera where we left him a few moments ago, Morny was gracious and reassuring to those whom he was about to imprison. "Dear Sirs, we all know that we are all betting our hides here," he had declared to his trusty men, gathered together around Napoleon at the Elysée. His trick having succeeded, he was appointed Minister for the Interior; he drafted the Prince-President's first declarations with a flair that would have earned him the Goncourt Prize for essays, then, as strategist of the reprisals, he advised, "Let the insurrectionists engage completely; let them build barricades, and then we can crush the enemy and destroy him." "It is only by complete abstention, by surrounding a district and by conquering it by famine or by debasing it by terror that one can start a civil war." On December 4, Canrobert's troops had an easy job. Thousands of deaths and arrests and innumerable deportations. "It was a fairly crude police operation," he would comment.

In *History of a Crime*, Victor Hugo wonders, "What is Morny? A cheerful, important man, a schemer, but not austere, having social graces and manners, content with himself, spiritual, and exhibiting a certain liberality." In a conversation with Mérimée before the coup d'etat, he speaks more sharply: "Morny, the racketeer, has spirit; he is very social, he is active in industrial deals, he put together the Vieille-Montagne business, the zinc mines, and the coal mines of Liege. I have the honor of knowing him. He is a crook." Pretty astute, but excessive. In the eyes of the masses, you are never completely a crook if you are successful. One only becomes a crook when one fails.

To clean up his image, the new minister hired a public relations consultant, a certain Monsieur de Guerronière. He earned his money: "Never shunning his responsibility, Morny remained, even under the most difficult circumstances, a gentleman and a great lord. As well as inflexible measures, he was able to create the most delicate process. He remained pleasant and polished, even while being threatened." Alphonse Daudet, the count' Secretary, more literary, described his boss as a Marquis de Mora. "No one knew better than he how to present himself in the world, how to walk across a room with dignity, to smile on his way to the Tribune, to lend gravity to futile causes, to treat serious matters lightly. That was his attitude in life, a paradoxical distinction."

In the free-for-all of the parvenus, Morny was hurt by his rivalry with the duke of Persigny,[6] a member of Napoleon III's brain trust. The confiscation of Orléans' assets, which he had guaranteed, enabled his adversary to oust him. Thrown out by the emperor, this corrupt man, faithful to his commitments, surrendered his portfolio, gave up the presidency of the legislative body, and found himself a mere deputy. True courage but a distorted outcome.

In 1852, he left government and took on managing the coal mines and forges of Aubière, transformed them into a public corporation, grabbed the majority of shares and pocketed two million francs while he was at it. His unhappy competitor, Mr. de Cabrol, chairman of the forging mills at Decazeville (and a sore loser), attacked Morny in the press. Morny responded with a suit for slander and the judges imposed hard sanctions on his attacker. Plonk, Minister for Interior,[7] would later say to Mathieu, his lawyer, "At the time when I was substitute in the First Chamber of the Seine, your client's name was a constant refrain. His celebrity bothered me. When one is Monsieur de Morny, one should neither win nor lose lawsuits, one should simply not have them."[8] That's an interesting way of seeing things.

Disturbed by the fuss that was being kicked up over the Aubière affair, Napoleon III berated his brother. "You are compromising your honor, and mine too."

"I have no more official function; thus, no one can associate your name with my companies."

"I am happy to see to your fortune, but I do not want any fiddling with the public funds."

"The public funds will never suffer from my actions. On the contrary. Everything I am doing is by way of progress and the final best interest of the country."

All the contractors, builders and speculators of the Second Empire, bankers like Pereire and Boucicaut, thought along the same lines, in a France that was hypnotized by luxury.

The empire was not a time of peace — the future would show that clearly — but an immense effort of industrial restoration and financial imagination. Railways and factories were being built, speculation was rife, and the statement, "Morny is involved in the deal" guaranteed the security and the profitability of the most insane speculations. When Morny was in "the deal," everyone was reassured. However, when he returned to power, everyone was worried. And return he did, by persuading Napoleon III to marry Eugénie de Montijo. Winterhalter captured in a portrait the agreeable nonchalance of her gaze, pitiful and pitiless at the same time, but he lacked the talent of Manet, whose sanctimonious and narrow-minded rendition of the Spanish-woman flutters her fan in Le Déjeuner sur l'herbe. This union earned Morny a renewal of favor with his half-brother, and the gratitude of the bride (of whom he was putatively the best man). She secured him the post of President of the Legislature, so ardently coveted. From the Hotel de Lassay he advised the Tuileries, often with great perspicacity, opposing the bloody and futile engagement in the Crimea (that was promoted by the empress).

Morny's lucidity never blocked his schemes. He whirled around, changed direction, juggled with France and the accounting books, and seduced women and bankers, until the day when a light Balzac-Stendhalian comedy slowed him down. In 1856, he was dispatched to Saint Petersburg for the coronation of Alexander II, in the capacity of extraordinary ambassador. He returned, married to a beauty from a famous noble family, Sophie Trubetskaya, who lived "on cigarettes and cancans."[9] She was eighteen years old and was, according to rumor, the natural daughter of Nicolas I and half-sister of the new tsar.

This event provoked the ire of Fanny Le Hon. Certainly, her lover had already been unfaithful, and certainly, they were getting bored with each other; but the grand dame of the banks was disinclined to serve as the carpet for a great love affair. She decided to get even. As Morny's associate, she laid claim to half of the profit he had garnered, that is to say six million francs; and the liquidation of this false community became an affair of state. Napoleon asked Rouher[10] to play Justice of the Peace. The minister examined the balance sheets, conducted a detailed audit and sent the emperor a painstaking description of all the misconduct perpetrated by the President of the Legislative Corps: trading favors, dubious profits, embezzlement and misappropriation, favoritism, corrupt practices. Fanny used her advantage to the full and, according to Alphonse Daudet, set a trap for her faithless lover. In their *Journal*, the Goncourt brothers reported an account by an overly talkative secretary. "Madame Le Hon summons Rouher to come to her, has him read the letters where the duke ridicules the bourgeois from Auvergne, and ends up giving in to him. Thus the arbiter chosen by Morny declared to him one day, to Morny's complete amazement, that upon his honor and his conscience, Morny owed three million to his ex-mistress. It was well-played by the woman."

Charles was outraged, and refused to be conned. Fanny insisted, threatening him with a public lawsuit. Would this be his complete undoing? Not wishing to be destroyed by a scandal, Napoleon paid off the courtesan of the empire. Less of a philanthropist than his deceased uncle, he had his brother reimburse him.

Soon, the light comedy turned to tragedy, with Morny as the central character. After sugar, the stock exchange, and the railroad, the count (who had been elevated to the rank of duke) saw the Mexican affair as an opportunity to win the bet of the century. In 1858, the dictator of the country was a general named Miramón. The coffers were.

empty. To avoid bankruptcy, he asked the Swiss banker Jecker (a kind of Stavisky in sombrero, residing in Mexico City), to lend him 75 million francs. In exchange, he issued 93 million in convertible bonds. The deal was going through, when the lawyer Benito Juárez (a Pablo Neruda character) revolted; he ousted Miramón and refused to return the borrowed sums.

At the brink of disaster Jecker, who had just become a naturalized French citizen, went to Europe and enlisted the support of London, Madrid and all the punters who had bought the bonds. Napoleon III (who had just demolished the Austrians in Italy) was under the impression that the United States was paralyzed by its War of Secession. He dreamed of creating a vast Latin and catholic empire anchored in the new world. Once established, the new State would be able to recover Louisiana, which his uncle had given away in 1803. Encouraged by the French ambassador in Mexico City, egged on by the empress (who was horrified at Juárez's anticlericalism), the Emperor made up his mind to intervene. In 1862, 35,000 French soldiers disembarked on the Mexican shores. More than 6,500 met their death there.

Looking to avoid the same trap, England and Spain signed a treaty with Juárez and withdrew. The shock of Puebla in 1863, where the Foreign Legion was covered in glory, obliged France to step up its war effort[11] at the very moment when Lincoln, newly victorious at home and faithful to the Monroe doctrine,[12] sent Juárez "military advisers" (the first in a long series of American interventions). Morny, recovering the clairvoyance he had displayed with regard to the Crimea, implored his brother to drop this escapade.

His advice was not heeded. In February 1867 the French battalions, badgered by guerrilla fighters, finally left Mexico, abandoned their partisans to the vindictive inclinations of their adversaries, transforming Emperor Maximilian, Miramón and his troops into "*harkis*"* of the New World.

On September 4, 1870, five years after Morny disappeared, compromising papers were discovered, left at the Tuileries by Napoleon III. Among them was a threatening letter from Jecker, still trying to get his money, to the head of the imperial cabinet. "You may not be aware that the duke of Morny was associated with me in this deal. He was to re-

*Harkis are Algerians who fought for France during the Franco-Algerian War and were given French citizenship

ceive 30% of the profits in exchange for getting the Mexican government to go along with the arrangements. As soon as this agreement was concluded, I had the full support of the French government and its delegation to Mexico."

Jean-Marie Rouart suggests that this could have been a prevarication that Jecker tried to use in order to make the emperor come across.[13] Others, less indulgent, think that Morny had pressured Dubois de Saligny, French ambassador in Mexico City, an acolyte to Jecker and an unrepentant saber-rattler, to encourage the intervention. At the end of this glorious epic, the natural son of Hortense should have reaped considerable profits on Jecker's bonds and, according to certain contemporaries, would have acceded to the Mexican throne (temporarily vacant after Maximilian's first refusal). Morny, an emperor? That would have been a fine revenge of the misbegotten. In spite of Persigny's malevolent insinuations, the mystery has never been cleared up. If Morny "was in on the deal," then by advising his brother to withdraw the troops, he put the interest of France before his own. A rigorous syndrome followed by Richelieu, Mirabeau, and all the others.

Its expansionist inclinations being obstructed, the hour had come for France, torn between the egoism of the bourgeois and the poverty of the proletariat, to face up to the real problems of a twilight century fraught with danger. Haussmann's Paris was cut in two by a line of demarcation between the opulence of the renovated West, and the East, a ghetto and a dumping ground for the poor. Louis Veuillot wrote, "These great streets, these great piers, these great buildings, these great sewers, whether their appearance was poorly copied or poorly conceived, embody something that smacks of sudden and dubious fortune. They exude boredom... And a people that is bored is capable of doing terrible things, and one cannot impose anything on it." Jules Ferry was harsher still. "Our affairs are being conducted by a spendthrift, and we plead that he be stopped," he concluded in 1868, in his *Comptes Fantastiques de Haussmann.*[14]

Napoleon now had to choose between democratization and tightening up his regime. An old *carbonaro*, he remembered the generous Utopias of his youth and would have liked to play Royer-Collard.[15] Unfortunately memories of the Terror, the aggravation of the class struggle, and the opposition of his narrow-minded entourage, held him back. Morny, who had stood by helplessly during the great defeat and the civil war, returned to the fore, saying, "It is time to extend some liberty, before they take it by force." That timeless statement is enough to redeem him.

How could this reactionary, who had organized everything and had experienced everything — repression, parliamentary humiliation, deportation, censure — issue such an appeal? Had he suddenly become the apostle of tolerance? Did "the duke de money" see liberalism as a source of profit? With Morny, anything is possible. A few months before his death, he instigated the new social program. Negotiated in 1864, shortly after the working class was given the right of coalition, it might have saved the empire. Almost as crafty a diplomat as his grandfather, he reconciled Paris with Moscow (which had not forgiven the Crimea). A committed and courageous pacifist, he sought to keep the soldiers from "performing miracles"[16] in the futile campaigns of Poland and Italy. If anyone had listened to this visionary jokester, France would not have confronted Prussia, alone, in 1870. As President of the Legislative Corps, he promoted (after Mirabeau but well before Edgar Faure), numerous ideas essential to modern parliamentarism. Emile Ollivier, head of the Third Party that came into being too late, would say of Morny, "No minister was comparable to him. He was not a statesman, he was *the* statesman."

Such a destiny for this man who dreamed of being Talleyrand but was only Offenbach! (Under the pseudonym of Saint-Rémi, Morny composed in partnership with Offenbach several comic operas that resembled the era's political vicissitudes.[17] The tireless Daudet related to Goncourt an incredible scene in which the duke and his co-author, huddled in his office, were "jumping on chairs," tapping out measures, and polishing their libretto while behind the door the ministers were quarrelling.

Morny died In 1865, in his room at the hotel de Lassay. His wife was at a ball. Holding the hand of Flahaut (who was in tears), instead of beseeching the Son who was hanging crucified above his bed, he was supervising the destruction of potentially embarrassing files that a servant was burning in the fireplace. Plonk, who sorted out his "large and complex estate," would comment that "he had many assets, and many liabilities." An apt reflection of Morny's image overall.

Footnotes

1. Hortense occasionally received news of him, and condescended to meet Charles in 1829 in Aachen. A short and unique visit.
2. Credit for this term goes to Peytel, a journalist and author of a lampoon against Louis-Philippe, *Physiologie de la poire* (1832). He was sentenced to death for killing his wife and their servant, her lover. Peytel was executed on October 28, 1839.
3. This man, who knew how to tame lady luck, launched the Grand Prix, allowing his horses to carry his colors from one triumph to another.
4. The seeds of the notion are found in the transformism theorized by the naturalist Lamarck (1744-1829).
5. The author referred to Saint-Petersburg's war of conquest, in which the writer Lermontov took part, who enflamed public opinion.
6. Persigny was the opposite of Morny. Zealous servant of the Bonapartism — to which it was converted by the reading of *the Memorial of St. Helena* — , the expression of his enthusiasm was heavy and awkward. After the elections of 1863, its attacks against Thiers weakened the governmental majority, and the emperor had to ask Persigny to withdraw itself.
7. Pinard, when he was a prosecutor, went after Baudelaire (*Les Fleurs du mal*) and Flaubert (*Madame Bovary*).
8. A tireless litigator, Morny engaged more than 100 lawsuits, almost always successfully.
9. I have a photograph of her, by the ubiquitous Nadar. A small pointed face, anemic, but with a certain mocking grace.
10. Called "vice-emperor without responsibility" by Emile Ollivier, this man of all ministries was an ardent servant of the Second Empire.
11. A city that was besieged in May 1863 for 63 days by the French. In Camerone, the Foreign Legion suffered heavy losses in permitting a supply convoy to pass, to relieve the defenders of Puebla.
12. In a message read to Congress in 1823, President Monroe recited a set of principles of foreign policy, affirming that the American continent would not be a territory of colonization.
13. *Un Voluptueux au pouvoir*, Gallimard Editions, 1995.
14. This violent attack against the prefect of the Seine and his dubious management precipitated his downfall.
15. French politician, d. 1845, who supported the constitutional monarchy all his life. Edited and presented to Charles X the address of the 221 who brought him down.
16. According to Marshal de Saint-Arnaud's atrocious expression.
17. Jules Claretie, critical severe of Offenbach and his popularity, spoke of his music like a disease: "To stop him was impossible. There was nothing one

could do against such a frenzy. Everyone was caught up in a nervous laughter; this lugubrious era" (like ours, today) "laughed piercingly, not like a merry companion, but like a sick man whose foot tickles."

Chapter 12

CLEMENCEAU

Georges Clemenceau, 1841-1929, was a statesman and a newspaper publisher during the Third Republic. Clemenceau headed the war-time government from 1917-1920; he was a major contributor to the Allied victory in World War I and helped draft the text of the Treaty of Versailles. While he was not in office himself, he devoted much rhetorical skill to bringing down other politicians.

> "A death's-head sealed in a gallstone. A Tiger rendered toothless, a Mongol made of rubber."
>
> Leon Daudet

> "His speeches are like a fencing bout: he riddles his adversary with direct hits. With his clear, lively, and decided voice, he imposes his views."

Short as our memories are, we may yet recall Clemenceau, a great Gallic figure known for probity, rigidity, and thunderous parliamentary addresses, savage patriotism and witty remarks. Clemenceau pursued Joseph Caillaux with a vengeful hatred, accusing him of giving information to the enemy, Aristide Briand, whom he suspected of siding with Germany, and Poincaré, "who knew everything, and nothing else." Clemenceau, icon of democracy, may be the only elected official from the regime that foundered with the 1940 defeat whose name is still remembered, when Fallières, Felix Faure, Paul Reynaud and Lebrun have become phantoms.

It is a rare politician from the Third Republic whose nicknames are not pejorative, and he was active himself in weaving the myth of his heritage as "Father Victory." During the massacres of World War I, he galvanized the French will to fight, and he fought for France's interests in the negotiations that followed. After the armistice, he took up the nationalist and revanchist refrain, "Germany will pay." Thus, the man "who served the fatherland well" erased his other nicknames from the time of the Panama scandal in 1892 and the strikes in Narbonne that he suppressed in 1907.

Clemenceau, who prolonged the 1916 massacre until Franz-Joseph (who was three-quarters senile) died, and until his son Charles (who was two-thirds retarded) proposed peace to the Allies. Clemenceau was associated with Pétain in the terrible suppression of the 1917 mutinies (whose pitiful victims waited more than 80 years to be rehabilitated). It was Clemenceau whose vengeful obsession imposed the Treaty of Versailles (that bore within it the winds that brought Hitler to power[1]), then the treaty of Saint-Germain, midwife to the perilous "misery of the small states of Central Europe," including the Yugoslavian hybrid that so disturbs today's peace.[2] Clemenceau the changeable, whose political orientation oscillated from far Left to the far Right (that of the Chamber of 1919); Clemenceau, whose lone-star reputation kept him from earning support in the presidential election the following year.

Born deep in the Vendée, this rough-hewn combatant was unquestionably a republican, even if his family came from royalist stock. Since the beginning of the reign of Napoleon III, Doctor Clemenceau was in the opposition's camp.[3] After the Sedan, this free-thinker was elected a deputy of Paris and, on the strength of his support from Arago, he became mayor of the 18th arrondissement.

And in that arrondissement, the guns of the National Guard were sleeping. Bought by subscription, they were the property of the people. The regular army tried to take them on the night of March 18-19, 1871. Things went wrong, and the story of the Paris Commune turned into a bloody drama. The soldiers refused to fight, and two generals lost their lives.[4] When our deputy swaggered over to help a casualty, he was chased away. Questioned about this later by a judge, he justified himself by saying that, "When I suggested to General Lecomte to have him taken to the hospital, he answered that the arrival of the transport could excite the troops." They did not need to be excited any further, and soon the Commune, the bloodiest and the purest of the French revolutions, devastated the capital and several other cities.

Clemenceau, seeking to mediate between the madness of the communards and the intransigence of the National Assembly, preached moderation to the young Adolphe Thiers[5] (whom Armand Carrel, founder of the *National*, had warned, "You will die of a kick in the ass"). God did not grant the journalist's wish, and the man with so much *toupet* paid no heed to Monsieur Mayor.

Clemenceau resigned as mayor and as deputy in 1871, and waited until 1876 to step back onto the political stage. Then he was elected to the Chamber of Deputies, where despite his blue-blood, he found his place among the radicals inspired by Lafargue (Marx's son-in-law) and Jules Guesde, at the head of the anticlerical battle. (He was so strongly anti-clerical that he when he addressed a letter to the Jesuit who shared the little garden of his ground-floor apartment on rue Franklin, he enjoined "Mister" — obligatory secularity — to prune the branches that were choking his roses. Once the tree had been pruned, he thanked him, restoring the title of "Father" to him. "I call you Father, for you showed me the light;" and he accepted this answer: "I call you son, for today, I opened the Heavens to you.")

Failing to obtain a Ministerial position, he joined the extreme Left and conducted a policy of destabilization within the Chamber, where his fatal and elaborate eloquence[6] made the leaders quake. His words scorched, and the "downfall of ministries" made people lose their positions and often their heads. Indefatigable, he denounced the costly colonial adventures of Jules Ferry, edging him toward the exit. Above suspicion himself, he pretended to be a new Incorruptible. But not for long. Events would overtake him.

Panama, in which Clemenceau was so deeply involved, Panama, a name that reeks of malarial swamps, nearly brought down the regime. (The regime was created by default, anyway, in 1870, and constitutionalized by chance in 1875;[7] it was rocked by supporters of General Boulanger,[8] and threatened by a flourishing trade in military decorations.) Scandal broke out amidst a climate of permanent crisis.

The new Republic, unsteady and unsound, was attacked on all sides. The monarchists (forerunners of today's French Action) called it "*La Gueuse*," ["the Harlot"]; they considered it inevitably "corrupt and stinking." The republican radical Right, personified by Barrès and Déroulède, called for an authoritative and purified State. They gained a following. The nihilist radical Left, building on the strength of the Russian model, preached revolution by blood and fire. In this noxious climate, the increasing anti-Semitism that had been germinating since the Restoration became a pivotal electoral issue. It would come to a head with the Dreyfus affair, which would divide France (although France had been a haven for the persecuted of Europe since the beginning of the century). General Boulanger's revanchism accentuated the political anarchy. The hunt for scapegoats on whom to blame the defeat opened in a climate of melodrama. Traitors were everywhere: at strategic posts in the army, in the ministries, the bank, the press. . . *Espionitis* generated paranoia and the epidemic ravaged anyone who might have had any kind of tie with the Kaiser: Protestants (the majority in Germany) and Jews, especially Jews, and Ashkenazi for the most part (and therefore indefinable, according to the physiognomist mania of "the patriots").

Panama was the dress rehearsal for the Dreyfus affair, and all the actors were the same. Barrès wrote *Leurs figures [Their Faces]*, a superb and repugnant book, presaging *Les Décombes* [*The Debris*] by Lucien Rebatet. Clemenceau, who managed to avoid falling into many of the schemes laid by Lesseps (who spearheaded the building of the Suez Canal and a first attempt at Panama), commissioned Zola's pamphlet in 1898 for his newspaper *L'Aurore*, and gave it the immortal title, "*J'Accuse.*" The main thrust was established: Panama and Dreyfus both had to do with the same manure; scandal would sow the virus of anti-Semitism, and it is in that light that the Affair must be analyzed.

Panama, that political-financial imbroglio, showed up La Gueuse's lack of maturity. Fascinated by its imperialist fantasies, it did not yet deserve democracy. After successfully breaking through the Suez isthmus, why not take a look at the junction of the two American oceans? Until this futuristic plan could be achieved, the merchant ships sailing from San Francisco or Valparaíso for Liverpool, Le Havre, Marseilles, or Hamburg, had to circumvent the new continent by Cape Horn, a maritime nightmare. The slender hips of Central America tantalized imaginative men and the contractors dreamed of digging a canal there.

In the positivist 19th century, nothing was impossible.[9] When the chemist Marcelin Berthelot claimed, in 1897, that "From now on, the world has no mystery," he was summarizing the vanity of an era. The Hegelian dialectic of the *Zeitgeist* and its faith in progress, together with Comte's positivist metaphysics and the activity (less eccentric than is often believed) of the Saint-Simonians, reinforced the scientific Utopias that were illuminated by the fairytale electricity and furrowed by iron. France, like England and Germany, strove to be outstanding in technology.[10] Its engineers — missionaries of civilization — were breaking ground in previously unknown fields; they were considered to be among the best in the world.

One of the most inventive spirits was Ferdinand de Lesseps. It was he who brought the Suez Canal to fruition, an idea that was born under the *Ancien Régime* and was revived for a time by Bonaparte. In

1879, when he launched a new company (in spite of his son's disap-proval), Lesseps, at 74 years old, confronted old age with all standards flying. The "Big Frenchman," still green, had remarried ten years earlier with an eighteen year old Creole who would give him nine children.[11] He was everywhere, and everywhere he exhibited an irrational confi-dence in his talents., carried along by his Egyptian success. Why ques-tion the technical feasibility of the Panama Canal? Nature would yield to his will.

There were indeed some debates within the "French Committee for Drilling an Interoceanic Canal," between the partisans of a level ca-nal and those who favored a design including locks; there was some infighting between proponents of the Panama route and those who thought it would be better to go through Nicaragua (a longer route, but easier to access). No real technical, financial, or geographical analysis was carried out, and no one much cared about the nature of the rocks, the climate, the marshes, and the malaria epidemics that would soon decimate supervisors and workmen.

The cost of the project was estimated at a minimum of 1,200 mil-lion gold francs. To avoid the public outcry that such a figure might create, Lesseps (an effective demagogue but a poor accountant) arbi-trarily cut the estimate by half. With 600 million in upfront capital, "The Universal Interoceanic Canal Company for Piercing the American Isthmus" was fatally dedicated to the failure. It offered the public an issue of shares valued at 400 million. The first disappointment: only 30 million were subscribed. No problem; the great adventure must go on. It would prove to the world France's genius and the supremacy of its entrepreneurial spirit. The Panama Canal would become the national isthmus that broke France.

The secrets cooked up within the stock exchange have not changed much since the *Belle Epoque*. When the public balks at under-writing a venture, a skilful campaign — and a good lure — recalls it to its duties. The Company secured the good graces of the press and gave the journalists reason to be kind. While the big banks did not invest much, they did open their trading counters — with the help of a com-fortable commission — to the long lines of hungry customers. Unli-censed financial go-betweens, merchants of influence whose job it is to heat up tepid investors, Marc Levy-Crémieux (an advisor to Lesseps), Cornélius Hertz and Emile Arton, his agents, and the man orchestrat-ing events, Jacques de Reinach (from the bank Kohn Reinach and Co.), emerged from the shadows. All four were Jewish, and they would feed anti-Semitism. At the forefront of the scene, Lesseps lied to force destiny's hand. He cited America's support, talked about work that was being completed on schedule, the rapid progress . . . all made up. This temporary optimism bore fruit and the 1880 share issue was a success. But it was not enough to feed this company, a compulsive eater, and he was soon forced to seek additional funds. In the meantime, the Company suffered many setbacks. The rock proved resistant, the climate maleficent, the malaria devastating. Lesseps poured 1.4 billion gold francs into this black hole, but the work hardly progressed. Short of money but never short of ideas, he gave up the more profitable single-level plan for a less expensive lock-based plan. To make people overlook this failure and to reassure the small investors, he thought to find a prestigious recruit. The man of the canal called upon the man of the Tower, Gustave Eiffel.[12]

This reinforcement was not sufficient to re-inflate a moribund treasury and the Company, this time, issued bonds in lots that required Parliamentary authorization.[13] To secure the good graces of some not very scrupulous elected officials, Reinach initiated them into the secret pleasures of the stock exchange and greased their not very circumspect palms. Clemenceau, whose name appeared for the first time in the deal, offered to add his own name to the list displayed by his political organization in Oise. Reinach accepted, then withdrew under pressure from his son-in-law (a radical deputy who did not like the looks of this family rivalry). All sorts of decorations and awards were being distributed, and Jules Grévy, the President of the Republic, tainted by the mischief with his son-in-law, Daniel Wilson ("the king of schemers"), resigned (his fortune already made) on December 1, 1887, yielding his position to Sadi Carnot. When it was time for Parliament to make a pronouncement as to the appropriateness of the new loan, Reinach and Hertz had their reward. The deputies proved malleable, and their votes stuffed the ballot boxes in favor of corruption. Two ministers, Baïhaut and Barbé, late to sign on, spoke out in praise of Lesseps, flattering the great man.

Since the Convention, the French had become used to the corruption of the deputies. Panama initiated them to a new type of political-financial delinquency, where under-the-counter payments were replaced by checks paid and deposited in broad daylight by people who regarded the universal vote as their armor and considered themselves to be above the law. Of the hoped for 720 million, only a third came in. Any rich scamp can buy people's consciences; but to inspire confidence was beyond the Company's capability.

In 1889, the court on the Seine ordered the Company's liquidation. A clean and honest bankruptcy? No. An affair of State. The small investors banded together and demanded to be repaid (so they could invest in the debt issued at the same time by Holy Russia). They preferred the tsar's paternal figure to the caricature of the *rastaquouère**in the white suit, reproduced *ad infinitum* on the posters put up by Lesseps's adversaries. Two years later, after some of the unfortunates driven to bankruptcy had committed suicide, a movement that one hesitates to describe as popular came into being. Under pressure from the subscribers who had registered their complaint eighteen months before, the Attorney General, Quesnay de Beaurepaire, and the Minister for Justice, Armand Fallières,[14] were constrained to order the opening of a legal investigation, with belated eagerness. In January 1892, the Chamber, emboldened, demanded that the government prosecute the responsible parties.

The Company's liability at the time amounted to 1.4 billion gold francs. Where had the money gone? In those days, when anarchists only threw pots and pans, the opening of the investigation was like a bomb going off and Henri Cottu, one of the administrators of Panama, gave Constans, the Interior Minister, a list of 104 names. *La Libre Parole*, the scathing paper of the far Right, revealed the nauseous underpinnings of the company. Everyone found in it whatever he most loved to hate. What did Drumont, the anti-Semite, see in Panama? Jews. What did Barrès, the future anti-Dreyfusard, see? Wops. What about Déroulède, the "nationalist" poet? Corrupt deputies. And the monarchists? A new misadventure of La Gueuse. Invective and hyperbole erupted in this "torrent of mud." The *chéquards*, who were running out of arguments, tried to hide behind the old excuse: our enemies are threatening democracy, through the honest representatives of the people. And these rascals managed to enlist the solidarity of some of the republicans.

When the sewers are overflowing, a man like Cornélius Hertz can show his worth. He was of Germanic origin and, to the anti-Semites, no one could be more corrupt and treacherous than a German Jew. Af-

* A pejorative and obsolete term for a wealthy foreigner

ter spending his youth in America, where his parents had emigrated, the young man returned to France and, in 1870, joined the army of Chanzy. He received the Legion of Honor and qualified for the Grand Cross for hypothetical services.[15] With peace established once again, Hertz gave up his medical practice, took an interest in telephony and electricity, launched a few companies, and even thought briefly about a tunnel under the English Channel (good material for a later Panama-type scandal). Having become familiar, in America, with the new discipline of lobbying, he had himself introduced everywhere, and became friendly with Adrien Hébrard (the director of *Le Temps*). Thanks to Clemenceau, he met General Boulanger, War Minister, and with him transacted various juicy and obscure deals in military supplies. To prove his gratitude, Hertz inserted his brother into one of his companies, "Electric Light," thus laying the foundation of Paul Clemenceau's immense fortune.

The two adventurers of the Hertz and Reinach escapade were made for each other. They recognized each other, hit it off, and joined forces in one of the most extensive scams of modern times. They bribed the members of Parliament, bought journalists, played with the interest rates, influenced the markets, adulterated everything.

Two crocodiles cannot share one lagoon for long, and the accomplices were soon tearing each other apart. Hertz claimed a ten million franc commission from Reinach, and deluged him with threatening telegrams; he badgered Clemenceau with cables, threatening to reveal everything if he did not receive his due. (One day I said to Edgar Faure, "One must never give in to blackmail." He gently corrected me: "One must never give in to blackmail *completely*.") Clemenceau exercised the same prudence and urged Reinach to be lenient.

On November 19, 1889, *La Cocarde*, a nationalist newspaper, pilloried Floquet. "A vulgar *chéquard* with the wrong friends." Reinach panicked; he persuaded Rouvier and Clemenceau to accompany him on a visit to Hertz (whom he suspected of being behind it all). The two men had hated each other since the day when Rouvier's government had succumbed under Clemenceau's attacks. This unnatural couple agreed to go to Canossa, where the master singer was expecting them. Then they dashed over to the Interior Ministry to persuade Constans to calm the press, whose virulence he had been stoking. Reinach could not take it anymore, and his corpse was found that evening — while Hertz sought to escape. Did he kill himself? Was he assassinated? The authorities were a little late in sealing the residence of the deceased, leaving his son-in-law time to do some housecleaning.[21] "Death is discreet," wrote Jules Laforgue. Barrès, less poetic, fed people's suspicions: "The demise of Baron de Reinach was discussed by several people in Paris before the event took place." In this syphilitic atmosphere, it is difficult to explain what Clemenceau was doing alongside such partners, in such positions.

Nothing could stop the scandal at this point. In the Chamber on November 21, Jules Delahaye, a fan of Boulanger, challenged the government, made accusations against Reinach, and demanded a new parliamentary inquiry. The Palais-Bourbon trembled under the onslaught. "I have discovered that these great frauds were defrauded, that these exploiters were exploited." "Names! We want names!" the auditorium howled. "If you want names, vote for the investigation." Nobody was tempted; of the 33 Members of the Commission, 17 were freemasons and Charles Floquet, President of the Chamber — a Brother — had received considerable subsidies for his election campaigns, under the colors of Panama.

For a month, the search for the truth went along parallel to an effort to filter all light away from the task. Thierrée, who had served as valet to "the suicide," gave the commissioners 26 check-stubs made out to the order of various intermediaries; Reinach, ever cautious, had taken the care to inscribe the first names and initials of the real recipients. A typhoon hit! The deputies were out for blood, and informants came out of every crevice.

On December 20, 1892, the heavily subsidized Charles Floquet opened the meeting. For three hours, there was a furious discussion over stripping the five least hapless deputies of their parliamentary privilege. Suddenly, a rumor started. Paul Déroulède, the President of the Patriots' League, supposedly was preparing to bring down Clemenceau. "Only the most obliging, the most devoted of friends could be behind this, someone who could associate as an equal, a peer, with the ministers and with the directors of the newspapers. You all know who he is, but no one will name him. . . . Ah, well, I'll name him: it is Clemenceau!"

Barrès would celebrate this eloquent betrayal as "A violent speech, fine-tuned, brilliantly played, sublime. . . " Déroulède had just forced the hand of the one person who thought he was untouchable. The

Chamber was in chaos but the deputy went on until he came to the obscure financing of *La Justice*, his victim's newspaper. "I say that Clemenceau is indebted to Cornélius Hertz... He gave enormous sums to *La Justice* and its political director. Why were these payments made, why this support? What transpired between this foreigner and this politician? One party gave everything and the other gave nothing in return? Indeed, one can only wonder whether what he expected of you, Mr. Clemenceau, was not precisely all these overthrows of governments, all these attacks on the men in power, all the trouble that you have created in the country's and the Parliament's affairs. How many people you have destroyed! Your career is built on ruins."

The crucifixion of Clemenceau would have been less perfect if Millevoye — another anti-republican deputy — had not added, "Cornélius Hertz is a foreign agent!" In the parliamentary language of 1892, that meant a spy in Bismarck's pay. And Déroulède fanned the flames: "Yes, Hertz is a foreign agent ... Let us denounce to the vindictive public, the most skillful the most frightening, the guiltiest of friends, the one whose deliberate and evil actions most of us in this Chamber deplored, without daring to reproach him (much less accuse him of crimes)."

"The slayer of ministries" wavered, then began again. "Yes, my newspaper was financed by Cornélius Hertz, that is the truth. And by many others whose names I could recite, if it were necessary, and these names are ones that you would be obliged to greet with honor. Yes, this newspaper received money from Cornélius Hertz. I did not at any time support the deals in which he may have been engaged. Did I turn over my newspaper to him? I call upon some of my partners who are here. Was this newspaper ever guided by any other inspiration that theirs, than ours?" Clemenceau draped himself in the tricolor. "This supreme insult, which I did not believe I deserved from my bitterest enemy: that I betrayed the French interest, that I betrayed the fatherland, that I brought to these benches a foreign influence of which I was the agent. To such a charge, there is only one answer I can make: Paul Déroulède, you lie!" This is a far cry from the sublime tirades that made him legendary. The Tiger howled; but he failed to convince.

Abused at the tribune, Clemenceau sought his revenge by duel; he would have to cleanse his honor with blood. He visited the expert Gastine-Renette, to improve his eye and his hand, and the meeting took place the following day, December 22, in the wee hours, at the Saint-Ouen race course. Six balls were exchanged, and every one missed.

While the duellists were missing each other, Andrieux[16] was also missing his target. Returning to London, he produced before the commission a new list of *chéquards* which he had just received from Hertz, who was definitely inexhaustible. The document had a providential hole just at the place where a certain name would have appeared. That of Clemenceau, his long-time friend? Justice pressed the former prefect to speak. He refused, and his protection kept his protégé out of the defendant's box in March 1893 (two months after the resignation of the government that had been discredited by the scandal, when the higher court tried the leaders of the Company and their accomplices). The corrupt members of Parliament denied the charges and all were acquitted, except for Baïhaut, Minister for Public Works, who admitted having received a million. Five years in prison. The confession gave the judge a clear conscience.

In 1893, after the board of inquiry was closed down, Rouvier, with a quiet cynicism, would comment that his colleagues had "used the Panama funds to defend the Republic." The notion gives food for thought. Meanwhile in June 1893, a letter was produced, on stationery from the British secret service, purporting to reveal the identity of their agents in France, including Clemenceau, "bought for 20,000 pounds." This coarse forgery, which Barrès himself denounced as ridiculous, did not mislead anybody and its author, a certain Norton, would be condemned by the court. During the debates, Judet and Marinoni, employees of *Le Petit Journal*,[17] revealed the deception, made up entirely to slay "the slayer." Then the newspaper, in its illustrated supplement, published a poisonous caricature, "Doing the Partnership Dance," showing Clemenceau dancing a jig on the stage of the Opera[18] while juggling bags stuffed with pounds sterling.

Le Petit Journal was not the only one to ridicule the one who had been judged. The voters of the Var discarded Clemenceau and elected in his place the worthy Jourdain, president of the bar of Marseilles. At the end of the legislative campaign in Salernes, the Tiger tried his last shot. "I had to borrow from a notary in Nantes to settle the debts from my youth. Where are the millions? I married off my daughter without a dowry. Where are the millions? I have been living in my current residence for six years and I have not finished paying the upholsterer to this day. Where are the millions?" Pierre Bérégovoy would say much the same thing.

More than a century has passed, and historians are still wondering. No check stub bears the name of Clemenceau, not even in code. No evidence incriminates him. Only his friendship with Cornélius Hertz worries the best-intentioned. "He was, I must admit, a complete scoundrel. Unfortunately, that was not clear to me at the time." That may be, but it is strange that the Tiger was so lacking in intuition when he entrusted his offspring to such impure hands: preparing to leave for Marseilles, which was devastated by cholera, he made the "scoundrel" his children's guardian.

Still, this trusting attitude did not convince everyone; he was reproached for having accumulated, his life long, high-priced objects and cheap women, and of having led a lifestyle that was not commensurate with his official resources. Impressed by these charges, I visited the modest ground floor apartment on rue Franklin. Little paintings, reproductions,[19] *The Rape of the Sabines* copied awkwardly by a laborious disciple of Poussin, antique photographs of Greek ruins decorate the walls of this friend of the impressionists and reveal the cultural tastes of a poor esthete. This austere petit-bourgeois interior exhibits no trace of the follies of Fouquet or the luxuries of Mazarin. And let's not forget, either, the humble rented Vendean cottage where he lived out his final years amidst his roses, his young mistress and his nostalgia.

The truth often leaves room for doubt, but I think that the awkward place occupied by Clemenceau in the Panama affair is explained by his passion for the press. It makes him corrupt through love. The need to have a newspaper, the obsession with the rotary printing-press, was expensive; but as a journalist above all, he never deviated from his line, and — with all due respect to Déroulède — his line did not betray his convictions. *La Justice,* founded in 1880 with Camille Pelletan, waged a campaign against Boulangism. *L'Aurore* immortalized Zola. *L'Homme libre* (muzzled by the censors, and reborn as *L'Homme enchâiné*) fought against the lethal inadequacy of French military leadership on the eve of World War I — "War is too serious a matter to be entrusted to the military," he wrote during the slaughter of 1914.

He could have added that freedom is seldom safe in the hands of moralists and that, often, courage forsakes virtue. He did not lack either. When the anarchist Benedetti, one of his writers, fired at him and missed, but broke a window pane, he turned to his accountant and said, "You will want to deduct the cost of that glass from this fellow's wages." The man replied, "But have him arrested, rather." "You don't put crazy people in prison," he retorted. As his attacker moved toward the exit, howling "Long live justice," he added, impassively, "You can see very well that he's mad."[20]

Footnotes

1. But what could he do, in the face of Lloyd George's narrow nationalism and Wilson's ignorance? Clemenceau supposedly told them, "With your agreements, your children will be at war twenty years from now."

2. Wilson knew so little about Europe that when the Polish deputy claimed Galicia, he answered: "And what else? Perhaps you'd also like Spain," thus confusing Galicia, the region to the north of the Carpathians, with the Galicia in north-western Spain.

3. Between 1860 and 1865, Clemenceau, a student in Paris, spent a total of sixty days in prison for his articles against the emperor's rigid policies. Blanqui, his friend, spent 27 years under lock and key.

4. General Lecomte and General Clement.

5. Adolphe Thiers (1797-1877), a statesman, journalist, and historian, became the first president (1871-73) of the Third Republic

6. Contrary to legend, Clemenceau was not a born orator. He became one through hard work and perseverance.

7. If the Orleanists and the legitimists had been able to get along and if the count de Chambord, alias Henri V, had had more political intelligence, the Third Republic would probably never have seen the light of day.

8. Clemenceau had thought Boulanger was a republican, and had him appointed minister of war; but when his demagogic and nationalist leanings became clear, and he became a magnet for both Bonapartist and monarchist support, Clemenceau took a strong position against the Boulangist movement.

9. Clemenceau, influenced by positivism, had translated John Stuart Mill's work on Auguste Comte.

10. The engineer was a quasi-mythical character in the *Belle Epoque*: he was at the center of World Fairs, feeding the dreams of the masses on the benefits dispensed by the god, Progress.

11. Public opinion would always support Lesseps, untouchable on his Egyptian pedestal. The press duly reported on the sexual escapades of the sprightly septuagenarian, tailed by the police into closed houses where he satisfied his voyeuristic inclinations by watching the erotic games of nymphettes. This mischievous trick earned him the (quite French) complicity of worthy people.

12. When the scandal broke, it was learned that Eiffel enjoyed a bribe of approximately a 150 million francs in today's value, upon which he paid some commissions to Reinach, among others. He would be jailed in Mazas, then at the Conciergerie, and was convicted of embezzlement. But his reputation remained intact, and when it was proposed to strip him of the Legion of Honor, his counsel resigned.

13. Already solicited and refused twice.
14. President of the Republic from1906 to 1913.
15. The Order was rescinded when the scandal flared up.
16. A former police prefect police force and a radical deputy. His principal merit was to have given birth to Louis Aragon, outside the holy bonds of matrimony.
17. A tabloid with a 1,200,000 press run.
18. The site was not selected at random; it allowed the caricaturist to evoke Clemenceau's liaison with the star of the stage, Héamide Heblanc, one of the "great horizontals" whose favors he shared with the duke of Aumale.
19. Even the canvas Monet painted for Clemenceau, *The Block,* in homage to one of his newspapers which bore the same name, is only a reproduction. The original belongs to Elizabeth of England and is at Windsor.
20. As a reminder of man's folly, this pane is displayed, under glass, at rue Franklin.

Chapter 13

EDGAR FAURE

Edgar Faure, 1908-1988, a lawyer and politician, was prominent during the Fourth Republic and in the early days of the Fifth Republic under De Gaulle. He was instrumental in France's de-colonization process and carried out a rapid and successful overhaul of the university system; he served as Premier in 1952 and 1955-56.

"My first government had forty members, it lasted forty days and I lost four kilos."

Edgar Faure

I miss Edgar Faure. I hesitated a long time before including him in the pages of a book dedicated to imperfection. I hope that by reading this chapter those who are superficial, those who are hasty, will discover one of the most sensible men of his time who, in a climate of constitutional instability, conducted a reasonable economic policy, a passionate cultural policy, and an open international policy.[1]

I met Faure beneath the palms of the island of La Réunion. This magician had a contagious spirit. After we returned to Paris, he telephoned me. "I would like, my dear Paul," he said to me with his slight lisp, "for you to come and see me, on rue Grenelle. I have a proposition for you." Such an invitation, coming from such a man, was irresistible and so, on the appointed day, at the appointed hour, I presented myself at his office. The Premier, in a dark suit, scarcely resembled that bather in baggy pants, rolling about in the surf. After an uncomfortable (for me) silence, he suddenly spoke up. "You probably know that old Roussac is ill." I did not know anything, but I commiserated. "I need a new associate and I think that you can do the job." While I digested my surprise, he paused and then added, in false humility, "That is, if you would condescend to work with me." The prospect made my head swell and I condescended, alright. "Then we need only agree on the division of labor. You receive the clients, you prepare the briefs and, of course, you plead the cases, because I detest doing that." Somewhat stunned by this Praetorian distribution, I hazarded to ask, "And you, Mr. President, what will you do?" "Me," he answered, somewhat put off by my incongruous curiosity, "I will keep the glue pot warm." The glue heated by his care bonded us forever.

The anecdote is a good illustration of Edgar Faure's approach: effectiveness through humor, with affected modesty and cordial cynicism. Only the combination of talent and energy had determined "this exceptionally gifted intelligence"[2] to enter politics. An obstinate collector of official responsibilities, a diverting joker with an encyclopedic mind, such was Edgar Faure. This pillar of the 4th Republic was instrumental in the birth of the future, but was held back by the disconcerting multiplicity of his own aptitudes. "Isn't it striking that the term ' statesman' is commonly held to be flattering, while 'politician' is sometimes viewed with reservations?" he asked, with his ironic clarity. No wonder I miss him.

From his father, a city councilman in a small town, he received a belief in political temperance, a horror of extreme opinions. His choice, so French, limited him to the nuances of a radicalism whose flexible and arcane innuendos we have lost today, one of those characteristics of humanism so dear to Alain. His independence often excluded him from the radical party. After one of his mishaps, as I congratulated him on his fresh appearance, he answered, "If I look OK, it is because I have a clear conscience." He always had a clear conscience. That was his strength.

From the Nuremberg trials to the Bicentenary of the French Revolution, working in the ministries and as President of the Council, writing detective novels[3] and an aggregation of Roman law, Faure fulfilled all the important roles without ever reaching the top. A lawyer, member of Parliament, singer and professor, he strewed his life with sophisms, witty remarks, and economic wonders (his budgets were the most balanced of the 4th Republic), diplomatic successes (peaceful decolonization, France's recognition of China, opening up to the East), political miracles (the reform of a university system in revolt), vision and mystery. How is it that this man of all seasons has sunk into purgatory? Why this lack of consideration?

Edgar Faure is close to Mirabeau in word and Talleyrand in flexibility. He recalls Clemenceau more than is commonly recognized, in his love of the Republic and his determination, even when in error.

Two men were instrumental in shaping his place in history: Pierre Mendès France (PMF) and Charles de Gaulle. The first, his peer, added the resonance of a prophet to his moral and intellectual qualities. The second, his opposite, grabbed the top spot on June 18, 1940, leaving nothing but merit badges for the others.

One cannot talk about Edgar Faure without evoking Mendès. Rivals bound by common experiences, they respected each other and appreciated each other. When their courses diverged, they defied each other but did not confront each other. Mendès mentions Edgar repeatedly in his memoirs, underscoring their political relationship and their spiritual fraternity. "We could each substitute for the other, as events proved." Then, commenting on one of PMF's speeches at the UN, Faure says: "I thought I was reading a successful expression of my own deepest thought." Both were advocates of a free France, both devoutly favored economic expansion, consumption and investment. They shared a noble idea of politics and its possibilities, persuaded that happiness and progress are inseparable.

Edgar Faure was never a demagogue who could stir up the crowds or attract media support. *La Nef* (his wife Lucie Faure's review) was not *L'Express;* her support was nothing compared to the flamboyant patronage enjoyed by others. Members of the same generation, the two men had paradoxical notions of modernity. Mendès knew no compromise; Faure was the living symbol of compromise. Mendès papered over his regrets; Faure inventoried them meticulously. Mendès persisted and failed; Faure wavered — but he resolved France's immediate problems.

There is a certain Mendès style: quick payback, and direct ties with the nation that he addressed every Saturday. Dealing with every event as it came, Faure never codified his style into a system. He collected ambitions. PMF collected hearts. Faure became a phenomenon, Mendès, a legend. The Left, which preferred Mitterrand over Faure, couldn't mourn him enough — forgetting that its own precipitousness, and its indecision, led to his failure.

On February 7, 1955, Mendès was overthrown. Faure succeeded him, determined "to bring France out of the 'dunce's corner.'" It was a delicate moment for the two friends, pulled in different directions by public affairs and their personal ties. The choice was not easy. "Some people reproached me, at the time, for agreeing to take his place. Should I have sacrificed the interest of France for the sake of a (poorly understood) notion of fidelity?" Accepting the inheritance was not treasonous; Faure extended Mendesism, he didn't end it.

In *L'Ame du combat* [*The Heart of Combat*], he did, however, adorn himself with well-deserved laurels, after the manner of Chateaubriand. "The results of my management can be seen clearly by looking at the status of the public finances. Without devaluation and without raising prices, my work enabled us to ensure two and half years of regular improvement in the indices of production, export and purchasing power." He could have closed this recital of his merits by invoking Nuremberg, de-colonization, and the university reform, important contributions to France's history. However, he deflected his well-earned glory with the humorous and self-evident truth that "The people are traditionally allergic to taxation." I am a too poor an economist to contradict him, and too sorely tried a taxpayer to disagree; but this approach often prevented him from receiving the credit he was due.

In Nuremberg, he represented France as assistant prosecutor. At the age of 37, he tripped up the defendant who was considered the most difficult to confound: the Minister for Foreign Affairs of the Third Reich, von Ribbentrop.

E.F.: "I would like to read to you the first paragraph of a letter from the German embassy dated June 27, 1942 and addressed to the chief of the Sicherheitspolizei in France. 'Hauptsturmführer Dannecker indicated to me that he needed 50,000 Jews from the free zone to be deported as soon as possible to the East, and that it was advisable to support the actions of Darquier de Pellepoix, General Commissioner for Jewish Questions.' Were you informed of this matter?"

V.R.: "No, I was not."

E.F.: "If your colleagues took such steps without keeping you informed, wouldn't that be because they were acting within the scope of your general instructions?"

V.R.: "All I know is that the general instructions were to carry out these tasks very slowly, and to manage things so that it would not be done suddenly but smoothly and evenly."

E.F.: "Smoothly, Mister von Ribbentrop?"[4]

Only Edgar Faure could have obtained such an admission.

Nuremberg was a special case; it did not make him lose his sense of law and justice. In Algiers, when the question arose of legalizing summary execution of militiamen, he protested. "Such actions seem fine in the fever of engagement, but I would in no case take responsibility for including them in a monument of French justice." When a petition was circulated seeking to have Philippe Pétain demoted, Faure bucked public opinion and rejected the idea.

Faure would display his courage again at a pivotal epoch in French history: de-colonization. This necessary break-up was the work of three men: Charles de Gaulle was the prophet, Gaston Defferre, the pioneer, Faure, the craftsman. In 1953, Paris deposed the legitimate King of Morocco and installed on the throne a mummy from the discredited Middle Ages, the *glaoui* of Marrakech. Faure condemned this maneuver, and tried to limit its consequences. He would pay a high price for his astuteness; a tide of calumny was loosed (preying on the fact that he had had ties with Muhammad V, in the days when he was a lawyer). However, this was not a politician playing with damage control, but a public advocate supporting one of his clients.

Faure stood up to a wild parliament, reminiscent of the atmosphere of the Panama scandal on February 6, 1934. They tried to keep him from speaking; insults were hurled; the usual conspiracy was invoked between the press, the multinationals, foreign diplomats and governments. Suddenly, the small man rose to his feet and forced his way to the podium. ". . . I would like to be sure that none of you will ever think that he has made his decision based on an incomplete understanding of what is my opinion, and my conviction." Then, using one of those formulas at which he was so adept, he averted a new war, the first Maghreb war for France. *"Independence in interdependence . . .* If not, you will see only blood and ruins."

He would speak out again after the aborted revolution of May 1968, the day when De Gaulle called him to the Education Ministry after the explosion, "an apocalyptic calamity." Paris was covered with barricades and its walls were covered with slogans. In 1968, the old ways were discarded, and the young knew better than their elders. "Revolution, after all, means a complete change of direction," Michel Serres wrote. First there was a face-off between the students and the state police. The students holed up in the Sorbonne, the high school kids in their schools. De Gaulle called in the youngest of the French leaders — Faure had just turned sixty — to save a moribund university system.

His profession of faith became the absolute weapon. "Since imagination did not seize power, those in power must have imagination . . . Revolution is not riot. There are brutal conservatives, even brutal reformers. There can be peaceful revolutionaries." Then, he pleaded the young people's case. "What is the determining element in one's education? I think it is not the tender solicitude that one experiences in consideration of one's childhood or even youth, it is the total fact, it is the person himself." Ignoring the hack politicians, he let the young people know that they were finally understood. What was youth? A passage. What had it become? A state. Thanks to Edgar Faure, youth now affirmed its right to exist and not to be assisted.

This reformer was also a great economist. As Secretary of State, Budget Minister, and Finance Minister for a few weeks (that was the fashion at the time) in 1952, then from 1953 to 1955, he achieved the highest growth rate of the 4th Republic. As a strategist and a manager, he reconciled technique and sentiment, the heart and the calculator. He proceeded like a chess player, moving each knight ahead at a different rate: as long as the prices were holding still, wages went at a walk, exports at a trot, and "the light brigade of discount and investment charged against immobilism." In 1954, taking advantage of the price stability inherited from Antoine Pinay, he fathered a new national plan accompanied by social protection measures and tax relief. The following year, and for the first time since 1926, the external trade balance was in surplus. Happy with that achievement, he came up with another crystalline formula, "expansion in stability." Another pleasing formula that, however, again deflects attention from his own contribution.

Edgar Faure himself was the greatest victim of this habit of crowning success with maxims in the form of a joke. "It is a great mistake to be right all the time." General de Gaulle made fun of everything, except his own person. Richelieu and Clemenceau resisted never directed their poisonous arrows against themselves. Edgar Faure was satisfied to play the fool, while he had a vocation to be a king.

Faure was the most eloquent lisper in French history. I have known many prestigious speakers; none of them had the elemental eloquence of Edgar Faure. Alas, he aimed too high to reach his mark. He charmed, without convincing, and he knew it. "When the people cease to understand, they cease to admire." His style excited their brains but neglected their hearts. The French did not understand that his skill was merely the vehicle for his conviction. Instead of waiting to grasp his message, they were looking for his latest pun. The people prized him without understanding him and the Parliament, even while giving him a vote of confidence, was wary of him.

President of the Council at a time when the president of the Republic was cultivating chrysanthemums, he governed the country but continued to live as an amused observer of the French comedy. He loved words too much to love people, and the man who shone so brightly at the republican banquets was never elected as Head of State. Faure had all the capacities necessary to occupy the supreme office but none of the qualities needed to get there.

To defend himself against charges of frivolity and inconstancy, he pleaded his own case at the risk of becoming a sophist. "A head of government is accountable for the constancy of his thought. Fickleness and imagination are not qualities he should cultivate. Sometimes, in my case, the irony of fate has exposed me to the criticism of levity, whereas one could rather accuse me of systematic stubbornness and a certain excess of obstinacy." It was true. But why, incorrigible, did he have to add, "It is not me who changes, it's the others"? Contrary to the general view of him, Faure was not overcome by the instability of the regime that was changing governments the way television viewers change channels. "I do not have any ambition for power," he would write in his memoirs; and, choosing to communicate by means that were detrimental to his ideals, he never came across as the man of the hour but as the illusionist of the moment.

The 4th Republic is overdue for a re-assessment. Viewed as a time of shifting sands and shifting directions, it nonetheless allowed France to forge a new unity after the division of Vichy, to regain the grand appearance appropriate to its rank, to rebuild its cities and its villages, to receive its share of the prosperity of the Thirty Glorious Years (of the post-war era), to make a success of the peaceful de-colonization of Tunisia and Morocco. After the 2nd Republic, the 4th Republic was, undoubtedly, the most virtuous. Admittedly, there were the wine scandals and a few others, but they were perpetrated by ordinary crooks without direct ties to the apparatus of State. The political parties lived spartanly and the election campaigns were held on tight budgets. The candidates, thanks to the devotion of activists who still believed and to the backing of discreet patrons, asked for votes as they did in the time of the Second Empire.

Faure has been accused, without any proof, of succumbing to

temptation while in power. Nonsense. Money interested him less than honors, and the only gold that he coveted was on the paneling in the national palaces. His standard of living was modest, and he left little enough to his family.

He was never compromised in scandals. He knew how to maintain a cordial but condescending distance from those who are always sniffing around for moral weakness. They would depart his office with a grin on their faces and with their envelopes intact. "Kindly show Monsieur out," he would say to his secretary, and she would graciously see the importunate visitor to the door.

When Faure became a lawyer again, of course wealthy customers, thinking that the judiciary would pay greater attention to a former minister, he promised to defend their cases himself. Of course, he sent to me in his place. One of them, disappointed, greeted me coldly; then, once the plea had been entered, he complimented me. "You are almost as powerful as the President. . . You have put them all to sleep."

Apart from these little jokes, Edgar Faure, the man of compromise, was never compromised. Faure's principal enemy was Faure. He thought that his little aphorisms would help him to accomplish the kind of jolt-free revival that Mirabeau envisioned. By the time he realized his error, it was too late. "It turns out that I am hopelessly inept at all that maneuvering and deal-making that comprise the politician's portfolio. . . My failure to attain the presidency clearly reveals this shortcoming, in which one can distinguish a certain disposition to naivety," he confessed. There is no better description of this indefinable man.

Footnotes

1. *Mémoires*, Plon, 1982, volume I: "Being right all the time is a great wrong."
2. Michel Serres, *Speech of reception to the French Academy* January 31, 1991, François Bourin.
3. Signed with his pseudonym, Edgar Sandé.
4. This episode is recalled by Arnaud Montebourg in his speech for the Conference of the training course in 1993.

Chapter 14

THE LAST-MINUTE GUEST

> "Let's not beat around the bush. Corruption is a cancer from which humanity must be delivered."
>
> James Wolfensohn
> *President of the World Bank*

They met one Sunday evening at a pub, to celebrate the publication of this work. It was a dinner of leaders: Jacques Coeur, the Concinis, Richelieu, Mazarin, Fouquet, Mirabeau, Talleyrand, Morny, Clemenceau and, naturally, Danton's head. Eleven characters in search of an author. Napoleon was late, like Grouchy; Edgar Faure was absent. "I'll have nothing to do with a place where pipe-smoking is prohibited. If any of your friends wants to join me, tell him I'll be at the *Deux Magots*" (roughly, "two bundles of money") "and don't try to read any symbolism into that choice."

Talleyrand, accustomed to such honors since birth, assumed a position at the head of the table, in his capacity as former bishop, and had cardinals Richelieu and Mazarin sit to his right and left. When everyone was seated, he addressed me. "Now you're your outrageous text about us has been read, let's hear the conclusion of your indictment."

With the devil's help, I apostrophized my guests. "You should be ashamed of having conducted the affairs of France in such a manner. You abused the confidence of the king, then of that of the people. What became of all the skill, the intelligence, the competence that made you first-rate seconds?

"One had to live, after all," murmured Mazarin.

"Your Eminence, you call that living, that unrestrained life be-

197

tween petticoats, money, and honors? Your capacity to fertilize a ground of which you are both the harvesters and the poachers, allows me to ask you the real question. . . "

At that moment, the door to our private dining room swung open under the impetus of an unseen hand. This was not the hand of God nor of the market, but of a late arrival — who bore a striking resemblance to François Mitterand. "May I join your company? It appears to me less strait-laced than those great minds that my wife so enjoys." His voice was melodious and the dramatic pauses in his speech trailed behind them the hypnotic vapors of incense. He turned his head toward me, and he challenged me. "You were just about o pose a fundamental question. . ."

"I was going to ask these gentlemen if it were possible to be, at the same time, a statesman and money man."

He cleared his throat. "Love of money is idolatry. Service of the State is a religion."

I cut this casuistry short. "Can one be virtuous in politics? Should one be?"

"The pure ones raise a storm, the others make waves. When a man believes himself above the others, neglects the flesh, mistrusts the worldly pleasures, he is taken for a god and compensates for the vacuum in his heart with the excess of his ambition. The dispensers of justice torment others and they torment themselves, for such is their true pleasure. Their love of power is both a mirror and a two-way mirror: the mirror reflects their idealized image, the two-way mirror makes it possible to watch others behaving licentiously. You should advise your guests to read Les Dieux ont soif [The Gods Are Thirsty] by Anatole France. They will see this terrible assertion: "When one starts to believe that men are virtuous, one is fatally led to kill them all.""

"That is the opposite of Christ's approach," said Richelieu.

"Still, you are not about to praise vice, shame virtue, and defend the wicked friends who crowded your anterooms?"

"We all had wicked friends, I have no lessons to learn from your guests. Remember Jacques Coeur and Ravant Le Danois, who embodied all that was rotten in the kingdom of his origin; Mazarin and Basile Fouquet, the depraved brother of the unfortunate Nicolas; Talleyrand had Dalberg, who succeeded in betraying more that Talleyrand did himself. Remember Hertz and Reinach, who contributed to Clemenceau's best and worst days. I will overlook Bonaparte's relationships;

and your commerce with Ouvrard, the corrupt banker."

"Let's talk about the scandals that transformed your reign into disillusion and that made you a corrupter through disillusionment."

"I didn't have any monopoly on scandals. The Fifth Republic was always having them and, alas, still is. The fault lies with men but also with imprudent and inadequate institutions. Elected officials have been taken hostage, and candidates are forced to act illegally. The 1958 constitution created an impasse on the financing of political parties and electoral campaigns.[1] It led to the birth of a new regime, without giving it the means of subsistence."

I stopped him. "The Fifth Republic found it normal, for decades, to cover its regular expenses through irregular practices. French policy was not established according to the working documents but by boards of directors at fictitious companies. Design offices serving the public works department became corporate welfare offices, and under-the-table payments took the place of the Tables of Law. Immediate needs took precedence over everything else, and image became all-important. Elections were won by the candidate who, in the absence of merit, had the greatest financial clout. After every presidential campaign, the people were told how much it had cost, but nobody asked questions and everyone got used to seeing financial delinquency coupling itself with democracy. France just waited for the next poll, to hear the candidates proclaim their sovereign contempt for money."

By no means deterred, he started again. "This election that you criticize made it possible to a man from Jarnac* to rule for almost as a long as the man from Corsica. However, I wonder whether the republic run by the upper echelons might not have been less corruptive than today's elective democracy that brought us General de Gaulle. No party, whether right or left, could manage the enormous expenditures to which you just referred. Nearly all of them have succumbed and it was not until the revolt of the judges that the French people stood up and took notice. You cannot evaluate the corruption of the Fifth Republic outside of this context. The corrupt of this era are the least guilty."

His assurance aggravated me. "You seem to forget that such practices made France the twin of Italy. The most praiseworthy motive does not erase the offence."[2] None of the diners rose to dissent. Every

---

* Mitterand's birthplace. He served longer than any other president in French history.

clan benefited from unclean funding, even if they had to share it with swindlers. However, the corruption of the Fifth was different from that of the preceding Republics. It resembled the *Ancien Régime* where the interests of the Prince merged with those of the State. Undoubtedly the institutions are responsible, but the majority of politicians are guilty, for having taken advantage of these practices, and for having allowed them to thrive. Fortunately, virtue is making a salutary and belated comeback that earlier times failed to generate.

"I am not trying to transform the indicted into innocent victims of institutional fate. But to be fair, the corruption in vogue at the end of the 20th century takes on a particular character, given its ties with public law. Our judges allow us to have a clear conscience by pursuing the most extreme cases, the ones with the worst luck , and the most dead, while the astute and the cautious gave lessons and distributed awards for good citizenship.

"It is even more serious since the media attacks stir up nationalist and racist reflexes. . . "

Mitterand cut me off again. "You seem to forget that I was the first to enact laws regulating the party funding that so troubles you."[3]

"I don't deny it. But why pair them with poorly thought-through amnesties, with contorted criteria such as the concept of personal enrichment? How can we differentiate between the cash that lines someone's pockets and that which fills the parties' war chests?"

He protested slightly; then muttered, "I think I fell far short of my ambitions and, generally, I agree with my critics. But I also ended the death penalty, I decentralized the government, and I took positions that were decisive for European unification. If I have any regrets, it's that I did not do everything in my power to reduce unemployment. You cannot change society through legislative decisions alone."[4]

He seemed so tired that I did not have the heart to contradict him, so I went on. "The decentralization that you just mentioned encouraged the growth of corruption. The old system inherited from Colbert and the Convention kept order, in a country where the presence of the prefect made life difficult for skimmers and pirates. When the civil servants were replaced by elected officials, decision-making powers and budget control were entrusted to men who were, often, inexperienced, whose appetites were difficult to control, whose failures were difficult to detect. The decline of morals coincided with the obliteration of

Jacobinism. It also coincided with the globalization of trade and consecration of the market as an idol in the service of the almighty cash. The Western world made corruption a strategic weapon and made it standard."

He did not even try to answer.

"But you may not realize the unforeseen developments of your posthumous destiny. In just a few years, your image deteriorated. In the first year after your demise, favorable new books came out every month, every week, extolling your successes. Then, imperceptibly, the tone changed. You were attacked, your entourage was ridiculed and a former Prime Minister stated that you preferred people who were 'somewhat limited.' In November 1998, he repeated it, accusing you of not being 'an honest man.' And public opinion was hardly moved at all. People did not even seem to be surprised."

"The deceased cannot defend themselves; but if you have a chance to talk with my accuser, ask him, if that is all true, what he was doing serving among 'limited people' and working for a dishonest man?"

Then, I quoted the president of the World Bank:[6] "Let's not beat around the bush. Corruption is a cancer from which humanity must be delivered."

Stunned by such a declaration, all the guests kept quiet. Little by little, it was getting darker, and the contours of the room grew blurred. I thought of the late arrival: what a strange fate. After having hoisted him to the heights of adulation, the people awaited the downfall of his memory. Nobody asked himself, "What would have happened if he had acted virtuously?"

The heroes and the anti-heroes of this book picked up my thoughts, and said, "Virtue?. . . but we all acted virtuously!" And they faded into the dust of the ages.

Footnotes

1. The first texts governing these financings go back to 1990.
2. In French law, the motive is not a component of an infringement.
3. The first laws governing the financing of the political parties and the election campaigns date from March 11, 1988 and January 15, 1990.
4. From his interview with Elie Wiesel.
5. James Wolfensohn.

Also from Algora Publishing:

CLAUDIU A. SECARA
THE NEW COMMONWEALTH
From Bureaucratic Corporatism to Socialist Capitalism

The notion of an elite-driven worldwide perestroika has gained some credibility lately. The book examines in a historical perspective the most intriguing dialectic in the Soviet Union's "collapse" — from socialism to capitalism and back to socialist capitalism — and speculates on the global implications.

IGNACIO RAMONET
THE GEOPOLITICS OF CHAOS

The author, Director of *Le Monde Diplomatique*, presents an original, discriminating and lucid political matrix for understanding what he calls the "current disorder of the world" in terms of Internationalization, Cyberculture and Political Chaos.

TZVETAN TODOROV
A PASSION FOR DEMOCRACY –
Benjamin Constant

The French Revolution rang the death knell not only for a form of society, but also for a way of feeling and of living; and it is still not clear as yet what did we gain from the changes.

MICHEL PINÇON & MONIQUE PINÇON-CHARLOT
GRAND FORTUNES –
Dynasties of Wealth in France

Going back for generations, the fortunes of great families consist of far more than money— they are also symbols of culture and social interaction. In a nation known for democracy and meritocracy, piercing the secrets of the grand fortunes verges on a crime of lèse-majesté . . . *Grand Fortunes* succeeds at that.

CLAUDIU A. SECARA
TIME & EGO –
Judeo-Christian Egotheism and the Anglo-Saxon Industrial Revolution

The first question of abstract reflection that arouses controversy is the problem of Becoming. Being persists, beings constantly change; they are born and they pass away. How can Being change and yet be eternal? The quest for the logical and experimental answer has just taken off.

JEAN-MARIE ABGRALL
SOUL SNATCHERS: THE MECHANICS OF CULTS

Jean-Marie Abgrall, psychiatrist, criminologist, expert witness to the French Court of Appeals, and member of the Inter-Ministry Committee on Cults, is one of the experts most frequently consulted by the European judicial and legislative processes. The fruit of fifteen years of research, his book delivers the first methodical analysis of the sectarian phenomenon, decoding the mental manipulation on behalf of mystified observers as well as victims.

JEAN-CLAUDE GUILLEBAUD
THE TYRANNY OF PLEASURE

Guillebaud, a Sixties' radical, re-thinks liberation, taking a hard look at the question of sexual morals -- that is, the place of the forbidden -- in a modern society. For almost a whole generation, we have lived in the illusion that this question had ceased to exist. Today the illusion is faded, but a strange and tumultuous distress replaces it. No longer knowing very clearly where we stand, our societies painfully seek answers between unacceptable alternatives: bold-faced permissiveness or nostalgic moralism.

SOPHIE COIGNARD AND MARIE-THÉRÈSE GUICHARD
FRENCH CONNECTIONS –
The Secret History of Networks of Influence

They were born in the same region, went to the same schools, fought the same fights and made the same mistakes in youth. They share the same morals, the same fantasies of success and the same taste for money. They act behind the scenes to help each other, boosting careers, monopolizing business and information, making money, conspiring and, why not, becoming Presidents!

VLADIMIR PLOUGIN
RUSSIAN INTELLIGENCE SERVICES. Vol. I. Early Years

This collection contains the latest works by historians, investigating the most mysterious episodes from Russia's past. All essays are based on thorough studies of preserved documents. The book discusses the establishment of secret services in Kievan Rus, and describes heroes and systems of intelligence and counterintelligence in the 16th-17th centuries. Semen Maltsev, a diplomat of Ivan the Terrible's times is presented as well as the story of the abduction of "Princess Tarakanova".

JEAN-JACQUES ROSA
EURO ERROR

The European Superstate makes Jean-Jacques Rosa mad, for two reasons. First, actions taken to relieve unemployment have created inflation, but have not reduced unemployment. His second argument is even more intriguing: the 21st century will see the fragmentation of the U. S., not the unification of Europe.

ANDRÉ GAURON
EUROPEAN MISUNDERSTANDING

Few of the books decrying the European Monetary Union raise the level of the discussion to a higher plane. *European Misunderstanding* is one of these. Gauron gets it right, observing that the real problem facing Europe is its political future, not its economic future.

EDITOR: BERNARD-HENRI LÉVY
WHAT GOOD ARE INTELLECTUALS?
43 Writers Share Their Thoughts

An intimate dialogue with some of the world's best minds, in the form of essays, interviews and responses to the oft-asked question, "What good are intellectuals?" 44 of the world's most respected authors reflect on life, death and meaning. Authors include: Nadine Gordimer, Ivan Klima, Arthur Miller, Czeslaw Milosz, Joyce Carol Oates, Cynthia Ozick, Octavio Paz, Salman Rushdie, Susan Sontag, William Styron, Mario Vargas Llosa, and others.

DOMINIQUE FERNANDEZ
PHOTOGRAPHER: FERRANTE FERRANTI
ROMANIAN RHAPSODY — An Overlooked Corner of Europe

"Romania doesn't get very good press." And so, renowned French travel writer Dominique Fernandez and top photographer Ferrante Ferranti head out to form their own images. In four long journeys over a 6-year span, they uncover a tantalizing blend of German efficiency and Latin nonchalance, French literature and Gypsy music, Western rationalism and Oriental mysteries. Fernandez reveals the rich Romanian essence. Attentive and precise, he digs beneath the somber heritage of communism to reach the deep roots of a European country that is so little-known.

PHILIPPE TRÉTIACK
ARE YOU AGITÉ? A Treatise on Everyday Agitation

"A book filled with the exuberance of a new millennium, full of humor and relevance. Philippe Trétiack, a leading reporter for *Elle*, goes around the world and back, taking an interest in the futile as well as the essential. His flair for words, his undeniable culture, help us to catch on the fly what we really are: characters subject to the ballistic impulse of desires, fads and a click of the remote. His book invites us to take a healthy break from the breathless agitation in general." —*Aujourd'hui le Parisien*

"The 'Agité,' that human species that lives in international airports, jumps into taxis while dialing the cell phone, eats while clearing the table, reads the paper while watching TV and works during vacation – has just been given a new title." —*Le Monde des Livres*

PAUL LOMBARD
VICE & VIRTUE — Men of History, Great Crooks for the Greater Good

Personal passion has often guided powerful people more than the public interest. With what result? From the courtiers of Versailles to the back halls of Mitterand's government, from Danton — revealed to have been a paid agent for England — to the shady bankers of Mitterand's era, from the buddies of Mazarin to the builders of the Panama Canal, Paul Lombard unearths the secrets of the corridors of power. He reveals the vanity and the corruption, but also the grandeur and panache that characterize the great. This cavalcade over many centuries can be read as a subversive tract on how to lead.

RICHARD LABÉVIÈRE
DOLLARS FOR TERROR — The U.S. and Islam

"In this riveting, often shocking analysis, the U.S. is an accessory in the rise of Islam, because it manipulates and aids radical Moslem groups in its shortsighted pursuit of its economic interests, especially the energy resources of the Middle East and the oil- and mineral-rich former Soviet republics of Central Asia. Labévière shows how radical Islamic fundamentalism spreads its influence on two levels, above board, through investment firms, banks and shell companies, and clandestinely, though a network of drug dealing, weapons smuggling and money laundering. This important book sounds a wake-up call to U.S. policymakers." —*Publishers Weekly*

JEANNINE VERDÈS-LEROUX
DECONSTRUCTING PIERRE BOURDIEU
Against Sociological Terrorism From the Left

Sociologist Pierre Bourdieu went from widely-criticized to widely-acclaimed, without adjusting his hastily constructed theories. Turning the guns of critical analysis on his own critics, he was happier jousting in the ring of (often quite undemocratic) political debate than reflecting and expanding upon his own propositions. Verdès-Leroux has spent 20 years researching the policy impact of intellectuals who play at the fringes of politics. She suggests that Bourdieu arrogated for himself the role of "total intellectual" and proved that a good offense is the best defense. A pessimistic Leninist bolstered by a ponderous scientific construct, Bourdieu stands out as the ultimate doctrinaire more concerned with self-promotion than with democratic intellectual engagements.

HENRI TROYAT
TERRIBLE TZARINAS

Who should succeed Peter the Great? Upon the death of this visionary and despotic reformer, the great families plotted to come up with a successor who would surpass everyone else — or at least, offend none. But there were only women — Catherine I, Anna Ivanovna, Anna Leopoldovna, Elizabeth I. These autocrats imposed their violent and dissolute natures upon the empire, along with their loves, their feuds, their cruelties. Born in 1911 in Moscow, Troyat is a member of the Académie française, recipient of Prix Goncourt.

JEAN-MARIE ABGRALL
HEALERS OR STEALERS — Medical Charlatans

Jean-Marie Abgrall is Europe's foremost expert on cults and forensic medicine. He asks, are fear of illness and death the only reasons why people trust their fates to the wizards of the pseudo-revolutionary and the practitioners of pseudo-magic? We live in a bazaar of the bizarre, where everyday denial of rationality has turned many patients into ecstatic fools. While not all systems of nontraditional medicine are linked to cults, this is one of the surest avenues of recruitment, and the crisis of the modern world may be leading to a new mystique of medicine where patients check their powers of judgment at the door.